V
S0-BZF-053
3 1502 00232 8928

851.1 REY

Reynolds, Barbara, 1914-

The passionate intellect

8 5/11
8 5/12
8 12/13

Helen M. Plum Memorial Library

Lombard, Illinois

A fine of 10¢ per day will be charged for overdue adult materials and 5¢ a day for overdue children's materials.

JAN 1990

The Passionate Intellect

Dante and the Leopard   Lino-cut by D.L.S.

THE PASSIONATE INTELLECT

DOROTHY L. SAYERS'
ENCOUNTER WITH DANTE

by Barbara Reynolds

with a Foreword by Ralph E. Hone

HELEN M. PLUM
MEMORIAL LIBRARY
LOMBARD, ILLINOIS

THE KENT STATE UNIVERSITY PRESS
Kent, Ohio, and London, England

© 1989 by The Kent State University Press, Kent, Ohio 44242
All rights reserved
Library of Congress Catalog Card Number 88-13930
ISBN 0-87338-373-7
Manufactured in the United States of America

Library of Congress Cataloging-in-Publication Data

Reynolds, Barbara, 1914–
    The passionate intellect : Dorothy L. Sayers' encounter with Dante /
by Barbara Reynolds : with a foreword by Ralph E. Hone.
    267 p. ; em. ill '
    Bibliography: p.
    Includes index.
    ISBN 0-87338-373-7 (alk. paper) ∞
    1. Sayers, Dorothy L. (Dorothy Leigh), 1893–1957—Knowledge—
Literature. 2. Dante Alighieri, 1265–1321, in fiction, drama, poetry,
etc. 3. Dante Alighieri, 1265–1321—Appreciation—Great Britain.
    4. Dante Alighieri, 1265–1321—Translations, English. 5. Italian
language—Translating into English. I. Title.
PR6037.A95Z85   1989   88-13930
851'.1—dc 19   CIP

British Library Cataloguing-in-Publication data are available.

851.1
REY

33015

IN FULFILMENT OF A PROMISE

Contents

FOREWORD

It was a pronounced providence that drew together Dorothy
L. Sayers, recently embarked on the translation of Dante, and Barbara Reynolds, then lecturer in Italian at the University of Cambridge. In the following pages we are introduced to many of the episodes by which the close acquaintance begun in August 1946 steadily
progressed into an enduring and reciprocally rewarding friendship.

Barbara Reynolds noted from the beginning that Dorothy Sayers'
work was a catalyst, "revitalizing" responses to Dante in England. No
doubt the fame of the detective novelist, dramatist, radio broadcaster, poet and critical essayist drew some readers out of curiosity to
the Sayers Dante translations. But the number of Penguin reprintings
alone indicates that Sayers' grasp of Dante gratified millions of readers not only in England but also throughout the entire English-
speaking world.

Dorothy L. Sayers on her own nourished the friendship with Barbara Reynolds over the years by accepting additional invitations to
address sessions of the summer school held by the Society for Italian
Studies at various English university centers; by requesting a preface
to her *Introductory Papers on Dante*; by voluminous correspondence
full of trial translations of Dante with pointed comments on verse
translation itself; and by varied purely social occasions. With aus-
picious foresight Sayers had prepared her friend to finish the work
she had only partly completed on the *Paradiso* by the time of her
death in December 1957.

The friendship did not prosper out of sheer cordiality, although there was an abundance of that. Sayers recognized the staunch scholar in Dr. Reynolds, and the scholar became a compatible resource. We need to remember that Barbara Reynolds, after completing the translation of the *Paradiso*, was to become the translator of Dante's *La Vita Nuova*, the translator of Ariosto's *Orlando Furioso*, and, after forty years' labor, the general editor of the *Cambridge Italian Dictionary*. She also has had an illustrious academic career in England and abroad.

The Sayers friendship constituted a legacy to Barbara Reynolds. She has lectured widely on Sayers. She has befriended any number of researchers studying the life and writings of Sayers. She has been the managing editor of *Seven*, which includes a focus on Sayers, since its inception. She is chairman of the Dorothy L. Sayers Society. And now she offers us a book on Sayers which absolutely no one else could have written. It draws upon unique personal relationships and reminiscences. But Dr. Reynolds has not told us merely about Sayers' Dante translations and lectures, long choosing and beginning late; she has told us about Sayers' radio broadcasts on Dante, her proposed Dante novel, her carefully planned study on the Beatrician vision; and she has discussed the part Charles Williams played in guiding Sayers in her Dante study. This book observes a brilliant mind meeting a Great Poet and becoming continuously awed, inspired and energized by his verse and vision. This book presents a sublime irony in a person who disavowed possessing a mystical temperament but nonetheless endorsed the Affirmative Way and brought her soul to support the Poetry of the Image, the Hierarchy of Love and the Co-inherence. Like all other heroes of faith, she being dead yet speaketh.

RALPH E. HONE

Redlands, California

PREFACE

Dorothy L. Sayers, the detective novelist who created Lord
Peter Wimsey, also wrote poetry, religious dramas and a number of
influential articles on the Christian faith. Her book entitled *The Mind
of the Maker*, published in 1941, which examines the concept of the
Trinity in terms of human creativity, is still highly regarded by both
theologians and students of literature. During the last thirteen years
of her life (she died in 1957, aged sixty-four) she was at work on a
verse translation of Dante's *Divina Commedia*, on which she also gave
a series of memorable lectures. These were later published in two
volumes: *Introductory Papers on Dante* and *Further Papers on Dante*.
After her death a third volume, *The Poetry of Search and the Poetry of
Statement*, made available lectures she had given on Tennyson, on the
legend of Faust, on allegory and on the art of translation. Her last
publication, in 1957, was a verse rendering of the eleventh-century
French epic, *The Song of Roland.*

Many readers of her detective fiction are unaware of these other
works. Many, on the other hand, acquainted for years with the three
volumes of Dante's *Comedy* published in the Penguin Classics, learn
with surprise that the translator is the same Dorothy L. Sayers who
wrote detective stories. Some resent this versatility. During World
War II, when the BBC invited her to write a series of plays on the life
of Christ, many fans of Lord Peter expressed disgruntlement that his
creator should have, as they put it, "gone all religious." Nowadays
too it is not unusual to hear this view expressed. The popular picture

of her is of a disintegrated writer, almost a split personality. Even among those who discern a line of development rather than of divergence there are some who deplore it.

In this book I attempt to show that the young Dorothy Sayers who brought her debonair, aristocratic sleuth into being in the pages of *Whose Body?* in 1923 is the same in essentials as the mature scholar-poet-interpreter who made Dante intelligible and relevant to millions of modern readers; and that to see this is to have a deeper understanding of her earlier works. In this I have been anticipated in some degree by Ralph E. Hone, who shows clearly in *Dorothy L. Sayers: A Literary Biography* how each stage led to the next in her creative and intellectual development. Mary Brian Durkin in her work *Dorothy L. Sayers* has also perceived that the study and interpretation of Dante was a fulfilment of all that had gone before.

In this book I also examine the effect which Dorothy Sayers' work on Dante has had. For a remarkable cultural event has taken place: since the publication of *Hell* in 1949, followed by *Purgatory* in 1955 and by *Paradise*, which came out posthumously in 1962, Dante has had more English-speaking readers in the last forty years than he had in the preceding six and a quarter centuries.

This was made possible by the availability of the Penguin Classics, an innovation in editing and publishing the impact of which has yet to be fully appreciated. Begun almost by chance by Dr. E. V. Rieu, who brought out his translation of Homer's *Odyssey* in 1944, the series was in its infancy when Dorothy Sayers, who began to read Dante that same year, offered him a translation of the *Divina Commedia*. How that came about is part of the story I have to tell.

It is a story which I am privileged to tell from the inside. I knew Dorothy Sayers for eleven years, while she was at work on her translation. I heard nearly all her lectures on Dante and was responsible for arranging many of the occasions on which she gave them. She entered into lengthy correspondence with me about Dante and we had many conversations. When she died suddenly on 17 December 1957 she had translated only twenty out of the thirty-three cantos of *Paradiso*; she had not begun on the notes or the introduction. I was invited by Dr. Rieu to complete the work.

It is now thirty years since Dorothy Sayers died. The period is long enough to provide a perspective. It is time to assess her contribution to both general understanding and specialized knowledge of Dante; to define what she set out to do, and why, and the extent to which she succeeded; and to show how this vast undertaking was related to the rest of her work, to her life and to her convictions.

I once said to her: "I don't think people have yet understood what it is you're doing regarding Dante. One day I want to write a book about it." I was half jesting, but she replied, seriously, "I hope very much that you will."

BARBARA REYNOLDS

Cambridge, England
13 December 1987

ACKNOWLEDGEMENTS

My first debt of gratitude is to the late Anthony Fleming, who gave me every encouragement and assistance in the early stages of this book. He not only supplied me with photocopies of his mother's letters which were specifically about Dante; he combed through a great deal of other correspondence for references which he thought might be useful to me. He read the first three chapters in draft and made many helpful suggestions. Unhappily, he did not live to see the work completed.

There are many others to whom I am grateful. Above all, I wish to thank the novelist and poet Sylvia Bruce, who read every draft, chapter by chapter, and gave me the benefit of her advice both as a writer and as a former copyeditor. She had already rendered me invaluable assistance in her latter capacity when I translated Ariosto's *Orlando Furioso* for Penguin Classics and I knew that I could look to no better guide. I acknowledge with gratitude the help of Philip L. Scowcroft, Research Officer of the Dorothy L. Sayers Society, who also read every chapter and kept an eagle eye on the accuracy of my facts. Walter Scott, another member of the Society, and Professor Brinley Thomas, a friend of long standing, gave me much helpful criticism. Professor Ralph E. Hone, author of *Dorothy L. Sayers: A Literary Biography*, another friend, accompanied me as I went along and heartened me with his generous help. I thank him for his permission to quote from his book and I am further grateful to him for his gracious Foreword.

There are also many to whom I turned for help and advice on specific topics. The late Patrick McLaughlin, who knew Dorothy Sayers well, gave me valuable insights into the relationship between Dorothy's own faith and her exposition of the *Divine Comedy*. Alice Mary Hadfield gave me helpful information relating to Charles Williams and kindly allowed me to quote from her own writings. The Reverend Dr. Brian Horne read through the chapters relating to Charles Williams as well as the chapter concerning Atonement Theology. On this I was helped also by the Reverend Lorna Dazeley, Deacon of St. Andrew's Church, East Chesterton, Cambridge, and by Prebendary E. C. C. Hill, Librarian of Lichfield Cathedral. To the Dean and Chapter of that Cathedral I owe thanks for permission to quote from documents relating to the performance of *The Just Vengeance* at the Lichfield Festival of 1946. For information about the staging of this play I am indebted to Norah Lambourne, who designed the scenery and who has drawn a diagram specially for this book. She also supplied photographs relating to the production which are included here and allowed me to quote from letters written to her about it by the director Frank Napier and by Dorothy Sayers herself. I wish also to thank Marcus Whichelow who acted in the play and Stewart Lack who saw it performed for allowing me to quote from their recollections.

The Reverend Walter Hooper most kindly sent me copies of correspondence between Dorothy Sayers and C. S. Lewis bearing on her work on Dante and traced the origin of a comment by C. S. Lewis which had been quoted elsewhere without identification. Ursula Bickersteth sent me copies of letters from Dorothy Sayers to her father, Geoffrey L. Bickersteth, of whom she also kindly supplied the photograph which is reproduced here. I thank her also for allowing me to quote from her father's introduction to his translation of the *Commedia*. Ruggero Orlando sent me a lively account of his conversations with Dorothy Sayers on the subject of Dante's metrical variations and also kindly allowed me to publish his photograph. Giles Scott-Giles, the son of Wilfrid Scott-Giles, and Wilfrid's sister Phyllis, provided much information and Giles most fortunately discovered the originals of his father's diagrams of *Hell*, which are here reproduced more clearly than would have been possible otherwise. He also kindly allowed me to quote from letters in his possession and supplied a photograph. The Confraternitas Historica of Sidney Sussex College, Cambridge, who twice invited Dorothy Sayers to address them, have kindly allowed me to quote from their records. For this privilege I was much indebted in the first instance to the late Dr. R. C. Smail and subsequently to Dr. Derek Beales. Colin Hardie kindly allowed me to quote from our correspondence about Dorothy Sayers' work on Dante. Kay M. Baxter also graciously allowed me to quote from a lecture I heard her give at a Dorothy L. Sayers Festival held at Wheaton College, Wheaton, Illinois in 1978. Dr. Edwige Schulte, who attended the British Council course for Italian teachers of English, held at Girton College, Cambridge in August 1954 and so heard Dorothy Sayers' lecture, "On Translating the *Divina Commedia*," most kindly traced for me the date of the Naples newspaper, *Il Mattino*, in which Cesare Foligno's tribute to Dorothy Sayers was published. James Brabazon, author of *Dorothy L. Sayers: The Life of a Courageous Woman*, permitted me to quote from this book (for which I am indebted also to David Higham Associates). William Anderson, author of *Dante the Maker*, generously granted me permission to quote a long extract from his remarkable book. Philip H. Vellacott allowed me to quote from his book *Ironic Drama: A Study of Euripides' Method and Meaning* and from his (as yet) unpublished work, *Oedipus and Apollo*. My kind colleagues in the Italian Department at Trinity College, Dublin, Corinna Lonergan and Clotilde Bowe, discovered an article in *The Irish Press* which was eluding me. Dominic Rieu kindly supplied a photograph of his father, the late Dr. E. V. Rieu, founder and editor of the Penguin Classics. Dr. J. T. D. Hall, Deputy Librarian of the Cambridge University Library, kindly answered my enquiries about Lord Peter's folio Dante. The photograph of Dorothy Sayers taken in 1937 was supplied by Dr. Kenneth Pickering. To all these friends I am most grateful.

I am grateful also to members of my family, my husband Kenneth Imeson, my son Adrian Thorpe, and my son-in-law Andrew Lewis, for their helpful comments and advice.

Finally, I wish to thank my publishers, the Kent State University Press, in particular my editors, Dr. Jeanne West and Dr. Laura Nagy, for their skilful editorial and technical advice. It has been a pleasure to work with them.

I acknowledge with thanks permission to quote from the following authors: Dorothy L. Sayers, granted by David Higham Associates on behalf of the Estate of Anthony Fleming, unpublished material © 1989 Harbottle and Lewis; Charles Williams, granted by David Higham Associates, unpublished material © 1989 Michael Williams; C. S. Lewis, extracts from unpublished letters © 1989 C. S. Lewis Pte Ltd., extract from "Rhyme and Reason" © 1963 C. S. Lewis Pte Ltd, reproduced by permission of Curtis Brown, London; E. M. Forster, excerpt from "What I Believe" in *Two Cheers for Democracy,* © 1939, 1967, reprinted by permission of Harcourt Brace Jovanovich, Inc.; Barbara Barclay Carter, extracts from *Ship Without Sails,* reproduced by permission of Constable Publishers.

The following newspapers have granted permission to quote from their pages: *The Sunday Times, The Stage and Television Today, The Birmingham Post and Mail,* and *The Irish Press.*

The illustrations contained in this book have been prepared for publication by Michael Manni Photographic, Cambridge. The photograph of Charles Williams was kindly supplied by the Marion E. Wade Center, Wheaton College, Wheaton, Illinois.

To the Wade Center I am also grateful for the Clyde S. Kilby Research Grant which was awarded me in 1986. It gives me great pleasure that my book is thereby associated with the name of my dear friend, the late Dr. Kilby, founder and first curator of the Wade Collection.

B.R.

A MIND PREPARED

> . . . the impact of Dante upon my unprepared mind was not in the least what I had expected.
>
> Dorothy L. Sayers

One of Lord Peter Wimsey's hobbies is collecting early printed books. This is the first thing the reader learns about him. In the opening pages of *Whose Body?* he is setting out to attend a book auction and has to turn back for the catalogue. A telephone call diverts him in the direction of his major hobby, detection, and he sends his man Bunter to the auction to bid for him. He is particularly anxious not to miss the folio Dante.

Dorothy Sayers was at work on *Whose Body?* between the summer and autumn of 1921.[1] She had not yet studied Dante, but she took the trouble to provide a learned footnote in which she identified the folio Dante which Lord Peter is anxious not to miss as the first Florentine edition of 1481 by Niccolò di Lorenzo. The footnote continues, "Lord Peter's collection of printed Dantes is worth inspection. It includes, besides the famous Aldine 8vo. of 1502, the Naples folio of 1477—'edizione rarissima,' according to Colomb."[2] Paul Colomb, Vicomte de Batines, brought out a three-volume bibliography of the works of Dante between 1845 and 1846. He describes the first Florentine edition (which Bunter succeeds in obtaining) as "veramente magnifica," the 1502 edition by Aldus as "graziosa e rara" and, as Dorothy Sayers correctly quotes, the 1477 Naples folio as "edizione rarissima." How did she come to know of Colomb's bibliography at this early stage?

In the spring of 1921, as a contribution to the celebrations of the sixth centenary of Dante's death, University College, London, put on a display of books, manuscripts, pictures, statues and medals relating to the poet and his works. Among the exhibits were early editions of the *Divina Commedia*.[3] Dorothy Sayers was then living in Mecklenburgh Square, within walking distance of Gower Street, where University College is. She could easily have strolled in there one day to see the exhibition. If she did, she would have seen that several of the items on view belonged to titled personages. The 1472 *editio princeps*, for instance, was owned by the Earl of Crawford and Balcarres, and two copies of the 1481 folio were owned by baronets. If the idea of making Lord Peter a bibliophile had already occurred to her, why should he not collect early editions of Dante?

In 1921 Dante was in the air. Translations of the *Commedia* were reprinted, articles about it were published in the leading journals, London University Press brought out a volume of essays by eminent Dante scholars in a deluxe edition, and the *Times* contributed a Dante supplement of sixteen pages, dated 14 September 1921, the six-hundredth anniversary of his death.[4] Whether Dorothy Sayers visited the exhibition at University College or not, her interest in Dante was undoubtedly aroused. She must have called in at the Reading Room of the British Museum (now the British Library) and enquired at the central desk about early editions of the *Commedia*. She would have been directed to Colomb's *Bibliografia Dantesca*, which was then on the open shelves. Leafing through the first volume, she chose three items for Lord Peter's collection. A few copies of the folio of 1481 contain nineteen engravings by or after Botticelli. No wonder he was so anxious not to miss it!

It was in keeping with the literary climate of the time that the horror of exhuming Sir Reuben Levy's remains in *Whose Body?* should be intensified by an allusion to *Inferno*:

> Two Dantesque shapes with pitchforks loomed up.
> "Have you finished?" asked somebody.
> "Nearly done, sir." The demons fell to work again with the pitchforks —no, spades.
> Somebody sneezed. . . .
> The sound of spades for many minutes. An iron noise of tools thrown down. Demons stooping and straining. . . .
> A mutter of voices. The lurching departure of the Dante demons— good decent demons in corduroy.[5]

But Dante provides more than atmosphere. His presence hovers over the novel and offers a substantial clue. Between the first reference in chapter 1 and the exhumation scene, which occurs in chapter 12, there are four others. In chapter 2 Lord Peter congratulates Bunter on obtaining the folio Dante and later in the same chapter he mentions it triumphantly to Charles Parker, the Scotland Yard detective, who comes to visit him. By chapter 5 the book has been brought round to Lord Peter's flat in Piccadilly and he promises to show it to Parker, who is having breakfast with him. At the same moment Bunter draws Lord Peter's attention to a review of a new book by Sir Julian Freke, the eminent neurologist, entitled *The Physiological Bases of the Conscience.* Lord Peter feels disinclined to "stodge through" the review and refers irritably to Freke's previous book on crime: "The fellow's got a bee in his bonnet. Thinks God's a secretion of the liver." However, he tells Bunter to order the new book from the library.[6] Reading it later, Lord Peter meditates on Sir Julian's argument: the knowledge of good and evil is an observed phenomenon, attendant upon a certain condition of the brain cells, which is removable. It is this statement which moves him to exclaim: "By Jove! that's an ideal doctrine for the criminal. A man who believed that would never— . . . ."[7] And suddenly he knows what has happened to Sir Reuben Levy.

In chapter 11, when plans for the exhumation have been put in hand, Lord Peter settles down to a perusal of his folio Dante: "It afforded him no solace. . . . Nevertheless, while communing with Dante, he made up his mind."[8] That is, he decides to convey an indirect warning to the murderer, thus giving him an opportunity either to leave the country or to give himself up. This moral resolve is formed by Lord Peter while under the influence of the *Divine Comedy,* a work uncompromising on the question of free will and individual responsibility, standing at opposite poles to Sir Julian's views on good and evil. When the two works are mentioned in the same context in chapter 5, the reader is given a meaningful nudge as to the implication of the difference between them. In accordance with the "fair play" rule of detective fiction, to which Dorothy Sayers attached great importance, this clue is presented simultaneously to the reader and to the two detectives.[9]

When Lord Peter goes to see Sir Julian, ostensibly to consult him

...e ponte donde li comincia a uedere la crä bolgia
Et indi potrebbe ueder tutta infino alfondo/
fe non fuffi pocha luce. IN SV LVLTIMA
chioftra:In fu lultima claufura: SI CHE E fuoi
conuerfi. Sta nella trasatione: et hauendo chia
maro quel uallone chioftro:perche ui fono richiu
fi ti peccatori:chome ne chiostri de monafterii fo
no rinchiufi e monaci et e conuerfi;/chiama quegli
conuerfi di tali chioftri. LAMENTI Diuerfi:
Perche erono uarii et ue muouono da diuerfe parti
SAETTORON ME: Mi punfono el cuore di
pietä: Et quefti lamenti mi faettauano ftrali:
equali hauuano el ferro di pianti. Efferro e
quefto che fa paffare lo ftrale. Adunque epiam
crono el ferro; perche quegli mi commoueuan a tanta
piu ad compaffione. Iuche mi commofie a tanta
paffione che per non gludire mi turai glorecchi
Allegoricamente dimoftra che come Vlixe fi tu
ro glorecchi a canti delle firene: cioe non uolle u
dire chofa uoluptuofa: Chofi io non uolli effere u
uincto da alchuna compaffione di quegli che me

ritano ogni graue fupplitio. QVAL DOLOR FORA. Tal dolor finendea in que peccatori quale
fi uede nellaghefto ne gia malaui fe tutti quegli di ualdichiana di maremma et di fardigna fuffino in una
foffa. Doue e/ da notare che dice dagofto: perche in quel mefe fono molti et difficiii morbi. Onde lu
uimile dice: Et augufto recitanes menfe poetas. Imperoche la corruptione dellaria et detta qua ne gi
di caldi: et pe uenti meridionali g'nera affai morbi: Et maxime nellaere grofso. Et per quefto nom
nu V.ldichiana et Maremma et Sardigna. Valdichiana e/ fra Arezo :et Cortona et Chiufi: et monte
Pulciano doue e/ la chiana fiume decto da la täni Clanis ftagna: Et rende laer grofso:et maxime ribol
tendo nella ftate la bellecta che rimane in fecco:Onde nafcono uari morbi. Sardigna laquale per excel
ftui caldi ha laer peftilente maxime ne luoghi piu propinqui all to.

Chofi parlammo infino alluogho primo
che dallo fcogio lalta ualle moftra
fe piu lume ui fuffi tutto ad imo
Quando noi fummo fu lultima chioftra:
di malebolge fi che fuoi conuerfi
potean parere alla ueduta noftra;
Lamenti faettoron me diuerfi
che di pianto ferrati hauean gli ftrali
ondo glorecchi con le man coperfi:
Qual dolor fora fe de gli fpedali
di ualdichiana tral luglio el fepembre
et dimaremma et difardigna enali
Fuffino in una foffa tutti infiem're
talera quiui et tal puzo nufciä
qual fuol uenir delle marcidë membre.

No difcendemo in fu lultima riua
dellungo ferogio ptir da man finiftra
et allor fu la uifta mia piu uiua

d   Imoftra che quando furono paffati el pon
te: et in fu la riua dila comincio a uedere
meglio gli fpiriti di quefta bolgia:equali eron nel
fondo puniti dalla luftitia: laquale meritamente

A page from Lord Peter Wimsey's folio Dante. "While communing with Dante, he made up his mind."

about nervous strain, he converses in the waiting room with a woman who has recently fled from Russia with her small daughter. The child has been ill as the result of starvation and the memory of horrors she has witnessed. But she is now much better, says the mother, for the great doctor does marvels and is moreover treating her without charge:

> "C'est un homme précieux," said Lord Peter.
> "Ah, monsieur, c'est un saint qui opère des miracles! Nous prions pour lui, Natasha et moi, tous les jours."[10]

The point is thus made that (like many of the sinners in Dante's *Inferno*) Sir Julian Freke is not wholly evil. A brilliant and potentially a good man, tragically flawed by a monstrous self-regard, he betrays a life-long friend without compunction. His written confession, addressed to Lord Peter, resembles in its self-justification and lack of remorse the "confessions" which Dante's sinners make. Like them, Sir Julian is also concerned for his good name. He asks Lord Peter to make his statement known "among scientific men, in justice to [his] professional reputation." Just so do Farinata degli Uberti and Pier delle Vigne, in cantos X and XIII respectively of *Inferno*, show concern about their reputation among the living.

More than twenty years were to pass before Dorothy Sayers embarked on the study of Dante. Yet already in 1921 her "unprepared mind" had seized on the essential elements in "the drama of the soul's choice," as she was later to call the *Divine Comedy*.[11] And at this early date, as the footnote about Lord Peter's collection shows, she took pleasure in learned research.

She had acquired a taste for it at Oxford. She was already widely read as a schoolgirl, when she won a scholarship to Somerville College. She also had a good knowledge of French, German and Latin, as well as a reading acquaintance with Greek. She had never studied Italian, but when she came to read Dante it did not take her long to understand the original. After all, she was a linguist. In many ways Oxford prepared her well for her eventual encounter with Dante. The degree in mediaeval and modern languages, in which she attained First Class Honours in 1915, offered courses in Old French and mediaeval French literature. She was taught in these subjects by Mildred

K. Pope, a tutor at Somerville since 1894. A distinguished scholar, Miss Pope was the first woman to hold a readership in the University of Oxford. In 1934 she was appointed to the Chair of French Language and Romance Philology at the University of Manchester. Lewis Thorpe, the Arthurian scholar who knew her in her old age, left this impression of her:

> I remember her well in her last years, when we both used to attend the meetings of the Anglo-Norman Dictionary committee. She was a tall and dignified person, severe in feature, always dressed in black. . . . I was filled with awe by this elderly scholar who had studied in the 1890s under Fritz Neumann in Heidelberg and with Gaston Paris and Paul Meyer in Paris. . . . When addressed directly, or when she chose to make a comment, her face would light up with enthusiasm, and she was clearly a most sympathetic and lovable person.[12]

The young Dorothy Sayers was deeply impressed by Miss Pope's dedication to learning. In later years they became friends and remained on terms of mutual affection and respect until Professor Pope's death in 1957. There is a delightful portrait of this unworldly yet wise, humane scholar drawn by her former pupil in the character of Miss Lydgate in the novel *Gaudy Night,* published in 1935. In the preceding year Professor Pope's monumental work, *From Latin to Modern French with Especial Consideration of Anglo-Norman,* had been published by the Manchester University Press. The subject is intricate and required a far greater typographic variety than any publisher could nowadays afford. In the preface the author thanks her printers, who, she says, have "borne with [her] inconsistencies and vagaries with exemplary patience." In *Gaudy Night* Miss Lydgate, a tutor in English, is at work on an equally monumental book on "the Prosodic elements in English verse from Beowulf to Bridges," containing a new theory of versification which demands "a novel and complicated system of notation which involved the use of twelve different varieties of type."[13]

In 1934 Somerville College held a dinner (a "gaudy") in celebration of Miss Pope's appointment to the chair of French at Manchester. Dorothy Sayers was invited to propose a toast to the University of Oxford. In her speech she showed how deeply she revered her former tutor and her scholarly ideals:

We in this college are this term bidding farewell to a woman who, to all who knew her, has always seemed to typify some of the noblest things for which this University stands: the integrity of judgment that gain cannot corrupt, the humility in face of the facts that self-esteem cannot blind; the generosity of a great mind that is eager to give praise to others; the singleness of purpose that pursues knowledge as some men pursue glory and that will not be contented with the second-hand or the second-best. Mildred Pope would be the first to say that Oxford made her what she is; *we* say that it is the spirit of scholars like her that has made Oxford anything at all.[14]

Miss Pope's special field of study was Anglo-Norman. It is not surprising, therefore, that works written in this dialect of Old French had a strong appeal for her pupil. She was fired by her studies with an ambition to translate the *Song of Roland.* Shortly after going down from Oxford she did so, in rhyme instead of assonance. But she was dissatisfied with the result. "I still have it," she wrote long afterwards. "It is very bad."[15] In the last year of her life she published a new translation, this time in assonance, as in the original. After more than forty years Miss Pope was still an inspiration to her, as she makes clear in the acknowledgements:

My first debt of gratitude is, of course, to my old tutor, the late Mildred K. Pope, with whom I read the *Roland* at Oxford, and to whom I owe such Old French scholarship as I possess. Unhappily, she did not live to see this translation published, but she gave it every encouragement and much practical help.[16]

Under Miss Pope's tuition the young Dorothy Sayers also read the Arthurian legends, to which she was much attracted, as can be seen from her first publication, a volume of poems entitled confidently *Op. I.*[17] Among the Arthurian characters who appear in it are Perceval, the Lady of the Lake, Merlin and Lancelot. In particular, the legend of Tristan and Iseult captivated her. She studied it with Miss Pope in the Anglo-Norman version by Thomas, edited by the great scholar Joseph Bédier, who provided in modern French prose the sections which are missing from the manuscripts, reconstructing them from other versions of the tale. She undertook to translate this work also, rendering it in rhymed couplets, combined with prose summaries of Bédier's linking passages. Entitled *Tristan in Brittany*, it has an introduction by George Saintsbury. It is dedicated to "M.K.P." (Mildred K. Pope).

Two long sections of this translation were published in 1920 in the journal *Modern Languages*. It did not appear in its entirety until 1929, by which time Dorothy Sayers was well known as an author of detective fiction.[18] But she had not lost sight of her scholarly attainments, nor did she wish her public to be unaware of them: on the title page she appears as "Dorothy Leigh Sayers, M.A., sometime scholar of Somerville College, Oxford."

The task was a learned one. In her translator's note she writes admiringly of Bédier's "noble work of reconstruction and interpretation," which she found a "delightful and intensely interesting study." But, characteristically, her response was not only intellectual: it was also imaginative. Erudition alone would not have satisfied her. By rare good fortune, she comments, Bédier "combines profound scholarship with fine poetic insight." The powerful love story stirred in her a creative empathy which enabled her, again characteristically, to relate this twelfth-century poem to human experience of all times:

> The fatal love of Tristan and Iseult is an absorbing passion, before which every consideration must give way; but the exasperating behaviour of the lovers conforms to the ordinary, human developments of that exasperating passion. . . . There is a kind of desperate beauty in this mutual passion, faithful through years of sin and unfaith on both sides, and careless of lies and shifts and incredible dishonour.[19]

Her skill in writing verse had already been tested beyond rhymed couplets. She delighted in fixed form. Her first volume of poetry contains a masterly and beautiful example of a lay, a series of poems linked in a complex structure, composed according to the rules set down for it by the fourteenth-century poet Eustache Deschamps.[20] She enjoyed mastering a craft. The skill of translating verse had fascinated her from her school days on.[21] Pleasure in complexity was also part of the satisfaction she later found in constructing a detective story. "It is almost as satisfying as working with one's hands," she said, and she compared it with laying a mosaic.[22]

All her life she was attracted by technique, especially a technique that was new to her. Her friend Muriel St. Clare Byrne initiated her in the craft of writing for the stage. *Busman's Honeymoon*, the play (later rewritten as a novel) which they worked on together, was an experiment in translating the conventions of detective fiction into those of the theatre. In accordance with the "fair play" rule, the play had to be so constructed as to allow every clue to be shown to the audience at the same time as it was shown to the detective. For this, the authors say, with unmistakable gusto, "it was necessary to invent a technique."[23]

Busman's Honeymoon had not yet been produced, or even cast, when Dorothy Sayers received an invitation to write a play for the Canterbury Festival of 1937. On the initiative of George Bell, dean of Canterbury, later bishop of Chichester, drama had been re-introduced into the Church for the first time since the days of Oliver Cromwell. This daring and imaginative experiment had led to T. S. Eliot's *Murder in the Cathedral* and to Charles Williams' *Thomas Cranmer of Canterbury*. It is not known why Dorothy Sayers was next approached. She had not then written any of her articles (later so influential) concerning the Christian faith. The very existence of *Busman's Honeymoon* (in any case a secular play) can then have been known only to a few. It is true that her sympathetic handling of Christian themes in several of her detective novels (as in *The Unpleasantness at the Bellona Club*, *Unnatural Death*, *The Nine Tailors* and *The Documents in the Case*) had won her an enthusiastic following among the clergy. It is possible too that her second volume of poems, *Catholic Tales and Christian Songs*, was known in cathedral circles. It contains, as it happens, a brief religious play, *The Mocking of Christ*.[24]

Charles Williams, who was later to play an important part in introducing Dorothy Sayers to Dante, had first met her in 1933, soon after writing to Victor Gollancz to express his admiration for *The Nine Tailors*. The two authors lunched or dined together in London from time to time and wrote to each other about books. Between 1935 and 1936 Williams was at work on his play for Canterbury. He may well have talked with her about it and may have learned that she was herself writing a play. She may have expressed views on religious drama: they would have been decided ones, if so. Williams may even have known of *The Mocking of Christ*. Whoever else may have put in a word,[25] the fact remains that Margaret Babington, the manager of the Canterbury Festival, wrote officially to Dorothy Sayers on

Dorothy L. Sayers in 1937, the year of *The Zeal of Thy House*.

6 October 1936, inviting her to write a play, saying that she did so at the suggestion of Charles Williams.

The result was not one play but two: *The Zeal of Thy House* (a play about the rebuilding of the cathedral quire in the twelfth century) and *The Devil to Pay* (a play about Faust), performed respectively in 1937 and 1939. Both plays, devised for production in the chapter house, presented formidable technical problems, which she applied herself to solving with typical enthusiasm and panache.

In the interval between the two Canterbury plays, she ventured into what was for her yet another technique: radio drama. Her nativity play, *He That Should Come*, imagined first in terms of a listening audience only and later adapted for performance on a stage, was broadcast by the BBC on Christmas Day 1938 on the programme (no longer in existence) known as "Children's Hour."

The success of this and of her other dramatic works led to an invitation from the BBC to write a series of plays on the life of Christ. Since, like *He That Should Come*, they were intended for "Children's Hour," it was agreed that the subject should be handled not liturgically or symbolically but realistically and historically. In her introduction to the published plays, entitled collectively *The Man Born to be King*, Sayers acknowledged her fascination with technique when she wrote, "This decision presented the playwright with a set of conditions literally unique, and of extraordinary technical interest." The task was, in a sense, one of translation. The Gospel story had to be recast in a form suitable for a new and, for this purpose, untried means of communication. The audience would be varied and vast (the BBC anticipated, rightly, that the series would attract adults as well as children) and the demands on the dramatist's skill were many:

> The rhythm of speech chosen to represent this ancient modernity has to be such that it can, from time to time, lift itself without too much of a jolt into the language of prophecy. . . . Fortunately, the English language, with its wide, flexible, and double-tongued vocabulary, lends itself readily to the juxtaposition of the sublime and the commonplace, and can be stepped up and down between the two along an inclined plane. . . . The smooth execution of this movement is the technician's job.[26]

She prepared herself for the work with zest. She read and reread the four Gospels in Greek as well as in the Authorized Version. Viewing the theology in terms of dramatic truth, she exulted in the discovery that from the "purely dramatic point of view the theology is enormously advantageous, because it locks the whole structure into a massive intellectual coherence."[27]

All these new experiences, first of the professional theatre in London, then of the performance of drama in a cathedral, followed by the process of adapting the Gospel story to the technique of radio drama, suggested to her an original and profound analogy. The embodiment of the words of a playwright in the flesh and voice of actors, in the skills of producers, stage managers, scenographers, costume designers and stage carpenters, and the impact of their combined creativity upon the audience was seen by her as an earthly instance, in the world of art, of the Incarnation of the Word and the power of the Holy Ghost. The image of the Maker began to dominate her mind. It had already found expression in the speech of the Archangel Michael which comes at the end of *The Zeal of Thy House*. Every creative act is three-fold, "an earthly trinity to match the heavenly":

> First: there is the Creative Idea; passionless, timeless, beholding the whole work complete at once, the end in the beginning; and this is the image of the Father. Second: there is the Creative Energy, begotten of that Idea, working in time from the beginning to the end, with sweat and passion, being incarnate in the bonds of matter; and this is the image of the Word. Third: there is the Creative Power, the meaning of the work and its response in the lively soul; and this is the image of the indwelling Spirit. And these three are one, each equally in itself the whole work, whereof none can exist without the other; and this is the image of the Trinity.

The play itself has a three-fold allegorical structure arising from the naturalistic level of the story, in which William of Sens, the architect engaged to rebuild the quire, falls from the top of an arch while attempting to fix the keystone. Disabled, he is obliged to hand over his work to be completed by a rival architect. On the first allegorical level, William's fall, resulting mainly from pride, is an image of the Fall of Man. On a second level, four archangels who are present throughout the action and, except at one crucial point, invisible to the other characters, represent Divine Providence or God's intervention in human affairs. On a third level, expressed liturgically, the play is interspersed and framed by versicles, responses, hymns and excerpts from the Book of Common Prayer, sung by a choir. The dream-like sequence in which William converses with the Archangel Michael and finally surrenders links the liturgical level with that of Divine Providence. Thus it may be seen that long before she began to read the greatest of all Christian allegories Dorothy Sayers had herself constructed an allegory of some complexity. (Even as early as 1913, while she was at Somerville, she had begun writing an allegorical epic, of which she completed the first canto of 700 lines.)

She expanded the final speech of the Archangel Michael into a book on the Trinity, which some consider her most profound and original work. This was *The Mind of the Maker*. It was intended as one of a series, entitled collectively *Bridgeheads*, to be brought out by various authors during the war and aimed, as the militaristic metaphor suggests, at securing a foothold on contested territory.[28] *The Mind of the Maker*, the first book of the series, explores the three-fold nature of an act of creation by a human maker as an analogy of the three-fold nature of God. Father, Son and Holy Ghost are shown to correspond respectively to the over-all idea of a work, the energy which brings it into existence, and the power which the work has upon those who respond to it. All three aspects, like the Persons of the Trinity, are distinct but not divided. This vision of the trinity of human creativity, as well as Dorothy Sayers' own experience of constructing an allegory and modulating with skill between the levels of meaning, had an important result: when she came to read the *Divine Comedy* her mind was exceptionally alert to its three allegorical meanings and their relation to the literal, above all to the coherence of the poem at all levels of meaning which, though distinct, are yet not divided.[29]

Her mind was alert also to the relevance of the *Divine Comedy* to the patterns of history. To understand why this was so it is necessary to recall that she began reading Dante in the midst of World War II. A book which she wrote during the first three months of the conflict, entitled *Begin Here*, reveals the range of her thoughts, many of which have a striking affinity with the ideas she is later to meet in the works of Dante. Examining the attempts to achieve world order in the past, she describes "the first structure of the Western-Mediterranean-Christian civilization," which she defines as "theological": "It referred all problems to one absolute Authority beyond history and beyond humanity; and as a scheme for the satisfactory fulfilment of the individual and the world-community it was and remains complete and unassailable." Why, then, did this structure break down?

> It did not fail because the theory itself collapsed when brought into contact with real life; but because the human instruments who had to carry it out failed to realise the implications of their own theory.
> In this tremendous conception of human life, nothing was omitted or

neglected; nothing was too great or too small for inclusion. It embraced the world eternal as well as the world of time; it provided minutely for the most trifling acts of daily life as well as for the rule of empires. . . .

Freedom was understood . . . in a . . . philosophic sense: the freedom to be true to man's real nature, that is, to stand in a right relation to God. As a stone, left free to follow its own natural law, falls to the ground, so the spirit of man, made free to follow its own natural law, flies to God. The stone, if set free, is not free to follow some erratic direction; it will only do that if compelled from without.[30]

Such passages might lead one to suppose that Dorothy Sayers had already begun to read Dante: there seem to be "echoes" here of his philosophic treatise, *Il Convivio*, of his work on world government, *Monarchia*, and of the first canto of *Paradiso*.[31] But it is not so. They are not echoes, but tones which are about to find a resonance and a resolution.

In 1943 Charles Williams' book *The Figure of Beatrice* was published by Faber and Faber. Dorothy Sayers read it, she said, not because it was about Dante but because it was by Charles Williams. It made her resolve to read Dante, but some months went by before she did so. We now from our point of perspective can see into her future. We move on along the line of time to the summer of 1944, to the month of August, when Hitler's guided missiles are screaming down on London and the Home Counties. It is a moment of crisis for Britain, for the Western World and for Christendom. We place Dorothy Sayers in our minds in the air-raid shelter in her home in Witham, Essex. She has taken something with her to read: Dante's *Inferno*. She is 51 years old. Her scholarly training, her wide reading, her many writings on the Christian faith, her varied professional skills, her personal experiences—all are poised, ready to respond. She begins to read: "Nel mezzo del cammin di nostra vita [Midway along the journey of our life . . .]."

In what way was Dorothy Sayers' mind "unprepared," as she said it was,[32] for what she was to find as she read on? Surely few minds can have been *better* prepared. What was it about Dante that took her so powerfully by surprise? The answer is to be found in her letters to Charles Williams.

"DEAR CHARLES . . ."

I am so grateful that while I breathe the air
My tongue shall speak the thanks which are your due.
Inferno XV, 86–87

Charles Williams, poet, theologian, dramatist, essayist and critic, was highly esteemed in his lifetime by a distinguished reading public. Among his admirers were T. S. Eliot, W. H. Auden and C. S. Lewis. On many people his influence was crucial and long-lasting. Those who met him acknowledged the fascination of his personality, particularly of his conversation. Largely self-taught, he was a man of many gifts, some would say of genius. The continuing interest in his work is shown by the growing number of books and articles written about him forty years after his death.[1]

Starting as a proofreader for the Oxford University Press at Amen House in London, he rose to be literary adviser and editor. In his spare time he produced seven volumes of poetry, four works of criticism, four books of theology, seven biographies, seven novels and twelve masques or plays. He also wrote articles and reviews and lectured on English writers to adult students attending evening classes. The enthusiasm he inspired appears to have been out of the ordinary.[2]

The inspiration of all his work was theology. Dorothy Sayers, as we have seen, first met him in 1933 and they became friends. She admired his writings, particularly his novels, "metaphysical thrillers," as they have been called, in which the supernatural and the natural intermingle with startling but believable effect. She was also much taken with his theological ideas. What these were and the extent to which they influenced her will be discussed in chapter 11 here. For the present suffice it to say that when she came upon a review of a new book by Williams it was natural that her interest should be at once aroused. The book was *The Figure of Beatrice.*

The reviewer was Desmond MacCarthy, the distinguished critic on the *Sunday Times.* Williams' exposition of Dante's mind, he wrote,

> brought home to me the rationality of Dante. I never had so clear a conception of the intricate coherence of the *Divine Comedy.* That poem ostensibly began with a personal experience, a falling in love in childhood, when neither the conscious spell of the senses nor the attraction of common tastes is strong. But having recognized that Beatrice was to his childish fancy what the ideals of religion became to his mature mind, he identified the two experiences not only as a poet, but as an interpreter of the nature of God and man.[3]

Here was a theme which was bound to interest Dorothy Sayers, even if the book had not been by Charles Williams. She bought it at once and read it straight through. It convinced her that "here was an Image, and here an Image-maker, with whom one had to reckon." It made her resolve to read the *Divine Comedy.* But she did not do so immediately. After all, as she said, "fourteen thousand lines are fourteen thousand lines, especially if they are full of Guelfs and Ghibellines and Thomas Aquinas."[4] Finally, in August 1944, she began.

The effect was dynamic. The work took so powerful a hold on her imagination that everything else receded, even the air raids:

> The plain fact is that I bolted my meals, neglected my sleep, work and correspondence, drove my friends crazy, and paid only a distracted attention to the doodle-bugs which happened to be infesting the neighbourhood at the time, until I had panted my way through the Three Realms of the dead from top to bottom and from bottom to top.[5]

The energy thus generated was first expressed in a flood of letters to Williams. Since it was *The Figure of Beatrice* which had set her off reading Dante, what more natural than that she should send him her impressions? The correspondence began on 16 August 1944. There are thirty letters in all, nineteen from Dorothy Sayers and eleven from Williams. Her last is dated 9 May 1945. Williams first replied

Charles Williams, author of *The Figure of Beatrice*.

on 24 August 1944; his last letter is dated 24 April 1945. Out of this brief exchange, lasting nine months, arose all Dorothy Sayers' work on Dante.

She begins by saying, "I have embarked upon an arduous enterprise for which you are entirely responsible." The embarcation date was 11 August and in five days she had read the whole of *Inferno*. She was using the Temple Classics edition, which provides a facing-page rhythmic prose translation, "slipping and scrambling," she writes, "between the original and the crib."

Her copy of the Temple Classics edition, in three volumes, had belonged, she thinks, to her mother, or was it her grandmother? At once she notices that the *Inferno* is slightly loose at the joints, the *Purgatorio* in excellent condition and the *Paradiso* practically as new. Was her mother, then, or her "highly religious grandmother," to be counted among the many readers who never venture beyond the *Inferno*? It did indeed look that way. The three volumes were evidently

in the rectory library at Bluntisham where she lived as a girl.[6] Why
had she never read Dante before? Because, she says, she knows just
enough Latin and French to make mediaeval Italian look easily read-
able and she had found herself being distracted from the translation
by "the lovely tooral-ooral on the opposite page." This suggests that
in earlier years she had at least dipped into these volumes, but had
made no headway, finding the translation uncompelling and herself
then lacking the resolve to tackle the Italian. She was later sufficiently
interested to go and hear a lecture on Dante by H. A. L. Fisher during
her first term at Oxford, however.[7] The family library seems also to
have contained an edition of the *Commedia* (or, at least, of the *Inferno*) with illustrations by Gustave Doré, and these she had looked
at: "I had never read Dante . . . but only quoted bits of him and
looked at Doré's illustrations to the *Inferno* (and I still think, whatever it may be the fashion to say about Doré, that he was a great
illustrator)." One illustration had remained vividly fixed in her
mind: that of the Simonists in canto XIX, upside down, "lamenting
with their legs." She had found this, she says, a supreme example of
unintentional humour, a reaction which suggests that she had seen
this illustration in childhood.[8]

   She had never read any books or essays on Dante before *The Figure
of Beatrice*. All she knew about him had come from quotations and
allusions in books and religious writings. This had not prevented her
from making allusions herself to Dante, nor from quoting from the
Commedia, as she did in 1941 in *The Mind of the Maker*: "en la sua
voluntade è nostra pace [in His will is our peace]."[9] As Desmond
MacCarthy wrote in his review of Williams' book, "It is a mark of the
greatest authors that we become acquainted with them without reading them, so numerous are the channels through which their spirit
seeps into the minds of men."

   Despite such general knowledge, or perhaps because of it (since
much of it was stereotyped), Dorothy Sayers was surprised by Dante.
The ideas she had picked up about him "were of a quite different sort
of writer and a quite different sort of person." She knew some of the
set pieces—"the canto of Paolo and Francesca, for instance"; and she
knew about "the tortures and the demons, and the politics, and the
boiled popes and so on." And she had expected "a good deal of
Thomist theology and mediaeval astronomy."

Her acquaintance with Dante, though second-hand for the most part, had inspired reverence: without having read him she ranked him above Milton. Indeed, her resolve to read him had been strengthened by a book on Milton by C. S. Lewis, *A Preface to Paradise Lost*, published in 1942 by the Oxford University Press. This prompted her to reread the greater part of Milton's poem. Having done so, she "cheerfully remarked to a friend that Milton was a thunderingly great writer of religious epic, provided it did not occur to you to compare him with Dante." The friend replied that she had never read Dante. Dorothy was pulled up short by such disarming honesty: "It then came to my mind that perhaps I had better read Dante, or else I might find myself condemned to toddle round for ever among the Hypocrites."[10] Her reaction to what she discovered has therefore to be considered not only in relation to her previous ideas about Dante but also in relation to the fact that she had just been reading Milton. Some of her first comments are inspired by her surprise at finding the two poets so different. In fact, if she had first read Dante in Henry Francis Cary's stately, Miltonic translation, instead of coming to him almost immediately in Italian, with the help of the Temple Classics crib, she might not have been struck so forcibly by the difference.

What astonishes her first of all is Dante's skill as a narrator. *This* is what her mind was unprepared for: "Neither the world, nor the theologians, nor even Charles Williams had told me the one great, obvious, glaring fact about Dante Alighieri of Florence—that he was simply the most incomparable story-teller who ever set pen to paper."[11] The discovery fills her with delight:

> I still don't know how he does it. After all, even without having read it, one knows what it's all about, and you wouldn't think there would be any real suspense about it. . . . In spite of which I found myself panting along with my tongue hanging out, as though it were a serial thriller, careful not to read the argument of each canto beforehand, lest it should spoil what was coming.

Here, from the very first letter, is the authentic Sayers response to Dante. Williams' book had served as the spur. Now she was galloping off in a direction of her own. What she needed and what he provided was companionship in her new adventure: "Unfortunately I have nobody to talk to here (my husband's comment would only be, 'What on earth do you want to read that stuff for?').'' And she continues:

> It is very arduous work tramping up and down and round all these circles, if one can't blow a little trumpet now and again to announce to somebody that one has got to a station;—a little tin trumpet, like the kind they blow on French railways to say the train has actually arrived. . . .

Almost the whole of this letter, ten pages long and continued over two days, is a joyful sounding of calls, not so much of a trumpet as the horn of a huntsman. She is fascinated by Dante's technique:

> In a way I know how it's done. I could take it to pieces and analyse the tricks. Just when you are getting tired, some "invention" occurs—an alarming hold-up at the gates of the infernal city, a pathetic story by Francesca or Ugolino, a pleasant aerial excursion on Geryon's back, a grisly laugh over the quarrelling demons, a picturesque apparition of giants, a sudden dab of bright colour when Dis appears in the middle of the grey ice, a smattering of science when they pass the Centre . . . but merely naming the tricks doesn't explain the achievement; it only makes one think one's self clever.

It should be remembered that these are first impressions, formed in five days' fevered reading and dashed off at top speed at the height of excitement. Later, emotion recollected in tranquillity will lead to more considered judgment. Reflection will show that the aerial excursion on Geryon's back is far from pleasant, and that "picturesque" is not quite the right word for the giants. But such early blemishes are of only minor importance. What is striking is the richly exuberant first response, combined with humility in face of what she recognized as superb craftsmanship. She knows she is a beginner, but she is learning fast. From her first letter on, all her quotations are in Italian and her comments show that she has no difficulty with it.

Since Milton is in her mind, she points out the drawbacks of his formal style which, compared with Dante's, lacks versatility:

> When one has started off in that key, the elephant is obliged to "wreathe his lithe proboscis"—what else can he do?—and the sudden domestic

reassurance, "no fear lest dinner cool," is bound to give one a slight shock, as of sitting down suddenly on a kitchen chair. But the style which carries one along and can practise the necessary art of sinking in verse is the style which can pass at will from the magnificent to the familiar without any jolt.[12]

Dante seems to her "bigger" than Milton, "a world-poet where Milton is an English poet . . . lumpy and heavy . . . like Rubens and, in some queer way, parochial." Dante has more artistic tact in that he avoids entering into unnecessary explanations; and he understands better than Milton the nature of courtesy. Adam's pompous language to Eve, "*whatever* Mr. Lewis says about the grand style," compares ill with the instance of what she calls "exquisite tact," where Dante, in canto IX of *Inferno*, alarmed by Virgil's anxiety, enquires of him delicately whether he really knows the way through Hell. In her letter of 17 August she recasts the dialogue as follows:

> Dante (in a detached manner, as one demanding information on a matter of purely historical interest): Do people from the First Degree ever come down into this depressing place?
> Virgil (with equal detachment): Well, it is unusual, but, as it happens, I have been down myself once before, to do a little job for Erichtho. (At which point Dante's façade must have given way slightly, and he feels he can add without being offensive): I know the way—don't worry.

Continuing in her first letter to Williams, she says that she has begun to read the *Purgatorio*, to which "I come," she says, "with a practically blank mind." In her second letter, undated but probably begun on 25 August, she says that she has finished it. That is, she has read sixty-seven cantos in thirteen days, an average of five cantos a day.

It was no "blank mind" that could respond so vividly to a first reading of the *Purgatorio*, as when she writes that the opening cantos are

> a sort of miracle . . . limpid and lovely and clean and enchanting, like one of those Italian pictures—or in fact like the real Italy, only more so.

Incidentally, of course, you can see Mount Purgatory with the terrace rings round it from top to bottom anywhere along the Adriatic coast.[13]

By her third letter, dated 31 August, she is already on the *Paradiso.* By 14 November she is more than two-thirds of the way through the *Commedia* for the second time. The speed is astonishing, the more so as it is not mere haste but an intense and lively eagerness. Her delight is two-fold: an unashamedly childlike pleasure in a story *and* a professional writer's recognition of the skill with which the narrative is handled. She acknowledges in her second letter that Williams has performed a valuable service in showing that the *Commedia* is not just a story but an experience: "All the same, it *is* a story and a piece of verse, so do not despise me for treating it as such—remembering that I am only playing the piano with two fingers." Her comments in the same letter on the episode of Casella in canto II of *Purgatorio* are an example of the two-fold attentiveness with which she reads:

> Terrifically moving . . . is Casella singing Dante's song while Virgil listens on that strange and lonely shore. And however right and proper the warnings you utter, dear Charles, about Francesca-like lingerings, I reserve the human right to say, Bother old Cato! I resent having Virgil bustled about by this disagreeable old Roman nuisance—and since the poor spirits seem to have had no particular occupation in the Ante-Purgatorio except to put in a few hundred years or so of waiting about, they might have been allowed to hear the song to the end.[14]

Then comes her professional appreciation of Dante's technique: "Poetically speaking, of course, the whole thing is brilliant—the 'trick,' I mean—for if there had been no such interruption, what an anti-climax and jerk to get the thing moving again!—and the fact that one resents Cato is a tribute to the success of the trick."

A major problem of structure soon caught her eye: the departure of Virgil and the change-over to Beatrice as guide. At first she is disposed to brood, a little sadly, on the fact that not even Dante has been able quite to escape the dreadful tendency of sympathetic characters to run away with the play, the killing-off of any charming person at the end of act 2 making it probable that the audience will spend act 3 in the bar. She still thought it a perilous passage four years later when, with considered judgment, the tumult of her first impressions calmed, she lectured on Dante's Virgil to the Virgil Society:

> It was necessary to the plot that Virgil should go; but his is one of those characters which tend, as one says in the theatre, to "run away with the play," and Beatrice's self can, in that poignant moment, hardly compensate us for his loss. Virgil fills the first two books of the poem; and in making him so central and so lovable and in then rending him clean out of the story, Dante took a risk which only the very greatest of artists could venture or afford to take. The whole structure of the poem quivers under the shock, and stability is only restored by the intense and concentrated brilliance of the scene that follows between Dante and Beatrice.[15]

Dorothy Sayers brought not only an eager response and a professional eye to her first reading of the *Commedia*. She was also a scholar, well read in the mediaeval romances. In the meeting between Dante and Beatrice she recognized the tradition of the *roman courtois*. Many readers find Beatrice intolerable at this point. Dorothy remarks that this is inevitable unless we have some previous acquaintance with Old French literature:

> Because, from the literary point of view . . . the harshness and the humiliation are in the tradition. This is Lancelot and the Charrette all over again with a difference; this, if you like, is the image of which that is the idol. Your young man came at your behest through the utmost hardships of what (originally) was some kind of other-world journey, and, having got him, you treated him like dirt, and rubbed his nose in it till all the by-standers burst into tears and protested.[16]

Many readers, coming from the enchanting description of Matelda singing and dancing and gathering flowers in the Garden of Eden on the top of Mount Purgatory, are disconcerted or bored by the pageant which precedes the entrance of Beatrice. Dorothy was at first among them: "It's a good pageant as mediaeval pageants go, but to be candid I feel that the colouring is wrong. . . . it's all indoor colouring, heavy, Hebrew, and opaque—golden candlesticks and peacock wings and rainbow streamers and a heraldic gryphon—grand in the Temple, but out of place in Dante's wood." Nor did she care for the transformations of the chariot which occur when the river Eunoë is passed:

> I admit to feeling it unfortunate that we should have to plough through all that rigmarole about the chariot. It's all right as these symbolic visions go, but any mediaeval writer can do those eagles and greyhounds and monsters on his head, from the *Song of Roland* onwards. No doubt it was necessary from the Church-and-Empire end of the thing, but it is one of the passages I shall skip when I re-read it. Happily, it is not very long, compared with the unconscionable lengths to which the mediaeval romancer was usually prepared to go with this kind of thing; and perhaps the trouble here is merely a change in literary taste.[17]

If she regarded herself as coming to *Purgatorio* with "a practically blank mind," she felt at an even greater disadvantage when she began reading *Paradiso* (although she humorously underplays herself throughout the letters). She notes first that if Dante has refrained from explanations in the two earlier sections of the poem, it must have been because he was saving them for the third. She does not object to this, for here, she maintains, is the right place for them. She nearly gives up on the moon; indeed, Dante's question about the markings on it and Beatrice's long scientific answer have discouraged many a reader who has got this far. Her immediate comment is that Dante started off by asking the wrong question. This seems, on the face of it, a trivial remark but it goes, in fact, to the heart of *Paradiso*, which is a gradual progression, by means of question and answer, in which Dante sheds error after error, intellectual and spiritual, until at last, "come stella in cielo il ver si vede [like a star in heaven the truth is seen],"[18] and his vision, cleansed and clarified, is empowered to see God.

Her comments on *Paradiso* show a ready awareness of the difficulties it presents for modern readers. There are gulfs to be bridged, prejudices to be overcome. People in the fourteenth century, for instance, were not so unscientific as modern critics tend to assume. Beatrice's explanation of the markings on the moon may not be correct in the light of modern physics, but at least she is not content to fall back on the mere citation of authorities. She has grasped the principle that an inadequate scientific theory must be exploded by scientific method. Dante's theory must be tested by experiment. "Take three mirrors," says Beatrice. She was not, Dorothy points out, in a position to say "take a telescope."[19]

Piccarda's famous utterance, "e la sua volontate è nostra pace [and His will is our peace],"[20] with which Dorothy Sayers has long been familiar, is now read by her for the first time in context. She seizes at once on the essential difference which it implies between modern and mediaeval concepts of happiness:

> I suppose there is nothing in Dante's heaven against which the contemporary mind rebels so uneasily as the reply to [Dante's question]. To be content *for ever* with a lower place, without either possibility or desire of "improvement" and "progress," has become quite alien to our way of thought; and we can't imagine "fraternité" without "égalité," or justice without uniformity. Were the Middle Ages wrong, or is it that our generation will so crowd the [Cornice] of the Envious that there will be no room to crawl?

In the same letter, dated 31 August 1944, she describes another jolt to the modern mind, which she herself experiences, in finding the inhabitants of Heaven

> so extremely and even fiercely concerned with Italian politics. Granted that all Heaven may blush crimson at the misbehaviour of Christ's vicar, one is apt to feel that so much brooding on earthly affairs and such gloomy denunciations of catastrophes to come, ought not to distract the minds of redeemed saints from their eternal bliss. I suspect, however, that this feeling comes, not from our taking Heaven more reverentially, but from our taking politics (for all the clatter we make about them) less seriously. In agitated moments we call Hitler "anti-Christ" and wonder that God doesn't blast him with lightning; but we don't genuinely feel that the angels are interested in Mr. Chamberlain and Mr. Churchill, or that St. Peter is liable to get all worked up over what the Archbishop of Canterbury is doing.

We find it strange, too, that the souls in Heaven have absolutely nothing to do, apart from their songs and solemn dances, except to "enjoy God." She acknowledges that this is well justified theologically but still thinks it is brave, from the poetic point of view, for

Dante thus to have depicted heavenly bliss. As the character in his story, he even finds it courteous and kind of the souls to interrupt their eternal contemplation for a moment in order to improve his mind. This brings her (again in the same letter) to a comparison between Dante's heaven and that imagined by Milton:

> The latter enjoys a morning and an evening and a variegated landscape with trees and streams and metalliferous soil; there is a thundering good battle to take part in, and a creation to watch, and a devil to circumvent, and a Fall to get excited about, followed by a number of strenuous astronomical and geographical tasks to perform. It is a magnificent outflanking movement; but Dante carries out a frontal assault on the main position. He will undertake to show you spirits and angels engaged in doing nothing in particular for ever and ever, amen, and persuade you that they like it. And he does.

Such a heaven, she continues, should forever blot out the popular legend of a grim and ferocious Dante:

> Was there ever a heaven so full of nods and becks and wreathèd smiles, so gay and dancing? or where the most abstract and intellectual kind of beatitude was so merrily expressed? Surely nobody ever so passionately *wanted* a place where everybody was kind, and courteous, or carried happiness so lightly. . . .

Her joy in the work is heightened by Dante's power of making pictures. She herself had the "painter's eye," and it should not be forgotten that her husband was an artist. Everything described in the *Commedia*, she remarks, except for technical difficulties with the *Paradiso*, could be drawn in line and colour. Dante's own use of colour in *Purgatorio* interests her from a craftsman's point of view. In the first canto, using "astonishingly few words," he creates an "extraordinarily pervasive colour-impression . . . that, of course, is where the genius comes in." She is enchanted by "the wonderful little bit of enamel-work in the Valley of the Rulers, with the setting sun just catching its carpet of flowers," and the angels with their green wings and the bright streak of the serpent gleaming through the flowers in the light between sunset and starlight.

It is the same with the Earthly Paradise. Except for the "vermigli" (vermilion) and "gialli" (yellow) flowers, no colours are named, but we sense them in the river, which is clear without sparkle and in the flowers which paint the grass where the lady comes, moving like a dancer. And in *Paradiso,* where everything is painted in continual gradations of light, what variety Dante achieves! But why, she complains,

> do the Temple Classics translators, having carefully established that *isplendor* and *risplendere* always in Dante mean "reflected splendour," insist on rendering them by "glow" or "re-glow," which suggest *neither* splendour *nor* reflection? "Sheen" or "re-sparkle" or almost anything would have been better than "glow," which always sounds dull and reddish and subdued, unless accompanied by some sort of adjective like "fierce" or "white-hot."[21]

We might be listening here to a technical conversation between craftsmen in an artist's studio.

Like many a delighted reader, she lists the well-known similes, rejoicing in their homely quality: "frogs, baby storks, birds feeding, a shepherd on a frosty morning, burning logs, organ-pipes, an animal in a sack, water in a basin, a child being scolded, a clock chiming, sailors caulking their ships, motes in a sunbeam. . . ."[22] Where did Dante learn to make his similes so concise and functional? Not from Virgil, certainly. Perhaps from Ovid? More probably from the Vulgate. After all, the range of literary models available to a mediaeval writer was not extensive. The explanation lay, she decided, in his use of fixed form, *terza rima* (triple rhyme), in the rigid allowance of so many lines per canto. This leaves no room for long, elaborate similes, "full of elegant amplifications which don't assist the argument." Sublime Dante may be, but he is also businesslike. He was a professional; he finished the work,

> and finished it exactly as he laid down the scheme for it at the beginning of the *Inferno,* all neat and ship-shape, with so many cantos per book, and so many lines per canto, all beautifully balanced and exact. No loose ends, no half-lines, no stravaguing digressions—and that, for the Middle Ages, is a feat in itself.[23]

Related to Dante's unpretentious style and homely similes was another element which surprised her: his sense of humour. Not just the grotesque humour of the devil-play in the *bolgia* (ditch) of the boiling pitch; this had long been acknowledged and, indeed, deplored. Dorothy Sayers noticed something more pervasive: a delicate spirit of comedy in which the poet conceives himself as a character in his poem. Her letters sparkle with the pleasure of this discovery. Later she twice committed herself to it in print: in the article ". . . And Telling You a Story" (1947) and in a lecture given in 1949, "The Comedy of the *Comedy*."[24] She was adversely criticised for this, but she was not alone in her contention that Dante had humour. Her earliest predecessor, among modern critics, was probably Professor Sannia, who in 1909 claimed that the popular tradition of a humourless Dante was a travesty and a libel. In 1921 Canon Lonsdale Ragg contributed to the centenary volume, *Dante, Essays in Commemoration*, an article entitled "Humour in Dante," in which he wrote:

> Dante was at once too great and too human to be devoid of this saving grace, though the very sublimity of his work tends to draw our attention away from the playful flashes, the subtler ironies, the masterly handling of the grotesque, and from that readiness to turn the flashlight upon his own weaknesses and to look at himself from outside which redeem him at once from affinity to the "cattivo coro" of those who "take themselves too seriously." (P. 227)

Benedetto Croce had said that there was laughter in *Inferno* as well as in *Paradiso* and Charles Roden Buxton in *Prophets of Heaven and Hell* considers that Dante and Goethe display more humour than Virgil and Milton. In 1944 Dorothy Sayers was not acquainted with these fellow spirits and for a time she believed herself alone in her view that Dante had

> conceived his own character from start to finish in a consistent spirit of comedy. . . . His self-portrait is saturated with a delicate and disarming awareness of himself as a comic figure. I do not think this is just a craftsman's device—I think it is, on the contrary, a sincere and touching humility.[25]

By 1949, when she delivered her lecture on "The Comedy of the

Comedy," she had located predecessors who agreed with her, and also several who did not. H. A. L. Fisher believed that "the poet was without humour," while Bishop Boyd-Carpenter pronounced, "He may be said with justice to be lacking in humour." John Jay Chapman wrote that "Dante's attempts at humour are lamentable," and Ernest Newman called the poet "the tight-lipped Dante, who probably never saw a joke in his life."

Nonetheless, by 1944 Dorothy Sayers's alertness to Dante's humour and to its implications already covered a wide range. In her first letter to Charles Williams she says: "The *Inferno* is a satire . . . it's like having a religious *Dunciad.*" In this she goes, with characteristic acumen, straight to the heart of the matter. Her view was corroborated by the distinguished Dante scholar and translator, Geoffrey L. Bickersteth, with whom she later corresponded and whom she ultimately met. In the introduction to his translation of the *Commedia* he says, "The first point to be grasped, or Dante's main artistic purpose will be entirely missed, is that in pattern his verse is neither epic nor dramatic, and still less is it lyrical. It was chosen because it admitted all these modes, but its norm is none of them: it is satiric."[26]

Not only could Dante laugh at himself; he could also laugh at evil. Not that he did not take evil seriously, but he could make it appear ludicrous. Here is an important difference, once again, between Dante and Milton. Milton has been accused of making a hero of Satan. But it is nonsense, Dorothy Sayers declared, to suggest that Milton was the dupe of his own genius. The grandeur is "all part of the Satanic set-up." Yet, despite the lines, "Him they found / Squat like a toad, close at the ear of Eve,"[27] Milton was not successful at depicting Satan as squalid. This was probably another drawback of the formal style. In Dante the "Satanic set-up" is stripped right off:

> con sei occhi piangeva, e per tre menti
> gocciava il pianto e sanguinava bava.

> [from his six eyes, and down his triple chin
> runnels of tears and bloody slaver dripped.][28]

Dorothy Sayers finds the last view of Satan ludicrous, his legs up, his head down: "Is he [i.e., Dante] being mediaevally naive about passing the centre of the earth? Or is that absurd and undignified last view . . . the terrific mockery that it might be?"[29] There is no doubt in her mind about the savage mockery of the Swindlers in the fifth *bolgia* of the eighth circle. This is the only piece of broad comedy in the poem and it is, she considers, brilliantly done: "Dante in the poem is desperately frightened and in real peril, but Dante the Poet is mocking his own fear as well as the pettiness of his enemies."[30] Technically, how right it is, she points out, to introduce the relief of comedy at this point, "to turn the laugh against Hell itself." Yet it is "a risky business to hold these malignancies up to ridicule, and a sarcastic tongue is not pardoned."

A more sinister humour (if humour it is) occurs in the picture of the Simonists, head-down in pot-holes, their legs lamenting. Earlier, looking at Doré's illustration, she had found this unintentionally funny. Reading it now in context, she is not so sure. It is not funny when one realizes that in Dante's time assassins were executed by being planted head downwards.

So the letters proceed, day after day, week after week, most of them over ten pages long, one of them running to twenty-six, the handwriting flowing and eager, the style intimate, informal and yet controlled. Everything she later said about Dante is here in embryo. Indeed, one can say that it is already to be found in the first three letters, written between 16 and 31 August. Since she began reading the *Commedia* on 11 August, the epiphany occupied twenty-one days. There it all is: the grasp of essentials, the acute observation of detail, the correlation of parts to the whole, the lively appreciation of character and plot, the vivid imagination which visualizes figures and movement, the dynamic delight of discovery, the craftsman's admiration for control of structure and pace: above all, a readiness to take Dante seriously, to recoil in horror from his portrayal of evil and to rejoice with him in his communication of joy.

But what, in the meantime, was Charles Williams making of all this?

3.

"MY DEAR DOROTHY..."

Given at the King's Court in Caerleon
Charles Williams

Charles Williams had told Dorothy Sayers that he liked getting letters. She took him at his word. Her first letter about Dante, ten pages long, reached him on 17 August. He replied on the 24th. He wished, he said, that he could write at length and as her exceptionally delightful and very interesting letter deserved. "But I am very old, my dear Dorothy!" He was fifty-eight.

By August 1944 the war had been going on for nearly five years and many people, young and old, were feeling the strain. In September 1939 the London office of the Oxford University Press had been evacuated to Oxford and the staff were billeted round the city. Charles Williams was offered lodging at 9 South Parks Road. Though a large house, it offered little privacy in wartime conditions, especially in winter when bedrooms went unheated in order to save fuel. Nevertheless, he continued to write, on a pad on his knee, in whatever time he could spare. His work for the Press took most of the day. In the evenings he lectured for the English Faculty of the University. During this period he managed to complete six full-length books, one of which was *The Figure of Beatrice*.[1] And he wrote hundreds of letters.

His reputation had preceded him to Oxford. In 1936 C. S. Lewis wrote to say how much he had enjoyed his novel *The Place of the Lion*. Williams replied that he had been on the point of writing to say how much *he* admired Lewis' *The Allegory of Love*. A correspondence developed and a friendship grew. On moving to Oxford Williams was welcomed into the group known as the Inklings, who met every week in Lewis' rooms in Magdalen College to discuss matters of literary interest and to read aloud from books they were writing. J. R. R. Tolkien, who was a member, read from early drafts of *The Lord of the Rings*. Other members were Nevill Coghill, C. H. Dyson, Owen Barfield, Major Warnie Lewis (C. S. Lewis's brother) and Colin Hardie, Fellow and Tutor in Classics at Magdalen College and an authority on Dante. Williams had enjoyed good fellowship at Amen House for many years. In his exile in Oxford the Inklings helped to make up for the disruption and loss of contacts which the war had inevitably brought about.[2]

His response to Dorothy Sayers was characteristically generous in the gift of time and energy which it represented. He first took up the question of Milton, with whom she had compared Dante, to the latter's advantage. It was to be expected that he would rise to this challenge, since he had championed Milton in the celebrated Milton controversy.

In 1934 Ezra Pound had drawn attention to what he was pleased to call Milton's misdeeds as a poet.[3] In 1936 T. S. Eliot in "A Note on the Verse of John Milton" questioned the poet's greatness. His gifts, Eliot maintained, were mainly aural. Withered by book-learning, he wrote English as a dead language. What, after all, did *Paradise Lost* offer? Some grandeur of sound, admittedly, but otherwise merely a glimpse of theology which Eliot found repellent, expressed through a mythology which would have been better left in the book of Genesis.[4] Eliot's indictment was deemed irrefutable by the Cambridge critic, F. R. Leavis, who remarked complacently, "Milton's dislodgement, in the past decade, after his two centuries of predominance, was effected with remarkably little fuss. The irresistible argument was, of course, Mr. Eliot's creative achievement."[5] In 1938 John Middleton Murry, in *Heaven and Earth*, also, "came out against Milton," as Leavis put it. Thereafter any lecturer or teacher felt at liberty to diminish Milton in the eyes of the young. And many did.

There was one who did not. All during this period Williams had been lecturing on Milton as part of his course on English literature at the City Literary Institute in London. Alice Mary Hadfield, who attended his lectures, recalls:

He made certain observations which had not been notably made before and will remain a permanent part of our knowledge. . . . In *Paradise Lost* he showed that Milton was not taken in by Satan and pride as his readers have been, and thereby released us to a whole and true understanding of the work. He pointed out that . . . far from being harsh and lofty, Milton's writing is warm and human, penetrating in psychological insight, and piercingly intelligent.[6]

Canon Roger Lloyd, who heard Williams lecture at Oxford on Milton's *Comus*, wrote, "What Mr. Williams said . . . had hardly been said in any university for years, and never with that lyrical, infectious enthusiasm. We listened, and were thrilled."[7]

During the winter of 1939, in the cramped conditions of his lodgings in Oxford, Williams wrote the introduction which the Oxford University Press had invited him to provide for the World Classics edition of *The English Poems of John Milton*, published in 1940. He entered the arena undaunted, welcoming combat:

We have been fortunate enough to live at a time when the reputation of John Milton has been seriously attacked. The result of this attack, which has come from various sources otherwise not noticeably sympathetic with each other, has been to distract the orthodox defenders of Milton, and to compel the consideration everywhere of his power as a poet. (p. ix)

In 1942 C. S. Lewis brought out *A Preface to Paradise Lost*, a revised and enlarged version of lectures which he had delivered the previous year. It contains a dedicatory letter to Williams, whose introduction to *The English Poems of John Milton* Lewis considers to be

the recovery of a true critical tradition after more than a hundred years of laborious misunderstanding. The ease with which the thing was done would have seemed inconsistent with the weight that had been lifted. . . . Apparently the door of the prison was really unlocked all the time; but it was only you who thought of trying the handle. (pp. v–vi)

Such, then, is the context in which Dorothy Sayers read Lewis' *Preface to Paradise Lost*, was moved by it to reread Milton and, when she eventually read Dante, to draw comparisons between the two poets. In his letter of 24 August 1944 Williams agrees with her that

Dante is "much bigger than Milton," but he puts in a word for the formal style, which she regards, he thinks, as "more pompous than it was ever meant to be. I am not quite certain that you are fair to either Adam or Eve. . . . I shall continue to hold that both these poets had a touch of lightness in them that we do not realize." He looks forward to hearing what she thinks of Dante's view of Beatrice and signs his letter, "Always yours adoringly."

This was invitation enough. She replied at once in a letter of twelve pages. A week later she began a third, which ran to fourteen, and may have taken several days to write, for it was not posted until 4 September. Williams replied to the second letter on a postcard, in playful Arthurian style:

> Given at the King's Court in Caerleon
> 1 September '44
>
> The King's Majesty heard with great joy the news contained in the dispatches received this morning from the distinguished commander of the Expeditionary Force. The King has caused these dispatches to be published throughout Logres, and has proclaimed a public holiday in His capital city of Camelot. He awaits with serene impatience the fuller information promised. The achievement of the City by all coheres in His complete intention. The Lord Taliessin permits himself to add his private congratulations, and so all the Lords of the Table.
>
> At the command of the King and
> by the hand of Taliessin.

En clair, this coded message means that Williams (Taliessin) has shared her first two letters with C. S. Lewis (the King). He in turn has talked about them with the other Inklings (having "caused these dispatches to be published throughout Logres"). They ("all the Lords of the Table") and Williams send congratulations, while Lewis hopes that she, and others after her, will read triumphantly to the end of *Paradiso* ("the achievement of the City by all coheres in his complete intention").

Dorothy Sayers enjoyed literary games. She had played an elaborate one in her childhood when she and her cousin Ivy had written to each other as characters out of the novels of Dumas.[8] She had played another as an adult in letters she had exchanged with her friend Wilfrid Scott-Giles about the origins of the Wimsey family.[9] With the greatest ease, therefore, she replied in like style:

> To the High Singer, Taliessin, at the Court
> of Camelot in Logres:
> Sir,
> Agreeably to the King's command, received by me this day at your hand, I have the honour to send you the further detail of the Empyrean expedition. That of the Purgatory campaign has, I trust, reached you already. I hope His Majesty will pardon the rough and familiar style of these despatches, for, to tell you the truth, we have none here can set hand to a pen but Dinadan the Fool, and he, being of but a rambling and feeble intellect, plays himself half the day and sleeps t'other.
>
> The troops are in good health and spirits, and desire me to thank His Majesty for His gracious and encouraging message, which I have caused to be posted throughout the camp.
>
> Given from the field this 4th day of September.
> D. L. Sayers
> O.C. Exp. Force

On 7 September Williams found the time to write her a letter of eight pages. "Marvellous!" he begins, "both the Achievement and the Record." Then he gets down to business. He is amazed at the speed at which she has read the *Commedia,* but is convinced that that is the way to do it. And now he has a plan to suggest: will she let these letters "or something like them" be printed? He is eager for her response to Dante to be made available to the general public: "I do very much want people to get all you say about the laughter and lightness and fun—of Dante. We want to break up the hideous monstrosity of the Catholic mystical poet which they envisage as part of their solemn culture. There are a score of touches in your letters which are invaluable." The letter does not make clear what he means by "they" and "their solemn culture"—academic interpreters of Dante, perhaps? He had by then been elected a member of the Oxford Dante Society. It may be that he disliked their approach to Dante, but "hideous monstrosity" is a surprisingly strong expression. At any event, he eagerly welcomes Dorothy Sayers' approach, whatever he is contrasting it with.

Will she consider writing him an "Open Letter"? He admires her "charming and intimate style," which he would much like to retain. If she will continue writing to him about Dante until Christmas, he will produce out of what she writes, without a word intruded of his own, exactly what he has in mind and send her the typescript to read: "O do, do! It's so necessary. . . . It's a solemn thought that you and I—with C.S.L.—are loosening the chain of generations—only by saying on and off 'How very good this is!' "

He is eager to enter into an alliance, believing, evidently, that current ideas about Dante are as mistaken as those about Milton. He envisages a role for her, on which he enlarges in a brief letter dated 13 September, suggesting that she should turn her letters to him into a pamphlet:

> I am convinced (and this seriously) that they might be of great use to a large and probably innocent public of whom a certain few might read (a) them and (b) Dante. And they might have their whole consciousness of Dante altered by reading you, and turned into a much happier and more truthful apprehension. It is this kind of thing which we need to encourage so much; less catholic culture and more poetic intelligence.

She began her reply at once, but it was interrupted by a visit to Chichester, where she attended a conference on religion and the arts in the company of architects, painters, sculptors, "with only T. S. Eliot and myself to represent the 'grand art'; and music was wholly absent." The pace had dropped a little and she had diverged from Dante to read C. S. Lewis' correspondence with E. M. W. Tillyard on "The Personal Heresy."[10] She enters into this digression at some length. Finally she refers to Williams' proposition. She begins with a jocular reproach:

> Let me inform you, dear Charles, that you (like every other literary bloke I ever met, including myself) are one of those who would boil the bones of his grandmother to make soup. I write you a series of innocent, carefree, personal letters about a great poet, and your immediate reaction is to contrive how they may be made into a pamphlet to improve other people's minds. (14 September 1944)

At this point she refers to "Topsy." This is not Harriet Beecher

Stowe's little slave girl in *Uncle Tom's Cabin*, the Topsy who "just growed." It is A. P. Herbert's Topsy, the scatter-brained débutante who appeared in the pages of *Punch* from week to week, making her naive but often penetrating comments on life and art. She was popular in her day and much quoted (though she has proved to have less staying power than her little American namesake, whom everyone remembers). She was gathered into two volumes, one of which, *The Trials of Topsy*, contains a letter to her darling friend Trix, describing a visit to the Lyric Theatre, Hammersmith, where she saw a performance of *Othello*. Since she arrived after the curtain had gone up and she was unable to get a programme, and since she had never read the play, she was able to bring to it an entirely fresh mind. In 1944 this amusing sketch was still well enough known for Dorothy Sayers to say without more ado, on the question of her own comments on Dante, "I am painfully reminded of A. P. H.'s 'Topsy'—who, you remember, once brought a virgin mind to *Othello*."[11]

The drawback of tidying up and filling in her letters with necessary information would be, she fears, that they would become self-conscious, unspontaneous, losing thereby whatever Topsy-like merits they may have. After all, she has not been writing them with a side-glance at posterity and the printer's press. At this stage she can see two possibilities: (1) that she should write a "Topsy's Guide to Dante"; and (2) that *he* should write something for the "innocent person," putting in all his "stuff" about Beatrice and the images in a shortened and simplified form and working in any bits of her letters which seem to him of value. They could then bring out a kind of "First Steps in Dante" under both their names and the Oxford University Press could publish it. She signs her letter "Topsy."

It would have been no easy task for Williams to provide a shortened and simplified form of *The Figure of Beatrice*. One wonders what the "innocent person" requiring an introduction to Dante would have made of his concepts of co-inherence and exchange, indeed of the whole theology of romantic love which is the subject of the book. Dorothy Sayers evidently had so clear a grasp of what this difficult book is about that she thought it could be reduced (and by its author) to simple terms.

In her letter dated 26 September, which at twenty-six pages took several days to write, she returns to the idea of what she continues to call "Topsy's Guide to Dante." She is now willing to go ahead with it, provided Williams is prepared to do the editing. Meanwhile she will continue to write, not an "Open Letter," but letters to *him*. And he, as he has promised, shall write letters to her about Milton, "and we will (for once) publish letters that are not exclusively occupied with knocking down each other's theories, converting each other to something, or displaying our own superiority to one another and to the subject!"

From 11–13 October she was in Oxford, staying at 9 South Parks Road. Her reason for going was to attend a meeting of writers and theologians who had been invited to prepare a year's cycle for the Church for use in country parishes. The group was known affectionately as "the theological bear garden." When the day's work was over, she and Charles Williams sat up late talking about Dante. There is no record of what they discussed in particular, but they probably got a little further with their plan for a joint book. They may also have talked about the *Vita Nuova*, for Williams lent her his copy. From her later allusions to it, they seem to have speculated as to why Dante's wife did not accompany him into exile. "Too many children for her to trail round," was Dorothy's guess. The question continued to interest her.

She left Oxford on the 14th, by a train "which was already full in every part before it was entered by myself and about 200 other people"—a vivid reminder of what travelling was like in wartime. She arrived home with a bad cold and spent two days in bed with a temperature, reading Dante's *canzoni* and the *Vita Nuova*. This was her first introduction to Dante's minor works.

One of the mysteries of the *Vita Nuova* is Dante's reticence concerning the death of Beatrice. He relates that she died but gives no details as to the circumstances, saying that for him to speak further of it would be inappropriate since it is not connected with the subject of the book. Various theories have been put forward to account for this surprising remark, none of them conclusive.[12] In between "fits of dozing and waking up with a start," Dorothy pondered the problem: "It does look as though something at some time happened which isn't in the *Vita*—if only to explain the surprising amount of interest she [i.e., Beatrice] takes in him in the *Commedia* . . . which assumes a relationship of the most personal kind" (letter of 16 October 1944). What that relationship might have been continued to interest her.

As for Dante's *canzoni* (odes), she finds them elaborate, beautiful, nightmarish and strange. She is struck particularly by the poems of the Donna Pietra group (so called because they are inspired by an infatuation for a woman named Pietra), above all by the erotic one beginning "Così nel mio parlar voglio esser aspro [Now in my words I would be harsh]." They have been said to be about philosophy, but she is inclined to doubt that the language of this ode was learnt in the divinity schools.

Two days later, on 18 October, she has looked up *The Figure of Beatrice* and found that Williams, too, doubts that this ode is about philosophy. This reinforces her belief that it is about physical love or "that, at any rate, its language derives from some experience of that activity." Her mind goes back to something she noticed about Dante from the beginning—his lack of constraint in regard to women, something she found lacking in Milton: "I do find in Milton (and C. S. Lewis can trounce me if he likes for this 'personal heresy') a certain discomfort about sex which imparts a discomfort to me. . . . I do not find this in Dante." In this view of Milton she may have been influenced by Robert Graves' historical novel, *Wife to Mr. Milton*, which was published in 1942. It is at any rate a view which she continued to hold, and later developed at some length.

Her discovery of the erotic ode, "Così nel mio parlar . . . ," confirmed her intuition of what Dante may have been like as a man. In a mock disputation, entitled "Bedworthiness," she conducts, as for a mediaeval Court of Love, a defence of Dante Alighieri as a sexual partner, "all glosses, intellectualisations and protestations notwithstanding." The evidence on which she bases her defence is the ode in question. The poet, as lover, after describing his sufferings as a result of his lady's coldness, imagines how he would act if she were to long for him as he for her. Seizing her golden hair which has so tormented him, he would be like a bear at play. Taking his revenge, he would dally, gazing into the eyes that have inflamed his heart. Then he would grant her peace with love.

The poem has been cited as indicating a streak of cruelty in Dante's nature. The most vehement expression of this view is to be found in

Giovanni Papini's *Dante Vivo* [*Dante the Living Man*]: "I do not believe that in all the love-lyrics in the world, even in those inspired by anger, we could find the expression of desires as atrocious as those in [this] famous *canzone*. . . ."[13] Dorothy Sayers had been to London and had picked up an English translation of this work in the Charing Cross Road. She read it on the train going home to Witham. It exasperated her. It is true, she wrote to Williams, that Dante "observes that having got the lady by the short hairs he would abandon courtesy and play bears, but what is bed for, if not to play bears in? Nor, I fancy, is anybody's hair going to be pulled out by the roots—any violence employed will be of the most agreeable kind" (letter dated 18 October 1944). One line, in her opinion, lifts the whole imagined episode onto a plane of lyrical loveliness: "con esse passerei vespro e le squille [holding her tresses I would stay till vesper and the evening bell had tolled]." This, she says, conjures up "the slow, languorous, lovely sound of the evening bells coming up hour after hour through the open window from a long, sun-soaked valley." This is the "trick which counter-suggests all the clutchings and bears and revenges . . . and ties up with 'piacere' and 'pace' [pleasure and peace]." She was later to translate this and the other Pietra poems.[14] (These translations are printed as an Appendix to the present work.)

Papini also exasperated her because he expressed distaste at finding Beatrice placed so high in Dante's heaven, "almost a rival of the Virgin Mary." Seeking illumination on this, she consulted Williams on the matter in his *Figure of Beatrice* and found:

> The original Beatrician experience—the knowledge of the quality of love off-springing from the quality of Beatrice, and the quality of Beatrice off-springing from the quality of love . . . was felt at first to be a unique thing. . . . It is certain that many lovers have seen many ladies as Dante saw Beatrice. Dante's great gift to us was not the vision but the ratification, by his style, of the validity of the vision. . . . It is everyone's or it is no-one's. . . . (Pp. 47–48)

This passage is an example of Williams' idiosyncratic mode of expression and of the nature of the difficulties which the book presents to many readers. Eager to get at his meaning, Dorothy paraphrased the passage as follows:

That which to [Dante] has been the God-bearing image is seen (in that place which is beyond time and space) [near] to the factual God-bearer, because to him it is so. But suppose, say, Dante himself had been to some other person the revealing image—possibly, let us say, to the Lady at the Window—then in *her* "Commedia" would *he* have been seen in just that heavenly place? (I think that is what you mean?) If so, all this theological agitation means nothing; in each man's paradise his particular image, whoever it is, is for him next in derivation from the Images—it was so for him and he sees it so for ever.[15]

On 4 November Williams replied to four of her letters. He made no comment on Dante's prowess as a sexual partner. His concern was rather with that other aspect of Dante the lover: his vision of Beatrice in Paradise. To Dorothy's enquiry about this he wrote what is his most important and characteristic reply. Attempting to make his meaning clear (but not altogether succeeding), he referred to his doctrine of interchanged hierarchies, according to which

the Celestial Hierarchy of the Blessed is not one and fixed but multifold and ever substitionary. . . . Beatrice is, for her proper moment, and not only for Dante but for all heaven, in the glorious function of the revelation [close] to the B.V.M. (who is the steady point of the means of union of the flesh with the Divine Word), but so, in the continually changing glory, is everyone else.

Twenty-four years previously he had expressed the same doctrine in a poem, a copy of which he now encloses:

> And as each soul or song one moment gains,
>   Fronting Phoebean deity face to face,
> His central pause, the universal strains
> Prolong his notes around in harmony,
>   And the whole City, bowing toward his place,
> Reverberates his name eternally.
>
> For there in turn republican all are
>   Our masters and we theirs; so interchange
> The hierarchical degrees afar;
> Waxing and waning, dwindled or increased,
>   In order as in right, all spirits range
> The whole ascent, now topmost and now least.

And for good measure he sends her a copy of his article "A Dialogue on Hierarchy," published in *Time and Tide* (2 October 1943). Dorothy replied on 6 November, in a brisk, matter-of-fact tone:

> Yes; one would like to know how Dante appeared to Beatrice in the eternal mirror. I don't think he was to her what she was to him; apart from that mysterious remark about her death, there is no evidence that she ever really noticed Dante much. But somebody else may eternally see him in that place.

This possibility remained at the back of her mind and issued later in a remarkable work, which is discussed here in chapter 13.

So their letters continued, without, for the moment, any clear sense of direction as regards the joint book they proposed to write. Occasionally, not realizing how over-worked he was, she urged him to write her the promised letters on Milton. On 10 November, perhaps to spur him on, she gave him her views on Denis Saurat's *Milton, Man and Thinker*, which she had just been reading. There was no response from Williams.

Then on 7 December comes a hint that things have taken a new turn: "I have fallen into the clutches of a monster—not the Leopard, Lion or [Wolf] but the Great-great-grandfather of all Spiders, or possibly an Octopus. . . . Some day, may be, I will lay before you the web it has spun." That is to say, she has begun to translate the *Commedia*.

A few days before Christmas Charles Williams received an unusual present: the first five cantos of Dorothy's translation of *Inferno*, accompanied by "many good wishes, indeed, and with all affection—but with an abashed front." He was astonished; he was fascinated; and he was eager for her to continue: "Do! now; in the first rush. Consider that you have done five already out of the 100 and the very little extra work that finishes it. Return to this sort of thing from your popular wildernesses. . . . I wait with thrilling expectation for the next batch" (21 December 1944). On New Year's Day he wrote to encourage her again:

> It would be very extraordinary if you succeeded in exciting people about Dante, and I am not sure that it would not do as much in the matter of the Lay Apostolate as anything else. After all, the result of a few more people

getting the right side of Dante might easily be that some of them got the right side of that Christian religion to which he has been so pretentiously and pompously attached. The indirect approach is as fruitful generally as the direct.

He has by now read most of her translation but has not yet studied the notes. He hopes to write her a sonnet in the grand style to celebrate the commencement of her undertaking.

Later in January she sent him cantos VI–IX, but received no reply. Her secretary wrote to ask if they had arrived and he apologised in a hurried note on 17 February, saying he had received, and read, the cantos: "Obviously the Inferno is where I ought to be." But he said nothing about a tentative suggestion she had put to him: if she can find a publisher for her translation, would he be willing to provide the arguments and notes, as well as a simple kind of introduction and the explanations he would use for, "let us say, some of those intelligent London students of yours?"

When several weeks had gone by and still no answer had come, she thought it best to make tactful enquiries (she had to do so twice) through his son Michael. On 24 April Williams replied, again apologising. He has not written the sonnet he promised (nor the letters on Milton, though he does not mention these): "I seem to have lost my knack of writing sonnets in the Grand Style, and indeed in present conditions, apparently, of writing verse at all." And now his son has passed on to him the message that she is waiting for a reply to her suggestion. He thought he had already made it clear long since that he would be glad to write an introduction to her translation, or, as he put it with disarming modesty, "I should be very glad indeed to be allowed to write a short preliminary chat to your translation if you did me the honour of asking me. You should tell me any points that you would particularly like brought out, and I will bring them out with enthusiasm."

This gave her the encouragement she needed. It dispelled a gnawing doubt that his silence betokened a withdrawal. Trusting that this was not the case, she had already been to see the editor of the newly launched Penguin Classics, Dr. E. V. Rieu, who had started the series off with his own prose rendering of the *Odyssey*. In March she had taken to his house in Highgate her translation of the first thirteen

E. V. Rieu, founder, editor, and translator
of Penguin Classics.

cantos of *Inferno* and read "great gobbets" aloud to him "over the
tea-cups." She tells Williams all about it in her letter of 9 May, written in a mood of high excitement. Dr. Rieu liked the translation and
was prepared to sign a contract. They had discussed the introduction
and notes and whatever further explanations would be needed. Dorothy had said firmly that though she was prepared to write a translator's foreword she would need help with the notes and that "the
obvious person to do the introduction was Charles Williams, since
he was the only living person who really understood the allegory."
"But will anybody understand Mr. Williams?" asked Dr. Rieu, who
had evidently read *The Figure of Beatrice.*

Dorothy is convinced, however, that Williams is the best person to
explain to modern readers what the *Commedia* is about. The young
especially need an interpretation that is relevant to their souls *now,*

"not one that is swamped for them in 'the mediaeval outlook,' or the development of literary form, or the history of the 14th century." And she puts to him her specific requests: will he provide introductions dealing with allegory, suitable to be prefixed to *Hell, Purgatory* and *Paradise*? And will he help her with the arguments and notes?

> And when we have done all this—supposing we all live long enough—we shall have hurled Messer Dante Alighieri at the heads of a larger number of people, and worse equipped to receive the shock than have ever previously stood up simultaneously to such a bombardment in this, or probably any other, country!

In her exhilaration she has forgotten to comment on the fact that the war is over. She does so briefly in a postscript, and asks: "When does the Household of Caesar [i.e., the Oxford University Press] think of returning to the City?"

Six days later Charles Williams was dead.

4·

A Poem Which Tells
a Story

"Begin at the beginning," the King said gravely, "and go on till you come to
the end: then stop."

Lewis Carroll

It was a bombshell. The sudden death of a friend is sad enough.
Dorothy Sayers had lost not only a friend but also an inspiring companion, a partner in a daring new enterprise. Margaret Douglas, one
of Williams' Oxford acquaintances, informed her at once of his
death. Dorothy replied on 16 May:

> This is very grievous news. Charles Williams was unique in his work and
> his personality; there is nobody who can take his place. It comes as a great
> blow to me personally. I was very fond of him and proud of his friend-
> ship; and especially at this moment, the work I am trying to do owed so
> much to him and to his encouragement and inspiration that I feel as
> though the whole direction of it had been cut off.

There were many bomb sites in Britain in 1945 but the survivors
somehow pulled themselves together, cleared away the rubble, salvaged what they could and started to rebuild their lives. As Dorothy
Sayers gazed ruefully round upon her own personal bomb site, she
saw that not everything was lost. Nothing could replace Charles Williams, as she said, but there remained the letters they had exchanged,
there was the memory, all the more vivid now, of their talks about
Dante, and there was still *The Figure of Beatrice.*

She had by now translated seventeen cantos of *Inferno,* just one half
of the *cantica.* That was a beginning, but the thought of the introduction and the notes, now to be done on her own, must have been

daunting. No doubt she talked the matter over with her friends Muriel St. Clare Byrne and Marjorie Barber, on whose judgment and encouragement she had many times relied.[1] There was also Dr. Rieu, who had already said, "As for the Introduction, I had much rather have one by you than by Charles Williams, having heard you talking about Dante as you did. I feel you could tell people just what they should know when they start in on their reading."[2] We do not know how soon she decided to continue alone. Possibly the hesitation expressed in her letter to Margaret Douglas was not prolonged much beyond the initial shock and grief. The absorbing task of verse translation has therapeutic value.

Meanwhile there was another task to be undertaken. Immediately upon Williams' death his Oxford friends decided to bring out in his memory the *festschrift* they had planned to present to him on his return to London. C. S. Lewis was to edit it. He wrote at once to Dorothy Sayers to ask her to contribute. This suggests that he knew she had recently been in contact with Williams.

Here was the opportunity to do what Williams had asked. She would produce from her letters, not exactly the "Open Letter" he had urged, but an article written *for* him and thus indirectly *to* him. And there would be ample material left over for the pamphlet he had also hoped for, in which Methuen were interested; but that could wait. Accordingly, on 24 May, nine days after Williams' death, she replied to C. S. Lewis' invitation, offering to contribute an article on "the sheer technical achievement of the story-telling" of the *Divine Comedy*. She explains why this is what she wants to do and remarks that the subject will fit in well with material already offered: Tolkien's "On Fairy-Stories" and Lewis' own "On Stories" were two of the items. Here was something salvaged from the bomb site. It would be her first publication on Dante.[3]

It was assumed that the book would be published by the Oxford University Press, but, owing to a misunderstanding, Lewis thought that Sir Humphrey Milford, head of the press, was dragging his feet. On 30 June Lewis wrote to Dorothy Sayers:

I have written to Sir Humphrey Milford about the Charles Williams volume. . . . he replies expressing his willingness to publish: but apparently he imagines we propose to let him do so at our expense. I have replied explaining that we had no such idea—we are seeking no remuneration, and will make over royalties to Mrs. Williams. (You agree, I presume.) I wait to see if this will shame him into making an offer.

She exploded with indignation: "Good God Almighty! And Charles served that firm faithfully nearly all his life! Pay? Pay? PAY? . . . Most publishers would be pretty glad to have our names on their lists at any price" (3 July 1945). "That's the spirit!" replied C. S. Lewis. But on 4 July Sir Humphrey replied, "Good gracious no! You misunderstood my letter. 'Terms and prices' only meant a question of royalty and publication price. Of course I realise that you intended a book published at our expense, and that was what I meant too." Lewis sent this letter to Dorothy Sayers, adding a footnote to his own (dated 6 July): "Best quality sackcloth and ashes in sealed packets delivered in plain vans at moderate charges." To which she replied on July 7:

> My menu for tonight shall be:
> HUMBLE PIE
> IPSISSIMA VERBA
> with sharp sauce
> FRUITS
> meet for Repentance
>
> washed down with
> WATER OF AFFLICTION

The volume, *Essays Presented to Charles Williams*, was published in 1947. It contained only six articles, of which the one by Dorothy Sayers was the second longest, two of them being no more than seven and nine pages long. Lewis, writing to her on 29 December 1946, said of her contribution: "It is a stunning essay and will, by itself, make the book memorable." He gave it pride of place as the first in the volume.[4] It was entitled ". . . And Telling You a Story."

In *Gaudy Night* Harriet Vane and Miss de Vine walk together in the moonlight at Shrewsbury College. They are discussing the difficulty of recognizing what one really wants to do:

"One has to make some sort of choice," said Harriet. "And between one desire and another, how is one to know which things are really of overmastering importance?"

"We can only know that," said Miss de Vine, "when they have over-mastered us." (chapter 2)

Dorothy Sayers had been overmastered by Dante. Replying to Lewis, who had first asked her if she wished to contribute an article on one of her own novels, she said: "I am very much at the moment in the presence of a *deus fortior me.*"[5] Also, she preferred not to make a mental switch from the work she was then doing to something else, especially during a period when, "owing to tiredness, and pressure of domestic duties, and lack of secretarial help, it is difficult to do more than one thing at a time" (24 May 1945).

Despite these handicaps, her enthusiasm kept her at a high pitch of creative energy. On 3 July she wrote to say that her article was turning into a young volume "because I haven't written on the subject before, and the froth of excitement keeps boiling up and over-running the stew. But I hope in time to reduce it to reasonable proportions." She sent off the article in December, apologising for its length. Lewis did not find it unduly long. He suggested omitting an autobiographical section at the beginning, to which she readily agreed. She complied with other minor points which he raised, but on one she stuck to her guns. She had called Dante's style lucid, but in a letter of 18 December Lewis exclaimed, "Great Gods!! Yes, I know it is in *places*— but *lucid* just like that! Whose style would you call obscure I'd like to know?" To this she replied, six days later:

I think I *do* mean "lucid"—just like that. I don't think his *style* is obscure—indeed what stumps the translator at every turn is its heart-breaking simplicity. . . . You ask: whose style, then, would I call obscure? . . . Well: I think Blake's Prophetic Books are obscure, because they rest on a mythology and a symbolical vocabulary personal to himself. . . . I find *Taliessin Through Logres* rather obscure in the same way. . . . In another way, Browning's translation of the Agamemnon is obscure, because in his anxiety to be literal he has done such murder upon English syntax that you can't make anything of the English unless you already know the Greek . . . [Dante] is often difficult, but that's another matter. Just as Eddington on relativity is difficult but his style is perfectly lucid.[6]

T. S. Eliot also found Dante lucid: "The thought may be obscure but the word is lucid, or rather translucent."

The Sayers article, though written as a tribute to Charles Williams, in fact owes remarkably little to him. Her comments, drawn largely from her letters, are all her own. In the eight months since his death she had become more sure of herself. Her ideas had developed from eager first impressions to well-substantiated commentary; and she made several new points which go beyond the letters.

The most interesting of these is her description of what she calls "mirroring," a point on which Lewis commented with admiration. What is in question is a stylistic feature in Dante which almost, she says, defies analysis. The change in style between *Inferno*, *Purgatorio* and *Paradiso* "mirrors" the nature of the change in spiritual experience: "There is, rightly, a grossness in Hell, and, corresponding to it, there is a certain crowded and close-grained quality in the workmanship. But as the soul ascends Mount Purgatory, it strips off grossness . . ." (p. 28). The poetry produces this effect in two ways: by a direct and an indirect mirroring. The direct mirroring, noticeable especially in the first eight cantos of *Purgatorio*, involves an immediate change of landscape, atmosphere and colour. From the gateway to Purgatory onwards, the second, indirect mirroring occurs:

> It may perhaps be best expressed by saying that the poetic technique itself begins to strip off its adventitious aids. . . . Growing as a tree grows, organically, into self-contained shapeliness, it dispenses with exterior props, and the poem, like the pilgrim, is crowned and mitred over itself. (pp. 28–30)[7]

In *Paradiso* the style is "transhumanized," insofar as such a thing is possible in a narrative. Landscape vanishes. The whole outward aspect becomes light, motion, geometrical pattern. The human outline disappears. Souls become lights, known by their pulsating brilliance and by voice and word. Precision and particularity are still there but we are made aware of them, no longer through externals, but through primary forms. The souls are apprehended as intellectual beings: "as God is One with His word, so they in their degree are what they speak" (p. 30).

Another passage which Lewis admired in the article concerns the difference between Virgil's concept of the Elysian Fields and Dante's concept of Heaven. The lines from book VI of the *Aeneid* which describe the region where the heroes and sages of antiquity dwell are celebrated for their nostalgic beauty:

Here an ampler ether clothes the meads with roseate light, and they know their own sun, and stars of their own. Some disport their limbs on the grassy wrestling-ground, vie in sports, and grapple on the yellow sand; some trip it in the dance and chant songs. . . . Their lances stand fixed in the ground and their steeds, unyoked, browse freely over the plain.[8]

And yet, says Dorothy Sayers, if we look down on this scene from the height of Dante's Heaven,

we . . . recognize it for what it is. Beautiful and peaceful, pathetic and fatigued, "all passion spent," it is only the upper circle of an immense despair. The *ben dell'intelletto* [good of the intellect] is here not lost, but it is arrested in an interminable adolescence. The endless games, the shining phantom horses, the odes and the choric measures are touched with the eternal futility, the eternal melancholy of Hell. (pp. 32–33)

She was delighted by Lewis' approval of this passage:

And, yes! I *thought* perhaps you would like the part about looking down on the *inania regna* [empty kingdoms] from the Empyrean. That just happened. I mean I happened to read through the VIth *Aeneid* when I was rooting around *Paradiso* for something, and it really gave me a sort of shock, taking them one after the other like that . . . one takes the beauty of the Elysian Fields for granted, somehow; it's one of the world's purple passages and one doesn't question it . . . But coming to it from *Paradiso* was like stepping down suddenly onto a bottom step that wasn't there. I think it was those nostalgic horses that smote me in the midriff. (24 December 1945)

She was later to develop and deepen her views on the subject of Dante's Virgil. In this article she already begins to notice why Virgil does not enter Paradise and what Dante means by this exclusion. Williams had prepared her mind for this in *The Figure of Beatrice*, as she acknowledges in a footnote: "Dante, as Charles Williams pointed

out, could not have let Virgil and the other great pagans into the
Christian heaven without making nonsense of their work: 'We have
more tenderness for them, but Dante had more honour.' "[9] With
acute alertness she notes that Dante pays a last tribute to Virgil towards the end of *Paradiso*. The earlier tributes are well known and
have been much quoted: the reverence paid by the four poets in the
first circle of *Inferno*, by Sordello and by Statius on Mount Purgatory,
the quotations from the *Aeneid* in the Earthly Paradise, the reference
to our "major musa" in the colloquy with Cacciaguida in the Heaven
of Mars. But Dorothy Sayers finds one more tribute: "By a touching
and beautiful act of piety he has taken Virgil's simile of the bees
visiting the flowers and transplanted it from the Elysian Fields to the
Empyrean itself" (p. 33, n.1). Virgil's lines are:

> ac veluti in pratis ubi apes aestate serena
> floribus insidiunt variis et candida circum
> lilia funduntur, strepit omnis murmure campus.

[even as when, in the meadows, in cloudless summertime, bees light on
many-hued blossoms and stream round lustrous lilies and all the fields
murmur with the humming] (VI, 707–9)

In Dante's *Paradiso* they become:

> sì come schiera d'ape, che s'infiora
>   una fiata e una si ritorna
>   là dove suo laboro s'insapora,
> nel gran fior discendeva che s'adorna
>   di tante foglie, e quindi risaliva
>   là dove 'l suo amor sempre soggiorna.

[As bees ply back and forth, now in the flowers
  busying themselves, and now intent to wend
  where all their toil is turned to sweetest stores,
so did the host of Angels now descend
  amid the Flower of the countless leaves,
  now rise to where their love dwells without end.]
(XXXI, 7–12)

This echo of Virgil may have been noticed before, but it is unlikely to
have been glossed so movingly as in this unassuming footnote: "So

long as poetry endures, one image of Virgil is established in that place where Beatrice, according to her promise, many a time speaks Virgil's praises to her Saviour.''

As she had told Williams, what surprised her first of all about Dante was the absence of the grand manner. The poem begins, she remarks, ''not like an epic but with the disarming simplicity of a ballad or a romance or a fairy-tale.'' Dante's debt to the classical writers has often been pointed out and he himself acknowledged it. She points to another, unacknowledged debt: to the romance writers of the northern tradition, whom he had also read, to stories of the achievement of a lady by means of an other-world journey.

She is amazed, too, by the poem's structure, knowing well enough, as she did from her studies at Oxford, ''the rambling and disjointed habits of the average mediaeval writer.'' Considering the mixture of elements which compose it, one would have expected the poet to choose a flexible construction which would admit as much variety and impose as little constraint as possible. But no, Dante ''deliberately chose for his material the most rigid form conceivable, because he was a superb story-teller and knew . . . that if you want the reader not only to follow but to accept and believe a tale of marvels, you can do it best by the accumulation of precise and even prosaic detail'' (p. 7). It is a story of adventure and, like all good stories of adventure, it exercises a spell by a special technique, ''the trick—and to some minds the scandal—of particularity'' (p. 10). Scandal or no, the particularity adds to the poetry a vivid conviction of fact. We know that the Inferno is there, just as, for the same reason, we believe in Robinson Crusoe's island. Macaulay had also pointed out that there is in Dante's Hell

the strongest air of veracity, with a sobriety even in its horrors, with the greatest precision and multiplicity of its details. . . . He is the very man who has heard the tormented spirits crying out for the second death, who has read the dusky characters on the portal within which there is no hope, who has hidden his face from the terrors of the Gorgon, who has fled from the hooks and the seething pitch of Barbariccia and Draghignazzo.[10]

This is true, Dorothy Sayers comments, but adds, characteristically, that it is not only Dante who has experienced all this. We too have been there with him and "can scarcely free ourselves from a dreadful conviction that one day we might even *go* there."

Dante, she observes, could not only tell a tale. He could also create living characters. His allegory is not, like so many others, "populated by droves of frigid abstractions and perambulating labels." Instead, he filled his poem with real people who do not cease to be themselves even though they symbolize or instance sins and virtues. One of the most compelling characters in the story is Dante himself, conceived, as she said to Williams, in a delicate spirit of comedy, "a brilliant expedient for which he has never . . . been given sufficient credit." By this means the narrator is prevented from becoming a self-glorifying bore, or else a mirror for fleeting impressions.

It took her eight months to write the article, to bring under control the "ebbrezza" with which the poem filled her. It comprises almost all that she had said in her letters. It also contains in essence a great deal of what she was later to develop in her lectures.

Dorothy Sayers' first public lecture on Dante was delivered in Cambridge in August 1946, at the invitation of the Society for Italian Studies. A committee had been set up to organize a summer school of Italian and accommodation had been secured at Jesus College. The chairman was Dr. George Purkis, head of Modern Languages at Colchester Royal Grammar School. I was then a lecturer in Italian at Cambridge University and the organizing secretary of the summer school. A meeting was held in London in the spring of 1946 to plan the lecture programme. The Williams *festschrift* had not yet been published, and the only member of the committee who knew anything about Dorothy Sayers' interest in Dante was Dr. Purkis; he happened to see an advance notice of her translation of the *Commedia* on the back of John Butt's translation of Voltaire's *Candide* (no. 4 in the series of Penguin Classics), which he had brought along to read on the train. "Why not invite Dorothy Sayers to lecture on Dante?" he suggested. "She'd be a draw." There was a stunned silence. The Cambridge professor, E. R. Vincent, looked dubious. "She can't do any harm, I suppose," he said gloomily.

So Dr. Purkis wrote to her, and she agreed to lecture. She offered a literary analysis of a single canto, something she had told Lewis she had in mind to do and which she had offered him as an alternative for the memorial volume. Advertisements of the summer school met with an unexpectedly good response. There were over six hundred applications for a maximum of two hundred places. On the evening of the Sayers lecture, 20 August, an additional hundred or so Cambridge residents had taken tickets, and the dining hall of Jesus College, where the lectures were held, was packed. The title of her lecture was "The Eighth Bolgia (*Inferno* XXVI): A Study in the Craft of Story-telling."

The canto of *Inferno* she had chosen is the famous canto of Ulysses. She had asked for it to be read aloud in Italian as a prelude. This responsibility was entrusted to Roberto Weiss, an Italian scholar learned in Renaissance studies, later professor at University College, London. Weiss bore a certain resemblance to Charlie Chaplin, though not in his ability to hold an audience. Dorothy Sayers, in a shimmering evening gown of silver lamé, stood on the dais of the high table which served as a platform, looking sibylline and majestic. Her chin supported on her elbow which rested on the reading desk, she gazed down expectantly at the little figure who seemed several yards below her. In a low voice, scarcely adequate for an audience of thirty let alone three hundred, he mumbled his way through the magnificent canto in a dreary monotone. Dorothy Sayers' face gave nothing away, though she must have been disconcerted by so dismal a performance. In fact, nothing could have served as a better foil to her own. The inaudible reader subsided into his seat and she began, "The *Divine Comedy*—and let us not forget it—is a poem which tells a story."

I was a young lecturer, eager to learn from my seniors, though it was not often I found them inspiring. As a student in Perugia I had heard the great Luigi Pietrobono lecture on Dante. Now, more than fifty years later, I can still remember his lovely reading of the line in canto I of *Purgatorio*, where Cato speaks of the water lapping at the foot of the mountain: "laggiù colà dove la batte l'onda [down there below where the sea belabours it]," his voice lingering on the liquid l's. But such moments had been rare. The famous English Dantists, Moore, Toynbee, Wicksteed, were dead. As a student at University College, London, I had been too young to hear Edmund Gardner, though I knew his works. The commentaries which accompany John

D. Sinclair's prose translation of the *Commedia* were models of excellence; and T. S. Eliot's essays on Dante were memorable. I had heard one outstanding lecture in January 1946, given at the British Academy by the Cambridge professor, E. R. Vincent. After six years of absence on war service he had reread the *Commedia* in the light of recent world events: the perspective revealed Dante as a living power. But on the whole it was a thin period, and I took my seat that evening not expecting anything out of the ordinary. I was mistaken.

Rereading her lecture now, I can see in it all the signs of a critical response which was to make Dante come alive for millions of readers of the Penguin Classics translation. At the time I knew only that I was listening to the most enjoyable lecture I had ever heard. Professionally it was impeccable. Every word was audible—quite a feat in itself in a hall not designed for public speaking. The style, appropriate to the audience, ranged from the informal and entertaining to the grave and impressive. Her powers of expression, understandably more skilled than those of the average academic lecturer, held us spellbound. But it was more than a question of handling words with skill: she had original and challenging things to say.

There are three cantos in *Inferno* which most people remember if they know anything about Dante at all: canto V, in which Francesca tells the story of her love for Paolo and of their murder by her husband; canto XXXIII, containing the story of Ugolino's death by starvation with his sons and grandsons in the tower; and canto XXVI, which contains the story of Ulysses. This for many readers is the most memorable of all. It was bold, therefore, to undertake to say something new about a canto so well known.

In Homer's *Odyssey*, Odysseus, after long years of wandering since the fall of Troy, returns home to Ithaca, slays the suitors of Penelope and resumes his royal duties. In Dante's *Inferno* we find him in the eighth ditch (*bolgia*) of the eighth circle among the Counsellors of Fraud, enveloped in a flame of fire, together with his associate Diomedes. At Virgil's command he tells the story of his last voyage, in which we learn to our surprise that he did not return to Ithaca but, on leaving Circe, set off with a depleted but loyal crew on a far journey, in which they perished.

Dante saw in the Ulysses story an image of man's restless pursuit of

knowledge, of an insatiable urge at whatever cost to explore the unknown. The poet recognized the nobility of such desire and acknowledged the temptation which it also had for him, but he saw its
dangers. His Ulysses is heroic, a compelling leader of men, but his
voyage is doomed. Forever damned and unrepentant still, Ulysses
proudly recites the speech by which he urged his crew to venture
beyond the Pillars of Hercules and into the forbidden waters of the
southern hemisphere, until at last they came within sight of a dark
mountain, higher than they had ever seen. A storm sprang up, whirl-
ing the vessel three times round; the prow went down, the sea closed
over them. The tale is told.

There have been many commentaries on this canto: allegorical,
theological, scholarly, literary, poetic. Tennyson composed a descant
upon it, seeing only noble courage in Ulysses' adventure, being
wholly taken in by the persuasive words to his crew:

> Considerate la vostra semenza.
>   Fatti non foste a viver come bruti,
>   ma per seguir virtute e conoscenza.

> [Think of your breed; for brutish ignorance
> Your mettle was not made; you were made men
> To follow after knowledge and excellence.]
>   (XVI, 118–20)

What Dorothy Sayers brought to the story was the *writer's* eye.
This above all made the lecture so striking. As though watching
Dante at work she showed how he achieved his effects. Why does he
begin the canto with a desolate, ironic cry against Florence? Because
he needs to set the scale and tone for what is to follow. But he also
needs to make us visualize *him* in order to get the action moving. So,
after the great image of wings beating over land and sea, Dante proph-
esies the doom of Florence and speaks of his own grief. He has now
got us looking at him, and at Virgil, who rouses him from his meditation and leads the way among the crags and boulders of Malebolge,
"the grim grey funnel of stone . . . carved in the eternal rock and
bridged by the colossal spurs, like the spokes of a cartwheel, along
which Dante and Virgil, and we with them, have painfully clambered

upon our perilous journey." In this three-dimensional description, which produces an illusion of physical participation, the key words are "and we with them" and "*our* perilous journey."

After the serene and lovely simile of the valley lit by fire-flies, which lifts us out of Hell for a timeless moment to an Italian hillside, Dante returns us to the eighth *bolgia* and we see the flames which flicker along its depth. We see them at the same moment as Dante, when we see *him* standing up dangerously on the bridge to peer down at them, so that, he says, "if I had not clung to a piece of rock I'd have gone over without being pushed." A nerve-wracking moment for Virgil, Dorothy Sayers observes as an aside, wondering if anyone has ever considered the journey from Virgil's point of view. It is the writer in her who wonders that.

Then came the most original contribution of the evening. When Dante learns that in one of the flames are the souls of Ulysses and Diomedes, he begs eagerly to be allowed to hear them speak. Virgil, as though pushing Dante to one side, says, "Let *me* address them, for they were Greeks and might despise your words." Why does Virgil say that? The question has puzzled commentators for centuries. Dante, being Italian, was a descendant of the defeated Trojans; but so was Virgil, being a Roman. But Virgil has sung of the Greek heroes in his poem, and he urges this as a claim on them. Yet there is more to it than that. Looking at it from the technical angle of a story-teller, Dorothy Sayers entered the workshop, so to speak, and saw what the craftsman was about.

In the story Virgil is already established as having special powers. He is engaged on a Heaven-sent mission. To overcome Charon and Minos, who challenged Dante's progress, he relied on words of power:

> vuolsi così colà dove si puote
> ciò che si vuole, e più non dimandare.
>
> [. . . thus it is willed where power
> and will are one; enough; ask thou no more.][11]

Further, as a man of the Middle Ages, Dante believed that Virgil was a white magician. He could command spirits. "Where Dante could only request, Virgil could compel them to speak." And, using his special power, he does so.

"I heard him speak," says Dante, "*in questa forma.*" These three words have usually been taken to mean "in this manner" or "with these words." But, said Dorothy Sayers, it is specifically "with this *form* of words," and what follows is a formal conjuration, consisting of an obsecration twice repeated, followed by the command: "Stand; speak." This is confirmed at the beginning of the next canto, where Virgil dismisses the flame, which cannot move until Virgil gives it his permission, the "licenza," the licence to depart: "Issa ten va; più non t'adizzo [Depart now; I vex thee no further]."

No one had spotted this before, not even Domenico Comparetti, the author of *Virgilio nel Medioevo*, who in fact denies that Virgil is shown to have magical powers in the *Commedia*.[12] Like all long-awaited solutions, it is obvious once it has been pointed out. Asked whether she had read Comparetti, Dorothy Sayers calmly replied. "No, I consulted a trained exorcist."

Here, I decided, was somebody I must get to know.

5.

NOT SO MUCH A PENGUIN, MORE A PHOENIX

. . . the phoenix dies and is then reborn.
Inferno XXIV, 107

It took a little time. The first thing to do was to make sure that Dorothy Sayers was invited to lecture at the next summer school. There was no difficulty about that. The organizers knew they were on to a good thing. She agreed to give two lectures in August 1947: "Dante's Imagery: Symbolic" and "Dante's Imagery: Pictorial."[1] From then on she was a regular feature on the summer school programme and could be relied on to draw a large audience.

I ventured to write to her, following up a tentative point I had made in conversation. She replied at once: "Now we're off! It's absolutely fatal to encourage me to write letters about Dante." The correspondence flourished. She quite often visited Cambridge, to address the University Italian Society and other literary groups. Before long she made it a habit to come to tea with me beforehand.

In the Cambridge of that period no woman, however distinguished, could be wined and dined or accommodated overnight at any of the men's colleges. The Professor of Italian, who was a Fellow of Corpus Christi College, gave a dinner in her honour once or twice in his private rooms, but what he could do for her socially was limited compared with what would have been possible had she been a man. As things turned out, this proved to be my good fortune.

After her lectures to undergraduates, which I always attended, discussion used to continue in the lounge of the hotel where she was staying. But conversation soon petered out in such impersonal surroundings. At last I plucked up courage and asked her if next time she would care to stay with me and my family. We lived in a somewhat ramshackle flat in the centre of Cambridge, opposite St. John's College, and I felt a little diffident about inviting her to say there. She replied, "I'd simply love to!" Thus it came about that we got to know each other well.

My husband, Lewis Thorpe, the Arthurian scholar already mentioned, who became Professor of French at Nottingham University, greatly enjoyed her company, and they held long discussions about Old French literature. We were her guests one year at the Detection Club dinner, held in London at the Café Royal, during the period when she was president. She took an affectionate interest in our two children, Adrian and Kerstin, remembering them at Christmas and birthdays and enquiring after their progress. When Kerstin at age seven had to undergo an operation for appendicitis, Dorothy wrote her a delightful letter and continued to show concern for her convalescence. Both children were quite at ease with this large, affable, famous person, who never talked down to them and who answered their questions with grave courtesy. They wrote letters to her and sent her their poems, which she kept. She was rather like an honorary aunt. Altogether, the hurlyburly of our family life seemed to amuse her and on some occasions she stayed with us for several days. Conversation about Dante usually went on into the small hours, to be continued the following morning over a late breakfast of bacon and eggs after the children had been got off to school.

"You don't write stories by talking about them," said Harriet Vane.[2] But for Harriet's creator writing was a shared activity. I used to think that her letters and conversation about Dante were by-products of her work. I now realize that it was the other way round: they contributed to the writing process and were part of it. She had always enjoyed sharing her ideas and they gained from being communicated. The Mutual Admiration Society which she and her friends had formed at Oxford[3] had provided creative stimulus, just as the Inklings group did for *its* members. Her outpourings about Dante to Williams, exceptional perhaps in their exuberance, were otherwise characteristic. Some writers prefer the privacy of a literary diary. Dorothy found this useful, too, but in her case it served a different purpose. The jottings in her Dante notebooks are mainly records of books read and passages noted. Here and there an idea is developed, but the impetus is less dynamic, the tone less eager, than when she is writing to a friend. Time and again, books, articles and lectures can be seen emerging from her letters. In a sense, her correspondents and those with whom she conversed about her projects were fellow workers. To my delight I found myself admitted to this creative circle.

One of her earliest listener-collaborators on Dante was Marjorie Barber.[4] She was at Somerville when Dorothy, already a graduate, was working for Basil Blackwell in Oxford. "Bar," as her friends called her, taught English at South Hampstead Girls' High School. She had learned Italian (though not as part of her degree course), but had not read Dante. In 1944 Dorothy invited her to spend Christmas with her and her husband "Mac" (Atherton Fleming) in their house in Witham, Essex. As a Christmas present Dorothy gave her a copy of *The Figure of Beatrice*, put a copy of *Inferno* and Laurence Binyon's translation of it into her hands and left her to read while she herself got on with cooking the Christmas dinner. Dorothy's "Dante mania," as she herself called it, had then been going strong for five months. It does not take much imagination to guess what subject dominated the conversation that Christmas at 24 Newland Street. Poor Mac must have had a boring time of it. "Look here, what *is* all this about Dante?" he once asked in exasperation, on seeing his wife with a copy of *Inferno* in one hand while she stirred a sauce with the other.[5]

Bar's reaction to Dante was similar to Dorothy's. Remarking first that his Italian was "lovely" and Binyon's English "stodgy," she expressed surprise at finding the style of the original so simple and direct. We can reconstruct some of their conversation, for Bar's very words are quoted at the beginning of the article that eventually evolved for the Williams *festschrift*:

> "It isn't at all what I expected," said the friend whom I had persuaded into having a go at the *Divine Comedy*; "I thought it would be all grand and solemn—you know—'Of Man's First Disobedience and the Fruit of that Forbidden Tree . . . Sing, Heavenly Muse,' that sort of thing. But it's like someone sitting there in an arm-chair and telling you a story."

Here is an example of a conversation leading to the written word. The casual remark of a friend seems to Dorothy to go to the root of the matter and it becomes the title of an article. From one of her letters to Williams we learn also that Bar commented "spontaneously" (presumably without being prompted by the eager, talkative Dorothy) on the simplicity of Dante's similes. She also said, "One's got to remember that the words with Latin roots, which for us are mostly 'noble' language, aren't that for the Italians—they're just common speech" (January 1945). This was an acute observation, which Dorothy bore in mind.

We know also that Dorothy and Bar discussed the difference between Dante and Milton. Bar knew Milton well and had "an especial reverence" for him. It was not only that the styles of the two poets were so different: they imagined very different Hells: "Even in damnation, Milton's devils can *do* something—dig for metals, build a palace, make a causeway over Chaos; but here [in Dante's Hell] there is only incessant restlessness without change. . . . The place is evil, with an evil stripped of its last shred of glitter" (" . . . And Telling You a Story," p. 13). "It is extraordinary," said Bar on arriving at the bottom of the eighth circle (that is, the tenth ditch or *bolgia*, where the Falsifiers sprawl in their repulsive afflictions), "when you look back from here, the upper part of Hell seems almost gay by comparison, with its rivers and cities and picturesque monsters." Dorothy's ready reply has become part of the same article: "The disappearance of ornament has much to do with this, by negative suggestion; and so also has the mere looking back—the looking *up* the four thousand miles of that colossal shaft." This has her very voice in it.

Christmas was over. Bar had gone back to London where she shared a house with Muriel St. Clare Byrne in St. John's Wood Terrace. She had resumed her teaching. Did she bring Dante into her lessons, one wonders? It seems likely, at least for the sixth-form pupils. Early in the New Year Dorothy went to London, where she still kept on her flat at 24 Great James Street. She called on Muriel and Bar and conversation about Dante continued. By the end of March of that year she had finished translating thirteen cantos.

It may have been Muriel who first told Dr. Rieu that her friend was translating Dante. Before he took on the task of editing the Penguin Classics he had been a member of the board of Methuen. Muriel had contacts with this publishing firm, but so had Dorothy, who might therefore have approached Rieu herself. However it may have been, he wrote on 8 March, expressing surprise to hear what she was doing and asking to see the result. She replied on the 12th, enclosing thirteen cantos and asking if she might visit him in his house in Highgate and read some of her translation aloud to him. "Miss Byrne and Miss Barber have endured this ordeal and still live." In the meantime she asks him to look at Binyon's translation. Her own, she considers, is much livelier. Binyon and other translators have, in her opinion, "far, far too much reverence for their author. . . . They insist on being noble and they end by being prim. But prim is the one thing Dante never is. . . ."

Dr. Rieu agreed to her suggestion and Dorothy set off to visit him, armed with her copy of the cantos. We have had her account of the event, as related to Williams. Here is Rieu's, as related to Betty Radice, who was to succeed him as editor of the Penguin Classics: "Dorothy Sayers had arrived in Highgate for lunch with her script of Dante, stayed to tea and then to dinner, still talking, and 'just when we were about to offer her bed and breakfast said she must go.' "[6] She left the thirteen cantos with him. He returned them to her on 8 April, saying:

> Now that I have had time to read your *Inferno*, I have no hesitation in repeating the admiration I expressed when you read it to us. It is full of fire, swift movement, poetry and vigour, and, above all, for my purpose, it is clear. . . . I have great pleasure in accepting your offer to translate the *Divine Comedy* for my series of Penguin Classics.

Since he had previously made up his mind that it should be translated into prose, his ready acceptance of a version in *terza rima* (triple rhyme) is the more remarkable.

In her first letter to him she had explained her reasons for sticking to the original rhyme scheme. It is the only form, she said, which can provide "the extraordinary swing from the great pounding line to the colloquial chatter, which may occur, breathlessly, in two consecutive stanzas. . . . No other form can . . . get the wonderful forward drive . . . which moves like a flowing tide, each new stanza riding in on the other's back." Blank verse, she considered, was "the most hopeless of all the forms for Dante'' because it "has none of the movement, and it makes it far too easy to be literal and timid; so that all you get is something that might have been good prose if it hadn't been hammered and twisted into ten-syllable lines.''

She returned to the question two years later, on 12 December 1947, when she sent Rieu an article from *The Irish Press*. Advance publicity, especially the announcement that she was using *terza rima*, had set the alarm bells ringing. She commented:

> I do not understand this extraordinary superstition about the impossibility of writing English *terza rima*. Any kind of verse is difficult to write well; but why should one particular form be invested with this kind of almost numinous noli-me-tangere atmosphere? . . . It is much easier to write reasonably good *terza rima* than reasonably good blank verse; and the difficulty of the rhyme is not comparable to the Spenserian stanza and is certainly no greater than that of *ottava rima*.

The article had appeared on 30 October 1947. The author was Francis MacManus, novelist, essayist and biographer. He took the view that nobody, not Shakespeare himself, could translate Dante. Anyone who tries is doomed to failure. Dante's genius and the genius of Italian are foreign to English. As for *terza rima*, it has been the death-trap of translators:

> Why do they do it? What a scorn of his fallen predecessors must be innate unconsciously in every new translator! But what must be in himself urging him on as in a play of the fates to his doom? He is betrayed not so much by ambition in letters, by vainglory, pride, self-confidence and the urging of friends as by the fascinating simplicity of the original. It is an illusory simplicity.

Despite such heavy-handed disapproval, Rieu did not lose his nerve. He remained a staunch supporter and a friend. He visited her in Witham and, despite continuous conversation about Dante, seems to have got on well with Mac, who did not always take kindly to visitors. On 19 November 1948 Dorothy wrote, "My husband is always asking when you are coming down to see us again. Do come some time— we can easily put you up for the night.''

Shortly before the publication of *Hell*, in the autumn of 1949,

Rieu telephoned to talk about further advance publicity. She followed up the conversation by a letter, dated 9 September, feeling that she had not made herself sufficiently clear on the telephone about a matter which concerned her deeply. She hopes he will not stress that it was only recently that she "fell in love" with Dante: "If I have not long been a Dantist, I am at least a Romance linguist and, to some extent, a mediaevalist. I was a scholar of my college, I am a Master in my University; I took First Class Honours, and, was, after all, a scholar and a poet before I was anything else." Significantly she sends him a copy of her *Tristan in Brittany*.

Another early companion in her Dante adventure was Wilfrid Scott-Giles.[7] An expert in heraldry, he first wrote to her in February 1936 to say that in his opinion the arms of the Wimsey family (sable, three mice courant argent, with a domestic cat as crest and two Saracens as supporters) had the appearance of antiquity. In the interest of history should not an opportunity be found to explain that the arms were in fact ancestral, and only by chance reflected Lord Peter's criminological pursuits?

Dorothy, obviously delighted, replied in similar vein, providing in mock seriousness an explanation of the origin of the arms. A correspondence developed, in which the family history of the Wimseys was gradually "discovered." Scott-Giles specialised in the mediaeval ancestors and episodes, Dorothy in the Tudor period. An excellent draughtsman, he made drawings of the arms, of the monumental brass of Gerald 1st Baron Wimsey, of the effigy of the tomb of the fifth Baron and of his equestrian seal. Mrs. Scott-Giles, who was also an artist, contributed a charcoal drawing of Thomas, tenth Duke of Denver. W. J. Redhead, the architect who designed the church of Fenchurch St. Paul in *The Nine Tailors*, made a sketch of Bredon Hall, showing the features described by the diarist John Evelyn, a description found among his miscellaneous unpublished papers.

The circle of researchers grew. When, two months after his first letter, Scott-Giles was invited to lunch to meet Dorothy for the first time, Muriel St. Clare Byrne and the novelist Helen Simpson were also present. They too had been drawn into the game. By the end of 1936 the four of them had assembled enough material for a pamphlet, *Papers Relating to the Family of Wimsey*, which they sent to their

Wilfrid Scott-Giles about to address the
Confraternitas Historica on the history of
the Wimsey family.

friends for Christmas.[8] In March of the following year, Scott-Giles, who had studied history at Sidney Sussex College, Cambridge, arranged a meeting of the college history society, the Confraternitas Historica, a body still in existence today. Until recent times, members, known as fratres, attended meetings wearing dinner jackets. And "for difference," as Scott-Giles might have said, they sported red socks.

With the utmost solemnity, as befitted a society which took its ceremonies seriously, Mr. Scott-Giles, Miss St. Clare Byrne, Miss Helen Simpson and Miss Dorothy L. Sayers, in that order, read four learned papers on the history of the Wimsey family. Some of this material was later put to use in the novel, *Busman's Honeymoon* (an expanded version of the play), while an account of their joint creation was eventually assembled by Wilfrid Scott-Giles in his delightful book, *The Wimsey Family*.[9]

At the beginning of 1946 Dorothy met Scott-Giles again and discovered that he was also a Dante fan. On hearing of her new interest, he gave her a miniature copy of the *Divina Commedia*, for which she wrote to thank him on 11 January, saying that she had made "a little leather purse for the wee Dante." She at once enlisted his help as a historian: what is his opinion in the controversy about Hugh Capet in canto XX of *Purgatorio?* Is it Duke Hugh or his son, who later became king? The question is complicated and they exchanged letters about it, examining the evidence and weighing the possibility that Dante might have confused dates and personages.

As they had enjoyed spoof scholarship together, so now, entering on the real thing in her Dante studies, Dorothy looked confidently to her old friend to enjoy this with her, too. He did not disappoint her. By 23 January he had already offered to read her translation as she went along, comparing it with others. She accepted his offer with joy:

> Hurray! You're the very audience I want—one who will compare my attempts, not with Dante himself (there will be only too many who can do that, to see how far I fall short) but with other translations, to see whether I have done any better. What I feel that most of them miss is Dante's dash and drive and *fun*. He is so lively, and they tend to make him stiff and portentous.

She hopes that she may also turn to him for help with the historical notes: "Most Penguin readers will be very ignorant about the Middle Ages in Italy, and it's a question of telling them *enough* to make the poem comprehensible, without swamping them with historical details."

Just as she had always visualised the settings of her novels, whether imaginary or realistic, so now she visualises Dante's journey through Hell, not as though looking on from a distance but as though she were there beside him every twist of the way. In one of her early letters to Scott-Giles, dated 17 April 1936, she had written, "Being a novelist, I have to make a sort of three-dimensional moving picture of everything." Three-dimensional and moving describe exactly the kind of picture she imagined for herself of Dante's narrative.

A striking example is her visualisation of the eighth circle of Hell. Arriving at Malebolge (Evil Ditches, or Malbowges, as she translates it), Dante describes the general plan of this structure:

> Luogo è in inferno detto Malebolge,
>   tutto di pietra di color ferrigno,
>   come la cerchia che dintorno il volge.
> Nel dritto mezzo del campo maligno
>   vaneggia un pozzo assai largo e profondo,
>   di cui *suo loco* dicerò l'ordigno.
> Quel cinghio che rimane adunque è tondo
>   tra 'l pozzo e 'l piè dell'alta ripa dura,
>   e ha distinto in dieci valli il fondo.
> Quale, dove per guardia delle mura
>   più e più fossi cingon li castelli,
>   la parte dove son rende figura,
> tale imagine quivi facean quelli;
>   e come a tai fortezze da' lor sogli
>   alla ripa di fuor son ponticelli,
> così da imo della roccia scogli
>   movìen che ricidìen li argini e' fossi
>   infino al pozzo che i tronca e racco'gli.

Her translation of this passage is an example of her ability to see an entire structure, almost as though she were there, walking about on it. It is not just a question of translating words. She has rebuilt Malebolge in English so vividly that it seems almost tangible:

> There is in Hell a region that is called
>   Malbowges; it is all of iron-grey stone,
>   Like the huge barrier-rock with which it's walled.
> Plumb in the middle of the dreadful cone
>   There yawns a well, exceeding deep and wide,
>   Whose form and fashion shall be told anon.
> That which remains, then, of the foul Pit's side,
>   Between the well and the foot of the craggy steep,
>   Is a narrowing round, which ten great chasms divide.

As one may see the girding fosses deep
　Dug to defend a stronghold from the foe,
　Trench within trench about the castle-keep,
Such was the image here; and as men throw
　Their bridges outward from the fortress-wall,
　Crossing each moat to the far bank, just so
From the rock's base spring cliffs, spanning the fall
　Of dyke and ditch, to the central wall, whose rim
　Cuts short their passage and unites them all.

(XVIII, 1–18)

The first ditch of the eighth circle contains the souls of Panders and
Seducers, who circle in two columns, facing in opposite directions.
This arrangement, says Dante, is like the method of traffic control
adopted in Rome in the year of the Papal Jubilee (1300), when those
crossing the bridge to and from Castel Sant'Angelo were divided into
two columns, each facing the opposite way. Dorothy, writing to
Scott-Giles on 25 February 1946, commented:

> I always delight in that little passage in the *Inferno*. It's one of the (to me
> rather few) places where one is reminded how long ago Dante lived. His
> theology has become up-to-date again; and then in *Purgatorio* XVIII,
> where he talks about reason "holding the threshold of assent," one feels
> he might have been reading Freud; and as for the variegated barbarities,
> and the confused party-politics, and the search for a just world-power—
> the whole thing is so exactly like modern Europe that one expects an
> allusion to Marx any moment—just as his stuff about Nature and Art
> (i.e., Land and Labour) being the only sources of real wealth makes one
> think of asking him to come and address a meeting on world-economics.
> And then, quite suddenly, one finds him praising traffic-control as an
> absolutely new and brilliant idea, thought out by the Romans to cope
> with the unprecedented holiday rush, and one says, "Golly! between him
> and us there is, after all, a great gulf fixed!"

She goes on to discuss the advantage of the arrangement in the first
ditch of Malebolge from the point of view of the narrator and of the
reader. Dante and Virgil always turn to the left in Hell (with one
exception, in canto X) and it is stated pointedly that they do so here.
So it is obviously practical to make the two columns of sinners keep
to the right, and Dante makes it plain that they do. Dorothy comments:

Clearly, it is much better that, as they go along, they should meet and see the faces of the spirits nearest to them. Therefore these spirits *must* be going round on the right side of the ditch. Then Dante and Virgil can go up over the bridge and look down at the people coming the opposite way—because, as Virgil says: "You could not see them from the bank, since they were going in the same direction as ourselves." By the other arrangement, Dante and Virgil would have had to get to the bridge and go over it *before* recognizing or speaking to any of the shades, and this would have been rather uneconomical for the narrative—especially as this is the first *bolgia* they come to, and it is advisable to get the geography clear in an orderly way, bit by bit.

The "geography" of her own novels was always well planned. She therefore knew the hand of a master when she saw it.

Wilfrid Scott-Giles was at that time writing a book about roads, for which he had drawn a number of maps.[10] In the same letter in which she expresses admiration for Dante's traffic arrangements, she asks, "When you have finished your book on roads, would maps of Hell interest you? . . . It is so important to have somebody who not only can draw but has read the poem." He replied at once: what kind of maps would be required and how many? She soon got down to details. She has already tried her hand herself at a few diagrams, which she will bring to show him when they next meet. Hell, she finds, is by far the most difficult for readers to visualise. Friends who have seen her sketches (Muriel and Bar, no doubt) say they are helpful: "What my friends like most is a great vertical section of Hell (*very* ill executed) which if well executed would be good—but Hell is so awfully *deep* that I don't know if it could be got on to even a double-spread." And the publishers are not going to be able to afford that at a shilling a volume! In fact, it is not even certain at this stage that Penguins will be able to afford any diagrams at all.

There is no need, Dorothy thinks, to be exact about proportions. Dante probably did not intend to be particular to a few miles, though enormous ingenuity has been spent by commentators in making calculations: "What is the good of working out the precise foot-pound pressure on the walls of the cavity when the whole thing is, in any case, a vision?" What is essential is to make clear to the *imagination* the three deep descents: from the circles of Incontinence to the circles of Violence, down the Great Barrier to Malebolge, and down into the

Well of the Giants and the Ice. This is exactly what Scott-Giles represents in his section map of Hell.

Dorothy was dissatisfied with the map drawn by the Duke of Sermoneta, whose *Tavole Dantesche* were often reproduced.[11] It leaves out, she complained, the Vestibule of the Futile, puts Limbo on the wrong side of the river Acheron, which is shown as merely crossing the upper circles, whereas she was convinced that it flowed right round; and it fails to show that Dante and Virgil make a half circle through the river Phlegethon, from the deep end to the shallow. All these points are shown correctly in the diagrams drawn by Scott-Giles.

It will be difficult, they confess, as they continue to put their heads together, in restaurants, or at the Oxford and Cambridge Club, to make Malebolge comprehensible. What confuses people, Dorothy finds,

> is the way the bridges are carried on a great rocky spur *above* the level of the general slope of Hell,—and also the reason why, to descend *into* the ditches, Dante and Virgil always cross the bridge first and go down on the lower side. The minute you see it drawn—even out of scale—it's as plain as a pike-staff.[12]

Scott-Giles' first sketch of Upper Hell was sent off half way through March. In an undated letter Dorothy thanks him for it: "This looks lovely. . . . The style of the drawing seems to me just right—bold and clear, with enough pictorial quality to keep it interesting without being affectedly 'quaint.' "[13] She is especially taken with the little drawing of Charon in his boat on the river Acheron. She knows she is being greedy, but could little figures of Minos, Cerberus and Plutus be worked in as well? (Scott-Giles obliged in a revised sketch.) She is puzzled about the rivulet which encircles the Noble Castle in Limbo. What is it? Where does it come from? "It can't just be a circle of stagnant water, because Dante distinctly calls it a 'fiumicello [little stream]'; but one can't have a circular river just running round after its own tail!" She thinks, though Dante does not say so, that this must be the seventh of the classical rivers of the Underworld, Eridanus, which in book VI of the *Aeneid* runs through the Elysian Fields. This would then mean that all seven rivers of antiquity were present: Acheron, Eridanus, Styx, Phlegethon and Cocytus in the infernal

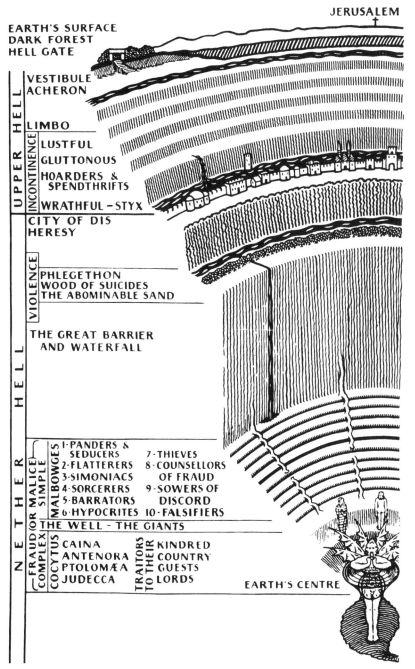

JERUSALEM

EARTH'S SURFACE
DARK FOREST
HELL GATE

UPPER HELL

VESTIBULE
ACHERON

LIMBO

INCONTINENCE

LUSTFUL
GLUTTONOUS
HOARDERS &
  SPENDTHRIFTS
WRATHFUL – STYX

CITY OF DIS
HERESY

VIOLENCE

PHLEGETHON
WOOD OF SUICIDES
THE ABOMINABLE SAND

THE GREAT BARRIER
  AND WATERFALL

NETHER HELL

FRAUD (OR MALICE)

SIMPLE

MALBOWGES

1·PANDERS &
    SEDUCERS
2·FLATTERERS
3·SIMONIACS
4·SORCERERS
5·BARRATORS
6·HYPOCRITES

7·THIEVES
8·COUNSELLORS
    OF FRAUD
9·SOWERS OF
    DISCORD
10·FALSIFIERS

COMPLEX

THE WELL – THE GIANTS

COCYTUS

CAINA
ANTENORA
PTOLOMÆA
JUDECCA

TRAITORS TO THEIR

KINDRED
COUNTRY
GUESTS
LORDS

EARTH'S CENTRE

Section map of Hell. Drawn by Wilfrid Scott-Giles.

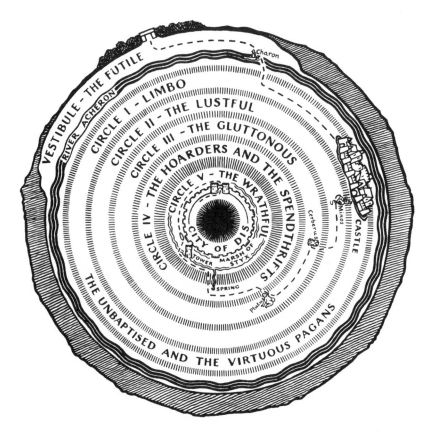

Diagram of Upper Hell—the Sins of the Leopard. Drawn by Wilfrid Scott-Giles.

regions, with Lethe and Eunoë in Purgatory. Eridanus must branch off from Acheron at some point, probably as an effluent or backwater: "After moating the Castle, it runs away either overground or underground, across the next three circles until it falls into the Styx." From the sketch of the castle ringed by the stream "we can easily suppose that it forks out of Acheron somewhere behind the square keep in the middle."

By 26 March she has received the first diagram of Nether Hell, showing the route of the poets from inside the walls of Dis to the Great Barrier. She is delighted with this, too: "Yes, indeed! this is a lovely one—extremely decorative; and that feel of slithering down

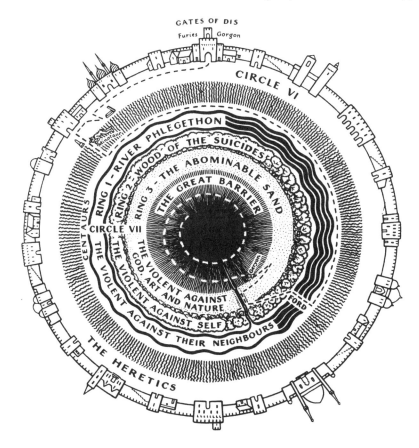

Diagram of Nether Hell, Circles vi and vii—the Sins of the Lion. Drawn by Wilfrid Scott-Giles.

the hole in the middle is just what I wanted to get." The walls of the City of Dis are lined with intriguing buildings, some of which might be understood to serve as taverns or public conveniences. (This was Scott-Giles' suggestion.) She replied:

I greatly appreciate your thought for the welfare of the inhabitants of Dis. At the pub, I fear, there can be but little good fellowship, and no questions asked but "What's your poison?" I don't know whether, strictly speaking, demons require a public convenience; but it occurs to me that this is perhaps the place where the "human ordure" mentioned in Bowge

3 is collected and dispatched by an underground sewer for the better immersion of Flatterers!

The tomb of Farinata, with its raised lid, is shown, as well as the vault of Pope Anastasius, behind which the poets sit to accustom themselves to the stench which rises from Nether Hell. There is a tiny sketch of the Minotaur, and Geryon clings to the edge of the Great Barrier between the seventh and the eighth circle.

There remained Malebolge and the Well of the Giants. How many lines of bridges cross the eighth circle? Dante does not specify. The Duke of Sermoneta's map shows nine. Scott-Giles settled for seven. What about the bridges over the sixth bolgia? Are they all broken? Again Dante does not specify. Dorothy thinks they are, since Malacoda's deception of Virgil has more point if so: there is then *no* bridge by which he and Dante can cross over and the escort of demons offered by Malacoda is no safe conduct at all. That is why Virgil is so angry. (Anyone wishing to read this exciting episode will find it in cantos XXI–XXIII of *Inferno*, pp. 201–14 of the Sayers Penguin translation.)

The diagram of Malebolge arrived at the beginning of April. This, too, met with Dorothy's entire approval. It was above all *clear*. Unfortunately, she is obliged to ask for an alteration in the lettering. The eighth bolgia (which was to be the subject of her lecture in Cambridge in August of that year) contains the souls of the Evil or False Counsellors:

> I have—stupidly—followed other commentators in describing the sinners in bowge 8 as "Givers of Fraudulent Counsel." Thinking it over, I believe that is a little misleading—it sounds as though they were deceiving the people to whom they gave the counsel. The right title is, I now think, "Counsellors of Fraud"—i.e., they did not deceive the people whom they counselled, but counselled *them* to deceive others. The point is subtle, but it seems important.

The alteration in the lettering was duly made.

In her lecture "The Eighth Bolgia" she referred to the souls contained in it as "the men who counselled fraud." In her note to canto XXVI in her translation she is more explicit: "The sinners in Bowge

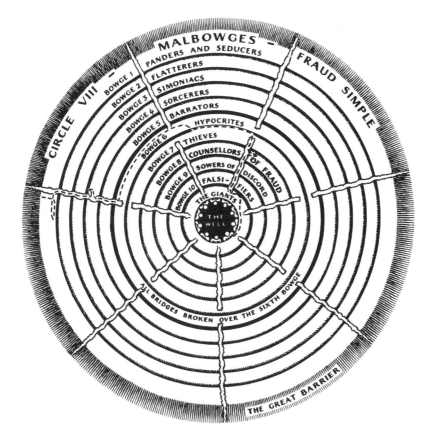

Diagram of Nether Hell, Circle viii. Drawn by Wilfrid Scott-Giles. "There is in Hell a region that is called Malbowges . . . " (Canto XVIII, 1–2).

VIII are not men who deceived those whom they counselled, but men who counselled others to practise fraud."[14]

Next, the Well of the Giants. This presented problems. How many giants are there? Six are mentioned by name: Nimrod, Ephialtes, Antaeus, Typhon, Tityus and Briareus. Probably all the Titans are there, but that would be a tall order in every sense! The real difficulty, however, was that Dante appeared to have been inconsistent as regards measurements: "Ah, yes, now we really are up against trouble, and not (I fear) of our making. Dante has been naughty, and made an inconsistency, hoping that nobody would notice." In canto XVIII of

Inferno, line 5, Dante says that the Well is "assai largo e profondo [very wide and deep]." In canto XXXI, lines 31–33, Virgil tells Dante that the giants stand round the well, the bank of which conceals them from the navel downwards. Nimrod, it has been calculated, is sixty feet high. If his feet are on the bottom of the well, it is only about thirty feet deep. In the same canto, lines 136–38, Dante says that Antaeus bending towards him to take him up in his hand looked like Carisenda, the tower in Bologna, when a cloud passes across it; and at the beginning of the canto he had said that the giants seen in the distance looked like towers. Both these allusions suggest a height of more than thirty feet.

At the beginning of canto XXXIII, Dante speaks of himself and Virgil:

> Come noi fummo giù nel pozzo scuro
> sotto i piè del gigante assai più bassi.

> [When we were down in the deep of the darkling well,
> Under the feet of the giant and yet more low . . .]
>
> (16–17)

From this Dorothy concludes that there must have been a ledge on which the giants stood, and that this was some way above the bottom of the well. On what, then, did Antaeus set Dante down? "I think that, after the top part of the Well, which was a smooth shaft, there must have been a longish climb down a *rough*-sided shaft, and that Dante went down backwards (as you go down a ladder) till he felt bottom, *assai più basso.*" Then, warned by a voice from behind saying, "Take care how you go," he turned round and saw that he was standing on the ice of the ninth circle. What the drawing needed to show, therefore, was "a drop 'under the feet of the giant'—but not sheer; possibly the cone shape resumes here, though rather steeply, so that the 'Well' would be the shape, more or less, of one of those things you strain soup through, with a straight band at the top and then a cone. . . ." Here followed a rudimentary sketch.

There still remained the problem of Satan and of the "little sphere" mentioned in canto XXXIV:

> tu hai i piedi in su picciola spera
> che l'altra faccia fa della Giudecca.

[Thou hast thy feet upon a little sphere
Of whose far side Judecca forms the skin.]
(116–17)

Some commentators think the sphere is ice on one side and rock on the other. Dorothy takes the view that it is a sphere of rock, on one side of which ice is deposited ("largely because it happens to be more convenient for the rhyme"). Satan is pushed through the sphere "like a knitting-pin through an orange." But how is the sphere attached to the surrounding rock? She suggests that it is not attached at all, except by ice, being simply held there at the centre of gravity, "like a glass marble in the neck of a ginger beer bottle, when we had such things."

By Easter the sketch of Circle Nine had arrived. Scott-Giles had ingeniously provided a double diagram: one, a circular map showing the poets' path across the four divisions of the frozen river Cocytus, with a bird's-eye view of the three heads of Satan; and two, an elevation of the well, with Satan's body and three faces seen from the front, two of them in profile. Two token giants, Antaeus and Ephialtes (in chains), represent the Titans.

Bar was staying with Dorothy for Easter. When shown the diagram of the elevation and asked, "Is it clear to you which is the level of the ice in this picture?" she looked quite blank and said "No." So it seemed, said Dorothy, that lettering was needed on the elevation. A study of the diagram will show that Scott-Giles has marked the spot where Antaeus set the poets down, the oblique shaft down which (according to Dorothy's theory) the poets climbed, and their horizontal route across the circle of ice as far as Satan's furry waist, to which they clung as they squeezed past him onto the other side of the little sphere. At the point marked "centre of gravity," the poets turned upside down and Dante saw the legs of Satan sticking upwards. Virgil placed Dante upon the rocky side of the little sphere, and from there on their path is indicated through the interior of the southern hemisphere, from which they emerged at last onto the shore of Mount Purgatory, "to look once more upon the stars."

In under five months the maps and diagrams of *Hell* had been discussed, sketched in rough, revised and finished. It had been strenuous work, but they had both enjoyed it. One letter from Dorothy, dated 2 April, ends: "Dear Dante! What a lot of fun he gives us, to be

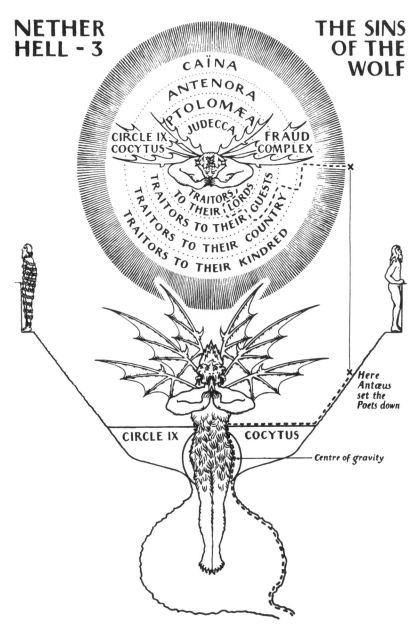

CAÏNA

ANTENORA

PTOLOMÆA

JUDECCA

CIRCLE IX
COCYTUS

FRAUD
COMPLEX

TRAITORS TO THEIR LORDS

TRAITORS TO THEIR GUESTS

TRAITORS TO THEIR COUNTRY

TRAITORS TO THEIR KINDRED

CIRCLE IX   COCYTUS

Here
Antæus
set the
Poets down

Centre of gravity

Diagram of Nether Hell, Circle ix—Treachery. Drawn by Wilfrid Scott-Giles.

sure!'' And another, dated 16 May, bewailing all the work involved in editing her translation, ends: "Oh, dear! Well, after all, it's great fun."

This was the spirit in which they worked. It was the same spirit in which ten years previously they had joyously "discovered" the history of the Wimsey family. Scott-Giles, modestly disclaiming the expertise possessed by Muriel St. Clare Byrne and Helen Simpson (and this at the end of a long impressive letter of mock-serious learning) said, "But thank you so much for letting me play!" And Dorothy, at the height of their creative impetus, wrote fondly of "our beautiful game." It was fortunate that circumstances brought two such people together again to work on Dante. They both belonged to the species *homo ludens*, for whom play is an essential element in creativity.

Suddenly, in the midst of all this, Dorothy announced that she was going to Lichfield and would be away for a month: "so that will hold up work on the Dante."

What was she doing in Lichfield?

6.

THE JUST VENGEANCE

. . . the living justice which inspires me . . .
Paradiso VI, 88

Lichfield Cathedral in Staffordshire is one of the oldest cathedrals in England. Its foundation dates from the year 700, when the body of St. Chad, who was bishop of the Mercians from 669 until 672, was enshrined in the earliest structure. The present edifice, built of dark red sandstone, with three spires and an exquisite west front resembling sculpted embroidery, was erected by the Normans, the year 1195 being regarded as the starting point.

On 20 August 1943, when the end of World War II was nowhere in sight, the Dean and Chapter of Lichfield met to plan the celebration of the 750th anniversary of the cathedral in 1945. They decided to organize a festival, which should include a pageant and a play, as well as services of thanksgiving for the preservation of the cathedral. It was an impressive act of faith. In March 1944, realism prevailing, it was conceded that the festival might have to be deferred until 1946, but it was still hoped that events would allow the celebrations to take place in the actual year of the anniversary. Events did not allow, and the festival was held in June 1946.

The Dean of Lichfield, F. A. Iremonger, knew Dr. James Welch, who had succeeded him at the BBC as director of religious broadcasting. It may have been Dr. Welch who suggested that Dorothy Sayers should be approached. He had worked with her on *The Man Born to be King* and he held her in high regard. On the other hand, this series of plays, which had made broadcasting history, and the plays she had written for Canterbury Cathedral, were in themselves sufficient recommendation. At all events, Dorothy Sayers was Lichfield's first choice as festival dramatist.

On 19 May 1944 the Dean went to London to meet her in order to talk the matter over. Early in June she wrote him a long letter, setting out the substance of their discussion and making further suggestions. By 9 June, Frank Napier, who was to produce the play, had visited the cathedral and had decided that a stage could best be erected at the west end.[1] Next, Dorothy formally raised a question which must have been in her mind from the outset and which she probably broached tentatively with the Dean at their first meeting: would there be any objection to the representation by an actor of the person of Christ?

At that period the Lord Chamberlain (the official censor) could not have permitted this to happen on any stage in any theatre in the United Kingdom. This legal restriction did not, as it happened, apply to broadcasting. In *The Man Born to be King* Jesus is a living character, portrayed in all his humanity by an actor who speaks dialogue provided by the playwright. Out of courtesy, the Lord Chamberlain had been approached and he had given permission for the part to be read over the radio on condition that no studio audience was present. In the case of a cathedral, authority rested with the Dean and Chapter. They raised no objection, provided the representation of Christ was made "under suitable conditions." This decision was unanimous, which says a good deal for the confidence which the author of *The Man Born to be King* had inspired among the clergy.

We know, then, that by June 1944 Dorothy Sayers had decided to introduce the person of Christ into her play, but that is all we know about it up till then. Theme, action, other characters had still all to be decided. She read up the history of Lichfield (the Dean having plied her with books). She noted a tradition that a thousand British Christians were massacred there in the reign of Diocletian and that the name Lichfield (interpreted as "field of corpses") was said to commemorate this event.[2] She noted also that workers in the Staffordshire potteries nearby had died of industrial pollution. Samuel Johnson and the Quaker George Fox were two famous persons associated with the city; she leafed through the latter's *Journal*. But none of this added up to a play. Such themes as war, the suffering of the innocent along with the guilty, reconciliation and forgiveness are likely to have occurred to her. But nothing yet took shape.

Then, as we know, on 11 August of that same year, she plunged headlong into the *Divine Comedy* and all else was forgotten, or so she says. Her statement that she "bolted meals, neglected sleep, work and correspondence" is the more startling when we learn what work she was neglecting just then. But the play was not really forgotten. At the back of her mind she was on the look-out for a central idea which should pull together all the disparate fragments she had gathered from her preparatory reading. On 31 August, having just read through to the end of *Paradiso* for the first time, she wrote the third of her letters to Charles Williams. In the course of detailed comments on the beauties of that section of the poem, she throws out an arresting remark. Certain lines in canto VII have caught her eye: she finds them "extraordinarily interesting": they seem, she says, "to get down to something absolutely central." She says no more about them then, nor in any other of her letters to Williams. He does not comment on them, either. But the seed of the play was sown.

The lines which had caught her attention are among the most cryptic of *Paradiso*. In canto VI the soul of the Emperor Justinian unfolds to Dante the scroll of Roman history. Of all its glories, the most sublime moment, he proclaims, occurred in the reign of the third Caesar, Tiberius, under whose authority Christ was crucified:

> chè la viva giustizia che mi spira,
>   li concedette, in man a quel ch'i' dico,
>   gloria di far vendetta alla sua ira.

> [For in that hand, the life which I respire,
>   The Living Justice, granted it to win
>   The glory of wreaking vengeance for His ire.]
>   (88–90)

Justinian, whom "God's justice inspires," represents the authority of Roman Law, under which Christ was condemned to death. He goes on to speak, appropriately, in juridical terms of the Atonement and of the paradox of the justice/injustice of the Crucifixion. In a court of law, a defendant, making his defence, was said to put forward an *exceptio*, or plea. If the plaintiff countered this, his reply was termed a *replicatio*, or counter-plea.[3] The plea that might be made in defence of the Crucifixion was that it was the appointed "vengeance" (atonement) for the Fall of Man. The counter-plea would then be that the plea did not affect the guilt incurred by crucifying an innocent man. Therefore, Justinian implies, the Emperor Titus justly avenged that guilt by destroying Jerusalem in A.D. 70:

> Or qui t'ammira in ciò ch'io ti replico:
>   poscia con Tito a far vendetta corse
>   della vendetta del peccato antico.

> [Marvel how plea meets counter-plea herein:
>   For afterward, in Titus' time, it sprang
>   To avenge the vengeance of the ancient sin.]
>   (91–93)

In canto VII Beatrice understands that Dante is puzzled by this apparent contradiction: if "vengeance" (atonement for the sins of mankind) was just in the first instance, how could it justly be avenged? She answers that, if the nature assumed by God in the Incarnation is considered, no penalty was ever so just as the Cross; but if the Person who suffered it is considered, no penalty was ever so unjust:

> Secondo mio infallibile avviso,
>   come giusta vendetta giustamente
>   vengiata fosse, t'ha in pensier miso;
> ma io ti solverò tosto la mente;
>   e tu ascolta, chè le mie parole
>   di gran sentenza ti faran presente.

> [My unerring insight sees thee in distress;
>   How the just vengeance justly was avenged—
>   That is the riddle which thou canst not guess.
> But I will solve the doubt which hath impinged
>   Upon thy mind; mark well! there's much to gain
>   For a great doctrine on my words hangs hinged.]
>   (19–24)

Thus Beatrice begins, using in line 20, as she does again in line 50, the very words, "giusta vendetta [just vengeance]," which were to become the title of the play for Lichfield Cathedral. And she continues, having expounded the doctrine of the Fall and the Redemption:

La pena dunque che la croce porse
s'alla natura assunta si misura,
nulla già mai sì giustamente morse;
e così nulla fu di tanta ingiura,
guardando alla persona che sofferse,
in che era contratta tal natura.

[Thus was the doom inflicted by the Cross,
If measured by the nature so assumed,
The most just penalty that ever was;
Yet judgment ne'er so monstrously presumed,
If we reflect who bore the punishment,
Being joined in person with the nature doomed.
(40-45)

Thus it is logical to say that the Crucifixion (the "just vengeance")
was justly avenged by Titus:

Non ti dee oramai parer più forte,
quando si dice che giusta vendetta
poscia vengiata fu da giusta corte.

[Henceforth no cause remains why he who saith
That the just vengeance was by a just court
Later avenged should take away thy breath.
(49-51)

Dante's concept of the Atonement is derived from St. Anselm,
who in his famous treatise *Cur Deus Homo?* (Why Did God Become
Man?) put forward in 1109 a juridical theory according to which man
had to repay a debt to God. Since man had nothing of his own which
he did not already owe to God, he had nothing worthy to offer in
atonement for his sins. Thus only God could pay the debt by Himself
becoming man.[4] This belief has been made familiar to us by the lines
in the well-known hymn by Mrs. C. F. Alexander which begins,
"There is a green hill far away":

There was none other good enough
To pay the price of sin . . .

Nevertheless, some readers of *Paradiso* find Dante's statement of
this concept too legalistic.[5]

Why was Dorothy Sayers so impressed by it? Verbal precision, of course, always appealed to her. The words "come giusta vendetta giustamente / vengiata fosse [how the just vengeance justly was avenged]" no doubt satisfied her as a writer with their powerful compression and alliteration. In 1948, in a lecture entitled "The Meaning of Purgatory," she spoke of canto VII of *Paradiso* as "one of the noblest statements of Atonement doctrine ever uttered."[6] The following year she referred to it again, in the lecture entitled "The Paradoxes of the *Comedy*":

> It is a matter for profound astonishment that this magnificent statement of Atonement theology should have been accused of Nestorianism—of the heresy, that is, which separates the two Natures in the one Christ. On the contrary, it asserts with almost Apollinarian emphasis that the two Natures are so inextricably united in a single indivisible Person as to make the sentence of the law at the same time wholly just and wholly unjust. In so far as it represents God's judgment of Man it is absolute justice; in so far as it represents Man's judgment of God it is absolute injustice; and it is not possible to qualify either of those pronouncements in any way whatever.[7]

Perhaps not, but there was something to be added, something she herself added in her play: man's response to God's sacrifice, a willingness to accept and offer up suffering in turn. She was well acquainted with St. Paul's teaching on the subject: God's redemptive act was perfect and sufficient, but man's imperfection and insufficiency endure. We must therefore be partakers of Christ's sufferings that we may partake also of his Resurrection. The relevant passages from St. Paul, together with the lines from *Paradiso*, are quoted in the introduction to the play: "the whole creation groaneth and travaileth in pain together" (Romans 8:22), and "Who now rejoice in my sufferings for you and fill up that which remaineth of the afflictions of Christ in my flesh for His body's sake, which is the church" (Colossians 1:24).

There also floated up in her memory the saying of Thomas à Kempis: "Whoso will carry the Cross, the Cross shall carry him." She now had ready for use Dante's presentation of the act of Atonement from God's side, balanced and filled out by the other statements, which presented the response from man's side. Together, these gave

her the theme of the play: divine justice and the suffering of the innocent.

The action, too, began to take shape. As Dante, the character in the
poem, is bewildered by Justinian's words, so modern man is bewildered by war, by the duty to kill, by what seems unmerited suffering.
She chose as her *exemplum* an Airman (he is never named) who has
been shot down in the recent conflict. At the moment of death he has
made, without realizing it, a momentous choice: he has responded to
the community, to his relationship with humanity, symbolized, for
him, by the city of Lichfield, where he was born and where he grew
up. In the *Divine Comedy*, too, "the drama of the soul's choice" is
momentous. Even at the moment of death a crucial decision can still
be made. Francesca da Rimini and her lover Paolo, at the moment of
their murder, chose self-justification and so damnation, which is self-
willed. On the Mountain of Purgatory, different in this from Hell,
Dante meets souls who, also dying sudden deaths, by murder or in
battle, had made the right choice in the nick of time. There is Buonconte da Montefeltro, for instance, the young Ghibelline warrior,
who, mortally wounded on the battlefield of Campaldino (where
Dante also fought), uttered the one penitent word "Mary"—and was
saved.[8]

The Airman in *The Just Vengeance* is a modern Buonconte. Confused, unable to reconcile himself to the suffering in the world, he
professes a humanist's belief in progress and tries to reject the past.
Like the souls on the Mountain of Purgatory, he is shown the truth in
a series of images, until at last he understands his relationship to
humanity and his descent from Adam and Eve. "Did you think you
were unbegotten?" the Recorder asks him.

Deliberate echoes of the *Divine Comedy* occur throughout the play,
including a translation of the first six lines of St. Bernard's prayer to
the Virgin:

> O Virgin Mother, daughter of thy Son,
> Lowliest and loftiest of created stature,
> Fixed goal to which the eternal counsels run;
> Thou art that she by whom our human nature
> Was so ennobled that it might become
> The Creator to create Himself His creature.[9]

There are echoes, too, of the Apostles and canonised saints, and of T. S. Eliot and Charles Williams. The two last were her predecessors in the innovation of re-introducing drama into the Church. It was fitting, therefore, that she should pay them both this tribute of quotation, especially to Charles Williams, to whom she owed her introduction to Dante.

The seed which had been planted in August 1944 germinated in her mind throughout the following autumn as she continued translating *Inferno*. By 12 January 1945 she had written to the Dean of Lichfield to make suggestions about music: she had by then decided to introduce a choir. The chapter agreed that she should approach William (later Sir William) Walton to ask him to compose for the play, but he declined and put forward the name of Antony Hopkins. Hopkins, then a young man in his mid-twenties, had been a star pupil at the Royal College of Music. He was already known as a composer of incidental music for radio and has since become renowned as a broadcaster in the series "Talking About Music." She met the young musician and together they planned the part the choir should have in the structure of the play.[10]

In May 1945 Charles Williams died and Dorothy got to work at once on her article for the memorial volume. At the same time she continued with her translation. Early in January 1946 she met her old friend Wilfrid Scott-Giles again and they began planning the diagrams for *Hell*, on which they worked with intense concentration over a period of five months.

She had also been making progress with the play. She had discussed it with her friend, the actor Frank Napier, who was to direct it, and he had asked Norah Lambourne to design the costumes and the scenic décor. Napier was making a scale model of the stage which would be built into the west end of the cathedral. By April 1946 costume designs were completed and approved by him and by Dorothy. On 2 May, she met Frank Napier and Norah Lambourne in London for further planning. On that same day she also managed to fit in a meeting with Scott-Giles to discuss the diagram of the Well of the Giants. She had by then finished her translation of *Hell* and was working on the notes.

Then on 16 May Dorothy announced in a letter to Scott-Giles that

The Director Frank Napier (*left*), with the young composer Antony Hopkins.

she would be in Lichfield for a month, "so that will hold up work on the Dante." Her absence may have held up work on the Penguin Dante, but what she set out to do in Lichfield was very much concerned with her work of making Dante relevant to the post-war world, as she and Williams had planned to do.

It is the opinion of her biographer, James Brabazon, that Dorothy Sayers was led astray from her true bent as a writer by her admiration for Williams:

> The thing that most vividly strikes any reader of this play who is familiar with the writing of Charles Williams is how completely she has succumbed to his influence. She has taken over his images, such as the City as the image of society; she has taken over his ideas, such as the emphasis on the timeless moment after death, when choices made while living are seen in the light of eternal reality . . . and in addition she has borrowed his verse rhythms and even his diction.

The image of the City and the emphasis on the moment of choice at

A scene from *The Just Vengeance.*

the point of death were taken not from Williams but directly from Dante, as Brabazon admits. But he considers that she was led astray by Dante, too:

> Dorothy knew well enough that the supernatural world was not her territory, and it is odd that she decided to venture into it. Dante and Charles Williams achieved the fusion simply because the fusion already existed in their own consciousness. In Dorothy's it was a theoretical proposition—and no amount of technique could turn that into an experience that could be communicated with theatrical power.[11]

James Brabazon, as well as being a biographer, is himself an author of drama and a producer; he has also been an actor. His opinion therefore has authority. However, I suggest that the words, "The thing that most vividly strikes any *reader* of this play," reveal a weak point in his argument.

Those who saw the play performed, those who were involved in the production and those who acted in it have a different story to tell.

Marcus Whichelow, who played the part of the Sailor, has told me what a deeply spiritual experience it was for him and for everyone concerned: "It was exactly right for the time. There we were; we had come through the war, but many of our friends had not. Like the Airman, we were bewildered. The play captured the atmosphere of the period and was above all *clear:* we knew exactly what it was all about. It united us all." [12] I have been told also that Raf de la Torre, the actor who played the part of Christ, was so profoundly affected by the play that he felt it had changed his life. [13]

In a lecture to the Dorothy L. Sayers Society Conference held at Canterbury in 1987 Norah Lambourne stressed the visual nature of the play. It was no "closet drama," dependent for its effects upon its verbal qualities alone. Quite the contrary. The director, Frank Napier, and Dorothy were in frequent contact by telephone, planning the acting and the staging, he working from his scale model and she adjusting the script as they went along. [14] Norah Lambourne described the scenery which she designed in accordance with the intentions of the author and the director:

> It consisted of a run of very tall flats with rounded tops and a great semi-circular arch behind which was the runner for the full length curtains. There was an inset scene for Adam and Eve which consisted of a "Tree of Life" with a wing flat on either side like a triptych. All the scenery was a deep blue with gold decoration—a stencilled gold border on the tall flats; the signs of the zodiac around the arch. The wing pieces for the tree of life were blue—the Heavenly Gates were gold with a cut-out design through which the light could shine.

In a letter to Norah Lambourne written on Christmas Day 1945 Napier made the following suggestions:

> The Chorus is the most foxing part. They are to present a panoramic view of the citizens of Lichfield through the ages and the Airman says of the world's muddle: "It was not our fault but the fault of the old people!" and this cry is taken up in turn by the next elder generation and the next, and so on. . . . From my point of view, I believe that the way to get the effects will be like this. The Chorus are on throughout in different groupings and I think I can get good results by changing the groups to bring out different colours at different moments to accord with the mood of what is

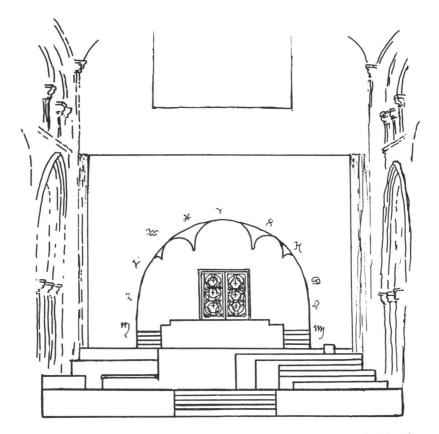

The front elevation of the staging for *The Just Vengeance*. Diagram by Norah Lambourne.

going on. . . . In fact the idea is to use the chorus as our paint box. . . . We can get a variegated effect by making them move around amongst each other, to indicate the varied life of the City.[15]

Viewers attested to the play's theatrical power. Lord Vivian, who was an associate of C. B. Cochran, came to Lichfield to see it and was enthusiastic. He told Cochran about it and urged him to join with him as "the management" and find financial backing to put it on in a London church.[16] Cochran was interested, but unfortunately he fell ill. Napier too fell ill and died. With this disaster the heart seemed to go out of the enterprise. Nevertheless, the BBC broadcast the play in

1947. The part of the Persona Dei was again played by Raf de la Torre, who was a member of the BBC Repertory Company.

There was no doubt about the success of the play at Lichfield. Critics were almost unanimous in their praise. The first performance, on 15 June 1946, was attended by the Queen (now the Queen Mother) and the Archbishop of York (Dr. Cyril Garbett). Dorothy Sayers, Frank Napier, Norah Lambourne and Antony Hopkins were presented to Her Majesty, who was enthusiastic. She expressed the hope that it would be produced in London as she would so much like the King to see it. Thirty years later, when Hopkins was again presented, the Queen Mother spoke of *The Just Vengeance*, saying "Do you know, I've seen so many things in my life but that Lichfield occasion stands out quite clearly in my mind."[17]

The festival had been planned to last eleven days, but the demand for seats for the play was so great that it was extended for another three nights. The critic writing for *The Stage*, who was likely to be an experienced judge of theatrical values, said:

> The technique is superb. The dignified simplicity of the stage rising in three tiers to the eminence where the Persona Dei first addresses the people before he descends among them in the figure of Christ is matched by the majesty of the rhythmic speech.
>
> The production reflects credit on Frank Napier for the impressive grouping of his figures and the imaginative use of lighting. All humanity is in Rowena Robinson's Eve, the essence of good nature in Percy Cartwright's Adam, and all the fearful hopes and distress of mankind in the Airman of Gordon Davies. Magnificent in voice and figure, Raf de la Torre stands, a commanding presence, over the woes of the world as Persona Dei. The whole company, amateurs and professionals alike, play with fervour, and the music, composed by Antony Hopkins, is in perfect keeping.[18]

The critic on the *Birmingham Gazette* wrote:

> Emotionally one of the greatest pieces of writing to emerge from the pen of a great writer, it shocked the audience into a silence noticeable by its continuity—there was hardly a rustle during the whole of the play's two and a half hours. . . . The acting was flawless . . . . "The Just Vengeance" is a feast of dramatic intensity which is satisfying to one's belief in

the existence of a spiritual and moral power behind the mystery of the Universe.[19]

The following eyewitness account of the play comes from Stewart Lack, who recalls his impressions after forty-one years:

> What comes immediately to mind, as one casts one's mind back, is the power of the opening sequence. The screams of the aircrash, the vibrant tirade of George Fox and the contrastingly quiet bewilderment of the Airman made a sudden and telling impact, derived not only from the incisive but sensitive playing of the actors but from the imaginative conception of the author.
>
> The rest seemed to flow naturally from these elements and from the questions which beset the mind of the Airman and which form the canvas for the development of the theme of redemption. It left one, I do remember, with a feeling of one's own inadequacy, and with a strong desire to identify with the Airman and share in his experience.
>
> Backing the direct effects of the play itself were the setting in the interior, calm and full of grace, of the cathedral, and the simple and unobtrusive staging against the west wall. The straightforward and undistracting costuming, lifted by the "Byzantine richness" of the liturgical parts, supplied the eye with a visual focus, which added to the aural and spiritual forthrightness of the language and thought. The discreet yet powerful presence of the music added the necessary and complementary fourth dimension.
>
> For me, as a comparatively young man of thirty-two, fresh from the war, and only dimly comprehending the world into which one was "launched back," this was one of the great dramatic experiences of my life, and one which, on reflection, probably had a more lasting effect on my personal pilgrimage than I would ever have realised at the time.[20]

This play, dramatic and visual, was not for reading but for hearing and *seeing*. The author has said as much in her introduction to the published text:

> I should perhaps add a reminder that the verse, as well as the whole architecture, of *The Just Vengeance*, is constructed for performance in a cathedral, rather than for reading in the study, and that the choruses assigned to the Choir were written for music. The circumstances called for a stylised presentation, moving in what may be called large blocks of action rather

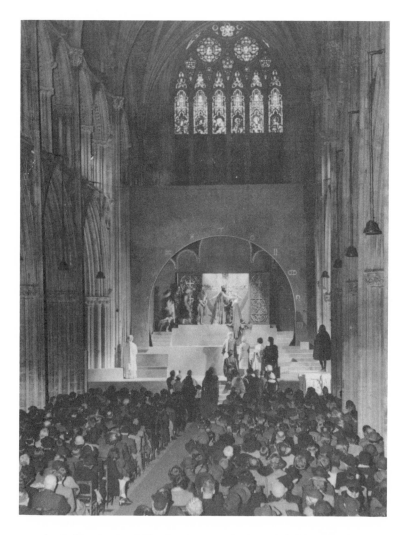

A performance of *The Just Vengeance* in Lichfield Cathedral.

than in the swift to-and-fro of dialogue; the emphasizing of important affirmations by repetitions; and a rhythm enabling the actor's voice to overcome those acoustical difficulties, which, in a large ecclesiastical building, no arrangement of microphones can wholly eliminate. (P. 10)

In this, her first attempt to convey one of Dante's most important concepts to a modern public, Dorothy Sayers had been able to command the attention of the Queen of England, the Archbishop of York, the Bishop, Dean and Chapter of Lichfield Cathedral, the company who put the play on—producer, costume and scenery designer, composer, actors and singers—and an audience of over 10,000 people. Never in the history of Dante studies can so impressive and memorable a statement have been made.

Long afterwards, talking to me about the play, Dorothy said, with a certain intensity in her voice, "It's the best thing I've done." In under two years Dante had inspired what she regarded as her masterpiece.

THE CITY OF DIS

The map of Hell is the map of the black heart.
Dorothy L. Sayers

Two months later, on 20 August 1946, Dorothy Sayers set out for Cambridge to deliver her first lecture on Dante. When did she find the time and energy to write it? "I feel horribly flat now the show's all over," she wrote to Norah Lambourne on 5 July. "And now," Dorothy said to her privately, "I've got this lecture on Dante to write. What on earth made me say I'd do it?"[1] Early in August she summoned the necessary concentration and wrote the lecture, "The Eighth Bolgia," with the result that has already been described.

In that lecture she had examined the power of the *Commedia* as a story. But she knew that the story, however enthralling, exists for the sake of what it signifies. Several months previously, while working on the notes which were to accompany her translation of *Inferno*, she paused for a moment while trying to find something helpful to say about the Giants, whose exact position had given so much trouble when it came to representing them in a diagram. "Why in the world," she asked herself, "did Dante put the Giants just here?" And, running over in her mind various other places where he might have put them, she suddenly had a vision of the whole depth of the Abyss. She saw it

perhaps as Dante saw it, but quite certainly as we can see it here and now: a single logical, coherent, and inevitable progress of corruption. . . . I saw the whole lay-out of Hell as something actual and contemporary; something that one can see by looking into one's self, or into the pages of tomorrow's newspaper. I saw it, that is, as a judgment of fact, unaffected by its period, unaffected by its literary or dogmatic origins; and I recognised at the same moment that the judgment was true.[2]

It is interesting to see what her note on the Giants eventually became. It occurs in the commentary to canto XXXI of *Hell,* in the section entitled "Images":

> From the point of view of the *story,* it is easy to see that Dante placed the Giants here, not merely to furnish a means of transport from Malbowges to the depth of the Well, but, artistically, to provide a little light relief between the sickening horrors of the last bowges of Fraud Simple to the still greater, but wholly different, horrors of the pit of Treachery. But *allegorically,* what do they signify? In one sense they are images of Pride; the Giants who rebelled against Jove typify the pride of Satan who rebelled against God. But they may also, I think, be taken as the images of the blind forces which remain in the soul, and in society, when the "general bond of love" is dissolved and the "good of the intellect" wholly withdrawn, and when nothing remains but blocks of primitive mass-emotion, fit to be the "executives of Mars" and the tools of treachery. Nimrod is a braggart stupidity; Ephialtes, a senseless rage; Antaeus, a brainless vanity: one may call them the doom of nonsense, violence and triviality, overtaking a civilization in which the whole natural order is abrogated.

In the Michaelmas term of 1946 Wilfrid Scott-Giles went to Cambridge and dined at Sidney Sussex College, where he met T. B. Blackburn, the Princeps of the Confraternitas Historica.[3] They spoke of the possibility of persuading Miss Sayers to give them another lecture, this time on Dante. In January 1947 Blackburn reopened the question, suggesting an evening in February. Scott-Giles made the desired approach and Dorothy replied, "Oh, dear me! I am frightfully tempted—any excuse for talking about Dante! Yes, I shall succumb to temptation."

February 1947 was a busy time for her. On the 19th she was due to talk at Wellington College (the boys' public school) on Tennyson's *Idylls of the King* and she had not yet written the lecture.[4] All the same, she was prepared to consider a topic for the Confraternitas. She has in mind, she says in a letter dated 22 January 1947, "a beautiful, gloomy exegesis . . . of the Inferno as the image of a corrupted society. . . . On the other hand, perhaps that is *too* gloomy (and too painfully topical?).''

It was in any case no moment for light-hearted spoof scholarship of the kind that had entertained the same Society in 1937. The war was over but the peace was grim. It was the period known officially as ''Austerity.'' Food was still rationed and so were many consumer goods. Petrol was restricted. The winter of 1947 was one of the coldest on record and, to make matters worse, there was a fuel crisis. Coal was in short supply. There were power cuts. Gas pressure for domestic use was deliberately kept low. The Ministry of Fuel and Power had appointed officials, called ''snoopers'' by the long-suffering public, who knocked at doors unexpectedly, with right of entry, to see if householders were using electric fires to keep themselves warm. If so, they were fined.

Thinking the matter over, during intervals in writing her lecture on Tennyson, Dorothy Sayers decided to offer the Confraternitas the ''gloomy exegesis.'' She had finished her notes on *Hell*, so the material was clear in her mind, needing only to be condensed and organised as a lecture. After all, as she wrote to Scott-Giles on 11 February:

> If the picture of a decayed and corrupted civilization should induce melancholy, it will be appropriate enough in present circumstances. Besides, I have found myself irritated by well-meaning Dantists who seem to think that if they can trace the arrangement of the Inferno back to Aristotle, they have said all that needs saying about it.

She wrote the lecture in two weeks. It was entitled ''The City of Dis.''[5]

The classification of sins in Dante's *Inferno* has been the subject of much learned research. The German scholar, Karl Witte, was the first to ask why the circles of Hell were not simply the circles of Mount Purgatory in reverse. He and others after him answered by pointing out that in Hell evil *deeds*, unrepented, are punished, while on Mount Purgatory evil *tendencies*, issuing in deeds which have been repented, are purged. W. H. V. Reade and others examined the influence of Aristotle and Cicero on Dante's moral distinctions. The doctrinal structure of the poem was the subject of studies by Edward Moore, Paget Toynbee and Philip Wicksteed, to name only the most eminent. In more recent times, Dante's philosophy of the active life and his doctrine of Empire had been discussed by Bruno Nardi, Etienne Gilson and Passerin d'Entrèves. All such work was of great interest to scholars but none of them, Dorothy Sayers complained, had thought it worth while to ask the following question:

> "However Dante arrived at this infernal arrangement, is it sound? is it relevant? does it correspond to anything at all within the living experience of you and me *now*? of the soul and state of Man at all times?" Because, if it does not, our enjoyment of Dante may be aesthetic or historical or political or antiquarian, or anything at all except poetically complete. . . . (P. 129)

The words "poetically complete" are an important challenge.

It is a challenge which has been made in another connection by the distinguished scholar and translator, Philip H. Vellacott. In his book *Ironic Drama: A Study of Euripides' Method and Meaning* he writes: "If no inference of personal attitude can be made connecting the words [a poet] wrote with our knowledge of human life and of the history of his time, his integrity as an author is under question and the whole study may prove a barren exercise." And again, in his forthcoming book *Oedipus and Apollo*, commenting on recent scholarly work on Greek tragedy, he writes:

> There has been abundance of scholarly criticism, which establishes a sound text, unravels syntax, elucidates expression, clarifies historical background and mental climate. Yet there is one aspect of understanding on which critics have spoken with an uncertain voice; and that is, the need to discover what moral canons, if any, the poet himself took as his standpoint in composing his plot. . . . The consequences of this failure have been far-reaching and sometimes destructive.[6]

This is exactly what Dorothy Sayers, in her more robust style, was saying:

> Our main business is to ask ourselves: "What did this poem mean in the experience of the poet? And what does it mean in our own experience?" So long as we keep these two questions clearly before us, we can ask any subsidiary questions we like, and it will all be to our profit. But unless we

ask those, and can answer them satisfactorily, the poem, as a poem, will be dust and ashes to us, however many little jackdaw pickings we manage to extract from the dump.

I do not mean, of course, that such pickings are useless. The historian's pickings are useful to history; the grammarian's pickings to philology; the theologian's to theology; and the scholar's to scholarship. But they are not useful to poetry unless we have first seen the poem in its native poetical significance. When we have, then we can use all these other things as aids to a fuller understanding; when we have not, then they serve only to bury understanding beneath the dust-heaps of antiquarian learning. (Pp. 127–28)

On the evening of 25 February 1947 Dorothy, accompanied by Wilfred Scott-Giles and his wife, stepped out from the Blue Boar Hotel in Trinity Street, Cambridge, and, braving the bitter cold in evening dress, walked up Bridge Street and along to Sidney Sussex College. They were received by the historian Dr. David Thomson, Tutor and later Master of the college, in his rooms in Garden Court. Dinner was served in a spectacularly decorated dining-room with gilded walls and a black ceiling. Among those present were the Master, T. Knox-Shaw; Dr. R. C. Smail, and two officers of the Society: the Princeps, T. B. Blackburn and the Pontifex Maximus, Norman Hunt.

Despite the limits imposed by rationing, the college kitchens managed to provide a lavish dinner, which must have been a welcome respite from the austerity of the world outside. Conversation at table is likely, surely, to have touched on Dorothy Sayers' theory that Sherlock Holmes had been an alumnus of the college,[7] as well as on her first visit ten years earlier. After dinner other members of the Society and their guests were invited to take coffee in Dr. Thomson's reception room and to meet the speaker. The lecture was given in the Combination Room, which held about sixty. There had been some misgiving that it might prove too small as so many people wanted to come. It was heated by an open fire, "whose vast dimensions would have roused the ire of Mr. Shinwell" (i.e., the Minister of Fuel and Power, later Lord Shinwell). But no snoopers knocked that night on the gates of Sidney Sussex College.[8]

The minutes of the meeting (from which the reference to the vast fire is taken) were recorded that evening by the Pontifex Maximus, Norman Hunt, who was then an undergraduate. Originally a freshman in 1939, he entered on his second year, after absence in the army, in October 1945, and graduated in June 1947, taking a double first-class degree in history. He was destined for a distinguished career, in which he served as constitutional adviser to the government, and Minister of State in the Department of Education and Science. Created a Life Peer, he was subsequently, as Lord Crowther-Hunt, elected Rector of Exeter College, Oxford. In his spirited account of the proceedings of that evening he wrote of Dorothy Sayers' "great eloquence and tremendous vivacity in describing the various circles of *Inferno*." He seems to have been struck by the parallels she drew between positions in Hell and positions held on earth in public life. From his careful minuting we learn that Scott-Giles' maps and diagrams were displayed. The audience was thus privileged to enjoy a preview of the illustrations that were to accompany the Penguin translation of *Inferno*. The lecture itself was a digest—all the more powerful in compression—of the notes which would expound it.

There they sat, the young men of Sidney Sussex College, on that icy February evening, elegant in their dinner-jackets and black ties, a few perhaps even sporting the red socks which were *de rigueur* before the war, the flames of a roaring fire leaping on the hearth. Why had they come? Was it just to see and hear the creator of Lord Peter Wimsey? Were they interested in Dante? Whatever the reason, they were different from their predecessors who in 1937 had enjoyed the symposium on the Wimsey family. Many of them—Norman Hunt was an example—had been through the war and had now returned to Cambridge to resume their degree courses. They probably had few illusions about the post-war world they would soon have to rejoin and help to reconstruct. The picture of society in necrosis which Dorothy Sayers was about to present to them was unlikely to surprise them. Her fear, expressed earlier to Scott-Giles, had been that it might prove only "too painfully topical."

She began by clarifying the question of allegory. The *Divine Comedy* is not primarily about the condition of souls after death. That is only the literal meaning, and, as she was to say in her introduction to *Hell*, "The literal meaning is the least important part of it. . . . The real environment within which all the events take place is the human soul" (p. 14). Maps and diagrams were on display that evening, but, useful as they were, "the truth of the *Inferno* is to be sought in the allegory and not in the literal story. The map of Hell is the map of the black heart; if we want to verify it, we cannot do so from books" (p. 130). The City of Dis, extended in time and space, is an image not only of things to come but also of things present: "Let us walk about the infernal city and tell the towers thereof; it may be that we shall recognise her public monuments, that as we pass through a street we shall say suddenly, 'I have been here before'; that we shall turn a corner and come unexpectedly upon our own house" (p. 131). Here was a spine-chilling beginning to a "journey of self-knowledge into the possibilities of depravity," as she defined the evening's expedition. It was not only as a writer of murder stories that Dorothy Sayers could induce a *frisson*.

The war had brought sharply into focus in her mind the religious issue underlying the conflict. This is clearly stated in the talk entitled "Creed or Chaos?" which she gave in May 1940. It begins: "Something is happening to us today which has not happened for a very long time. We are waging a war of religion. Not a civil war between adherents of the same religion, but a life-and-death struggle between Christian and pagan."[9] James Brabazon describes her state of mind as follows:

> Dorothy's patriotism, her sense of history and her sense of romance, deep-rooted qualities all three of them, responded to the image, romantic and yet for once real, of the little peaceable island standing as a bulwark against tyranny; and not only tyranny, in Dorothy's eyes—heresy was involved as well. (P. 176)

For the Nazis had committed the sin against the Holy Ghost: they had chosen to see evil as good. In her article "What Do We Believe?" published in the *Sunday Times* one week after war had been declared, she had argued that what we believe will inevitably issue in deeds.[10] That is why she undertook, as a kind of self-appointed war work, the task of emphasizing—what few people, not even the Church, seemed to regard as important—the connection between belief and behaviour.[11] Ralph E. Hone in *Dorothy L. Sayers: A Literary Biography* calls attention to the range and intensity of this work:

> Nothing less than the practice of her own preaching accounts for the incredible pace of Sayers' involvement during the first year of World War II. Her publishing record was amazing. She lectured widely and participated in numerous conferences and committee meetings. She spoke on radio. She traveled up and down the island. She scolded—in print—a king and a former teacher, cabinet ministers and newspaper men, a bishop and the rank and file of church members, politicians and status-quo-ers, theologians and featherbedders, literary critics and the uninformed. With a Pauline glare, she reproved, she corrected, she instructed in righteousness. (P. 102)

Long before she read Dante she had personified the ill doings of society in figures of the Seven Deadly Sins. They put in a brief appearance, as though for an audition for a morality play, at the end of her article "Christian Morality,"[12] and they reappear in full panoply in the talk "The Other Six Deadly Sins," which she gave to the Public Morality Council on 23 October 1941. She explained the title by saying, "I am reminded of a young man who once said to me with perfect simplicity: 'I did not know there were seven deadly sins: please tell me the names of the other six.' "[13] The seven deadly, or mortal, sins—pride, envy, wrath, sloth, avarice, gluttony, lust (to list them in the order in which Dante arranges them on the Mountain of Purgatory)—were deemed by the Church to cover the entire range of human corruption. They were all equally deadly, not least because they could all assume beguiling disguises. When Dorothy came upon them in Dante's poem, she recognised, there drawn by a master hand, what she herself had depicted in lesser degree. Her mind leapt in creative response. Here was the greatest Christian poet saying for her, with immense power, what she had been trying to tell people through the years of war. One of her favourite maxims was that a writer must "serve the work." After her discovery of Dante, it was *his* work that she would serve. It is significant that for her first volume of lectures on Dante she chose as an epigraph the following lines from *Purgatorio*:

> Poichè di riguardar pasciuto fui,
>   tutto m'offersi pronto al suo servigio,
>   con l'affermar che fa credere altrui.

> [And when I'd feasted eyes on him, I threw
>   My whole self at his service, pledging him
>   Such vows as hearers must give credence to.]
>   (XXVI, 103–5)

If we compare her article "The Other Six Deadly Sins" with her lecture "The City of Dis" we see at once the new dimensions which her encounter with Dante has produced. Already in 1941 she had known how to apply the concept of a basic sin to a wide area of social behaviour. Gluttony, for instance, is shown in "The Other Six Deadly Sins" to be not merely individual self-indulgence. It is the voracious consumption by society of manufactured goods, the "barrage of advertisement by which people are flattered and frightened out of a reasonable contentment into a greedy hankering after goods they do not really need." She had herself taken part in stimulating such hankering when she had worked as a copy-writer in an advertising firm. That she felt uneasy about it had already been shown in her novel *Murder Must Advertise*.

In Dante's *Inferno* the Gluttons lie prostrate under drenching rain and snow, mauled by Cerberus, the three-headed dog:

> Grandine grossa, acqua tinta e neve
>   per l'aere tenebroso si riversa;
>   pute la terra che questo riceve.
> Cerbero, fiera crudele e diversa,
>   con tre gole canina-mente latra
>   sopra la gente che quivi è immersa.

> [Huge hail-stones, sleet and snow, and turbid drench
>   Of water sluice down through the darkened air,
>   And the soaked earth gives off a putrid stench.
> Cerberus, the cruel, misshapen monster, there
>   Bays in his triple gullet and doglike growls
>   Over the wallowing shades.]
>   (VI, 10–15)

Commenting on this image in "The City of Dis," she said:

> Like all the sinners we have so far met, the Gluttons are people of whom
> our present civilization is inclined to think highly. They have an engaging
> egotism; they demand so amiably and seem to get so much out of life that
> we feel they have hit on the right attitude to the world of things. They
> have, in fact, a high standard of living—and that, we agree, is the thing to
> aim at.

They represent a civilization which equates material possessions with
beatitude. Would it have surprised Dante, she asked, to find such a
civilization as ours "waking to the realization that, having pursued
these ideals with all its might, it was inexplicably left cold, hungry,
bored, resentful and savage? Probably not, for he described Gluttony
so" (p. 135).

In "The Other Six Deadly Sins" she had drawn a rakish picture of
Covetousness or Avarice. Disguised as "Enterprise," it had been endowed with glamour on a large scale:

> a swaggering, swashbuckling, piratical sin, going about with its hat cocked
> over its eye, and with pistols tucked into the tops of its jack-boots. Its
> war-cries are "Business Efficiency!" "Free Competition!" "Get Out or
> Get Under!" and "There's Always Room at the Top!" . . . Covetous-
> ness is not incarnated in individual people, but in business corporations,
> joint-stock companies, amalgamations, trusts. . . . (P. 75)

She recognised the image of Covetousness in Dante's description of
the Hoarders and Spendthrifts, who trundle heavy boulders round
and round, crashing against their opposites as they meet half way.
Scholars have found this picture interesting from a philosophical
point of view, noting that Dante has learnt from Aristotle that avarice
and extravagance are opposite forms of the same sin. But Dorothy
Sayers recognised in it an image of perverted society in conflict with
itself: "The greeds of either sort combine in gangs. . . . Even as
gangs they are barely distinguishable—the economy of accumulated
thrift and the economy of conspicuous waste are counterparts of one
another and issue in the same economic deadlock" (p. 136).

In "The City of Dis," as in the notes and commentaries which accompany her translation, she stresses again and again the modernity of Dante's pictures. Confronted with the Usurers, who squat on the infertile, burning sand, an environment they share with the Blasphemers and the Sodomites, she observes:

> nineteenth-century commentators, brought up in the tradition of financial autonomy and the sacro-sanctity of banking, were aghast at this astonishing listing in one doom of unmentionable vice and irreproachable finance; they could only suppose that Dante's genius had been entangled, willy-nilly, in a net of mediaeval nonsense.

But to us, "looking at a world full of dust-bowls, unemployment, strikes, and starvation, yawing hideously between over- and underproduction, the connection between usury and the barren and burning sand does not, perhaps, seem altogether too far-fetched" (p. 142). The Flatterers, immersed in excrement, may seem to some readers to suffer an exaggeratedly repulsive punishment. But to Dante flattery was the prostitution of language, the falsification of words for gain. Our modern parallels, said Dorothy Sayers, are advertisement, journalism and propaganda: "this is the filth and ordure of the falsifying intellect, steeped in its own slime" (p. 143).

Step by step she took them, those young Cambridge men of 1947, down through the circles of Hell, pointing inexorably as she went to connections with the world outside. First came the Vestibule, containing the souls who chose neither good nor evil. How subtle, how mediaeval, we may think, this in-between area, impossible to visualise, like counting angels on the point of a pin! Dorothy Sayers brings the concept into focus:

> Here are the people who never come to any decision. Do we despise them? or do we admire their wide-minded tolerance and their freedom from bigotry and dogmatism? They dismiss everything, but come to no conclusion. . . . They will commit themselves to no opinion, since there is so much to be said on the other side. . . . They shrink from responsibility, lest it should bind them; they condemn nothing, for fear of being thought narrow. . . ." But surely," they cry, "*all* experience is valuable! All good and evil are relative! All religions are the same in essentials!" (P. 132)

"I had not thought death had undone so many," wrote T. S. Eliot, echoing Dante.

The circle of the Lustful is the circle of shared sin. It contains that famous pair of lovers, Paolo and Francesca, concerning whom it is usually said that Dante's heart was in conflict with his moral judgment. But Dorothy Sayers, agreeing in this with Charles Williams, sees in them an instance of mutual indulgence. The image is a sexual one but the sin is not limited to sex: "One indulges one's children to their hurt. . . . One writes and speaks no matter what foolishness, because one's public turns up an eager face and must not be disappointed . . ." (p. 135).[14]

The City of Dis is an image of *progressive* corruption: one step leads on inevitably to the next. Indulgence, which begins so tenderly with the yielding of Francesca to Paolo, is followed by greed, antagonism, wrath, obduracy, violence, fraud and, finally, in the Circle of Ice, to treachery.

The ninth circle, the last and lowest of Dante's Inferno, consists of the frozen surface of the river Cocytus. It is divided into four concentric rings or zones, which correspond to four categories of treachery. These are distinguished by the bond between the traitor and the betrayed. The first, Caina, contains the betrayers of kindred; the second, Antenora, the traitors to cause or party; the third, Ptolemea, those who betrayed the sacred trust of hospitality. The fourth and last, Giudecca, is the ring of those who betrayed God and the City, spiritual authority and temporal authority. It is dominated by the towering figure of Satan, three-headed in monstrous parody of the Trinity. In each of his three mouths he crunches a supreme example of this basest of all sins: Judas, who betrayed Christ, Brutus and Cassius, who betrayed Caesar: "Here, in the heart of cold, in the place that knows neither obligation nor community nor coherence nor exchange, treachery devours treachery for ever" (p. 149).

The lecture was received with "enthusiastic applause" and discussion continued afterwards for over an hour. It probably continued later on, too, when Dorothy Sayers and Mr. and Mrs. Scott-Giles, having emerged once more into the cold, regained the lounge of the Blue Boar. Dorothy always needed to unwind after a lecture. She and Wilfrid had that evening launched their Penguin on a specimen public. Exhilaration is likely to have kept them up talking for some time.

If they talked about the last circle, the icy weather they had braved on their journeys to Cambridge must have given an edge to their conversation. In her letter about travel arrangements, Dorothy had said:

> I shall travel to Cambridge direct from Witham without doubling back on London. . . . Of course if by that time we find ourselves already in the Lowest Circle, wholly covered in ice, or with only the head emerging, or if the trains have stopped for lack of coal, or if the loosing of the waters has swept the permanent way into the Ouse, or anything of that sort, we shall be sunk—but we will hope for the best.
>
> Up to the present, we have been living about on the edge of Cocytus, with occasional returns to the Third Circle; but the ominous appearance of seagulls in the back garden suggests that the next stage will be at least Caina; and I seem already to feel on my numbed face the diabolic and icy wind which freezes up all the water-pipes. (11 February 1947)

It was not only the external weather that was relevant. Across the road from the Blue Boar was Trinity College, where a climate of treason had frozen more than water-pipes.[15]

Long before she read Dante, Dorothy Sayers held clear views as to the priority of public over private loyalty. This was the theme of her novel *Gaudy Night*, published in 1935. It is written into the book's very structure and is worked out in several of the key conversations. Intellectual integrity, adherence to the truth, no matter what the personal cost, are paramount. In this she agreed with C. P. Snow, whose novel *The Search*, on the same theme, is one of the major clues in the plot of *Gaudy Night*.

Another novelist, E. M. Forster, had expressed a different view. In his wartime article, "Two Cheers for Democracy," published in *The London Mercury*, he had written:

> I hate the idea of causes, and if I had to choose between betraying my country and betraying my friend, I hope I should have the guts to betray my country. Such a choice may scandalize the modern reader, and he may stretch out his patriotic hand to the telephone and ring up the police. It would not have shocked Dante though. Dante placed Brutus and Cassius

in the lowest circle of Hell because they had chosen to betray their friend Julius Caesar rather than their country Rome.[16]

Forster has misunderstood Dante. It is not treachery to friendship that is represented by Brutus and Cassius in the fourth ring of Cocytus, but treachery to supreme temporal authority, to Caesar the chosen founder of Empire. It is true that Dante places treachery to guests lower than treachery to party or cause, but this is not the distinction which Forster had in mind. It may be that he attributed to Dante Shakespeare's view of the friendship between Brutus and Caesar (though Cassius does not come into this category). However we try to account for the confusion in Forster's mind, there was none in the mind of Dorothy Sayers:

> In the last region of the thick-ribbed ice they cannot even speak. They are wholly immersed, unable to communicate. The last semblance of community, the last vestige of humanity is withdrawn from the "social animal," man. This is Giudecca, the circle of Judas, the circle of those who betray the ultimate bond of deliberately sworn allegiance. (P. 148)

It is said of a certain Trinity College graduate, the traitor Guy Burgess, who defected to the Soviet Union, that he was so moved by that statement in E. M. Forster's article that he learned it by heart and would recite it to anyone who would listen. It was a pity nobody told him that Forster had got Dante wrong.

8.

ALIVE ON MEN'S LIPS

Eppur si muove.
Galileo

The translation of Inferno, starkly entitled *Hell*, was published in November 1949. In three months the whole of the first impression, 50,000 copies, was sold out.[1]

One of the first people to read it was the historian G. M. Trevelyan. He was particularly impressed by the introduction, which he had seen in advance. In his function as Chancellor of the University of Durham he put forward the name of Dorothy L. Sayers for an honorary Doctorate in Letters. The offer was made, and accepted. It was the only public honour she was ever to receive. In 1943 the Archbishop of Canterbury, William Temple, had asked her if she would accept a Lambeth Doctorate in Divinity in recognition of what he considered the great value of her work, especially *The Man Born to be King* and *The Mind of the Maker*. After some hesitation she had declined, feeling that the title "Doctor of Divinity" would limit her freedom as a secular writer, and might also lessen her effectiveness with the general public when she wished to write on religious topics. But the offer from Durham was different. Here was a university paying tribute to her as a writer and especially, in view of her latest undertaking, as a poet and a scholar.

The degree was conferred on 24 May 1950. No doubt she was duly wined and dined at Durham, but the occasion called for some further, more personal celebration. Like many creative people (T. S. Eliot and Edmund Crispin, another detective novelist, come to mind), Dorothy Sayers loved cats. That year she acquired a handsome tabby. In jubilant mood and with a characteristic mingling of the domestic and the professional, she named her new household companion George Macaulay Trevelyan.[2]

The publication of *Hell* widened the circle of her correspondents. Among them was Geoffrey L. Bickersteth, who became a friend. An Oxford graduate in "Greats" (i.e., classics) and Professor of English at the University of Aberdeen, he was also a distinguished Italianist. His verse translations, accompanied by substantial commentaries, of the poetry of Carducci and Leopardi, have been much admired.[3] In 1932 he had brought out a verse translation, in *terza rima*, of Dante's *Paradiso*. He was still at work on his translation of the rest of the poem when he heard of Dorothy Sayers' rival enterprise. With characteristic generosity he wrote to send her his best wishes. In her reply she said that she knew of his translation of *Paradiso* but had decided not to read it

> because such extracts from it as I have already seen are so good that if I did read it I should be certain, either to be unconsciously influenced by it, or, still worse, to be so conscious of having to avoid its influence that I should contort my own translation merely in order to be different. (15 January 1948)

She *had*, however, read Binyon's translation (which Bickersteth admired), but she found his rhythm and syntax too Italianate. Furthermore, to her mind, "Binyon, in common with most of his predecessors, fails to reproduce what are to me the three outstanding qualities of Dante's verse: speed, humour and flexibility." She hesitated, when the time came, before sending Bickersteth a copy of *Hell*: it was so different from everything he liked in Binyon's version. However, she plucked up courage and was rewarded by a letter of "generous and ample praise." Her translation, he said, was "tingling with life." The phrase delighted her. Here was just the response she had hoped for: "I am so very glad that you find the thing 'tingling with life.' That, as you so well realise, is what I wanted first and foremost, and I think I can bear any amount of criticism or disagreement, provided the judgment ends up 'eppur si muove'!" (November 1949).

She was delighted also with the comment of a Cambridge under-graduate which I passed on to her. I had been talking about her translation with a group of pupils and one of them said: "I'm enjoying it so much! It makes me laugh and I just go on and on reading. I wonder if I *ought* to enjoy Dante as much as that?"[4] Dorothy found this more encouraging than any amount of approval from the wise and learned:

> If only they will "go on and on reading," that is the great thing. Perhaps I have made them laugh at Dante when they "ought" to be trembling at the thought of Hell!—but if they don't *read* and don't enjoy what they read, they will never even begin to learn to shudder. *Oderint dum metuant* is a shocking bad principle where poetry is concerned, even the poetry of Hell.[5]

C. S. Lewis, too, was encouraging. Like my Cambridge pupil, he read on and on compulsively. It was against his literary conscience to go at such speed, but, as he wrote on 11 November, "this tells us one thing about your version: you have got (what you most wanted) the quality of an exciting story." He had by then read nineteen out of the thirty-four cantos. Four days later, having finished the remaining fifteen, he wrote again:

> I've finished it now. There's no doubt, taking it all in all, it's a stunning work. The real test is this, that however I set out with the idea of attending to your translation, before I've read a page I've forgotten all about you and am thinking only of Dante, and two pages later I've forgotten about Dante and am thinking about Hell.

On the same day, 15 November, I myself wrote to convey a similar experience of eager, compulsive reading: "*Greed* is the only word which describes my sessions with it; indeed it has thrown all my timetable out of joint."

"Tingling with life," "I just go on and on reading," "an exciting story"—these are unexpected reactions to Dante's *Inferno*. Yet they had been Dorothy's own when she first read the whole work in the original. She had now succeeded in communicating and sharing them. Some of the ways in which she achieved this came in for criticism. Bickersteth, for instance, taxed her with occasional "amplify-

ing and colouring"—his courteous terms for padding. She acknowledged this but also in part defended it as unavoidable

> because the English words are usually shorter than the Italian . . . And
> also, English verse does tend, more than that of the Latin languages, to
> rely on its epithets for its effects, and if deprived of them seems to pro-
> duce an impression of baldness which doesn't exist in the original. (No-
> vember 1949)

Bickersteth had also found fault with what he considered an excessive
over-running of lines, that is, of allowing the meaning contained in a
single line in the original to overflow into the next. In the same letter
Dorothy admitted this as a defect:

> I am well aware of a lot of faults. The excessive over-running of the lines,
> which you mention, is largely a fault of inexperience, and you will find
> much less of it in the *Purgatorio*, as I learn better how to handle the *terza
> rima*. Here and there I have still had to resort to it—chiefly where a Latin
> tag, or an awkward Italian name, or a tiresome bit of technical astronomy
> has dictated the rhymes. But I have avoided it as much as possible. Dante
> does use it sometimes, but in the *Inferno* I used it too much.

C. S. Lewis had also raised doubts. In his first letter he wondered
whether her "metrical audacities," though nearly all effective in their
places in *her* poem, were "like anything in Dante." They made Dante
seem like Browning, though that was "certainly better than making
him like Milton" (as Cary had done). Her colloquialisms, he judged,
would be a target for criticism (and he was right). He approved of
many of them, but here and there they seemed to him to suggest "not
intimacy and directness, but flippancy." All the same, he considered
her "strong, exciting view of Dante . . . worth any number of timid,
safe versions." He concluded, "The sheer work of the thing, the un-
tiring quality and inexhaustible cleverness (there are hardly any
creaks) fill me with astonished admiration. How do you keep it up?
Oh—best of all—it *frightens* me more than any translation I've seen."

Like C. S. Lewis, I, too, found the translation startling and I also
wondered if it startled me in the same way as Dante's original; but, as
I wrote to her, "It throws the original into relief and makes you look

at it more closely." I was struck above all by the sense of *enjoyment* which she conveyed: "I think the key . . . is that you do what you like. . . . You so obviously enjoy looking into Dante, and so the reader enjoys it with you." This, I thought, accounted for the exhilarating vigour of the commentary and notes, which I found as compulsive reading as the translation itself. She replied on 18 November: "You are, of course, perfectly right—I never do anything (I mean, I never *write* anything) that I don't like writing, or about anything or anybody that I don't like." In the same letter she said that she had just thought (too late, alas!) of the perfect quotation for the title page of *Hell:* the passage in *Pride and Prejudice* where Elizabeth Bennet explains to her father why she has become engaged to Mr. Darcy:

> "We all know him to be a proud, unpleasant sort of man; but this would be nothing if you really liked him."
>
> "I do, I do like him," she replied, with tears in her eyes; "I love him. Indeed he has no improper pride. He is perfectly amiable." (Chapter 59)

Dorothy had previously described Dante in a letter to Scott-Giles on 23 January 1946: "I like his personality—he *isn't* all grim and sour; he's humorous and charming—though I admit he didn't suffer fools gladly." Continuing in her letter to me she said, "I wish it had occurred to me earlier! It so exactly represents my feelings . . . it would have been such fun for the critics and the academics," whose pigeon-holes, she thought, "will be badly fluttered."

One academic whose pigeon-hole was relatively unfluttered was Cesare Foligno. Formerly Professor of Italian at Oxford University, he was then living in retirement in Naples. In a long and favourable review, published in *Studi Danteschi* (1951, volume 18), he acknowledged her scholarly credentials and welcomed her attempt to make Dante accessible to modern readers. His considerable knowledge of English poetry enabled him to make an informed judgment of the verse. He defended her use of half-rhymes and, occasionally, of eccentric rhymes, which are plentifully used by Byron, after all; and he had no objection to padding, providing it was skilful, recognizing that, since English was a more monosyllabic language than Italian, fill-in words and phrases (*zeppe,* wedges) were sometimes necessary, even in blank verse. He much preferred her translation to that of

Binyon, who in his opinion failed to produce anything like an English echo of Dante's verse "quale esso suona a noi [as it sounds to us]."

Dorothy Sayers did not usually write to reviewers, except to correct matters of fact, but, making an exception in this case, she wrote to thank Foligno for his article, which she found "very kind and fair." That was on 25 July 1952. By then she had seen the reaction of most of the English and American critics. Many, she remarked, had been carping, but the difficulty was that, for the most part, Dante scholars could not judge English verse, while scholars who could judge verse knew little of Dante; some even disliked what they did know. What encouraged her were the many letters she kept receiving from members of the general public, who wrote to say such things as "I don't know any Italian, and I tried Dante in So-and-so's translation and couldn't get on with it, and I've read your *Inferno* eagerly from beginning to end and am looking forward to the *Purgatorio*." She quoted a schoolmistress in a London high school (undoubtedly Marjorie Barber) who found a sixth-form girl with her nose in a Penguin book and was told in excited tones: "Oh, Miss B. . . , I've just got down to the Eighth Bolgia!"

These were the kind of readers for whom the Penguin Classics had originally been intended. Whatever the scholarly or literary world thought of it, the Sayers translation of *Inferno* was reaching more general readers, young and old, than any previous translation had ever done. As she said in her letter to Foligno, her aim had been to achieve exactly that, namely:

> to present Dante . . . to the (literally) thousands and ten-thousands of my countrymen to whom he is a sealed book. Most of them are incredibly lacking in literary background. They know no Catholic theology, no history, no classic mythology to speak of. Many of them have even lost touch with the Bible. They are brought up on science and psychiatry and television—the new reading public of an illiterate age. At all costs he must be shown to them as a living poet, who has something vital to say to them here and now. . . . Somehow one must bridge time and space and come back, not with a "crib" but with an English poem that people will *read*. If one has not done that, one has done nothing.

Objections were raised by several reviewers to the use of *terza rima*.

We have seen already from the remarks of Francis MacManus what a prejudice there was (and still is) against its use in English.[6] On this matter Bickersteth agreed with Dorothy Sayers, as also with Binyon: only triple rhyme will do. It is important to understand, however, that Bickersteth's views on *terza rima* are more subtle and perceptive than those of other translators, or their critics. In the introduction to his own translation of the *Commedia*, he states that Dante's use of it is different from that of any other Italian poet and different, too, from triple rhyme as written by any English poet, especially Shelley, who imposed on it the rhythms of blank verse. Dante uses rhyme not only to link the lines of every canto in an unbroken chain, a device essential to the structure; he uses rhyme also to point and guide the meaning. As a result, the argument of a whole passage can be caught by glancing at the rhymes. Further, the rhyme affects the cadences, enabling the reader to attune to the music of the poetry. Thus *terza rima*, as Dante uses it, is essential to structure, meaning and sound. I do not believe that critics hostile to the use of it in English translations of the *Commedia* have paid Bickersteth's observations the attention they deserve.[7]

The main reason which is urged against the use of *terza rima* in translation is the alleged scarcity of rhymes in English as compared with Italian. But, as Sayers pointed out in an important and unheeded passage in her introduction to *Hell:*

> English is "poor in rhymes" because it is remarkably rich in vowel-sounds. Of these, Italian possesses seven only, all "pure" and unmodified by the succeeding consonants. For English, on the other hand, the Shorter O.E.D. [Oxford English Dictionary] lists no fewer than fifty-two native varieties, shading into one another by imperceptible degrees. This phenomenon results from the fact that most English vowels are diphthongs to start with and nearly all are subtly modified by a following consonant, particularly by a following "r." Indeed, in Southern English, this self-effacing consonant when it appears at the end of a word seems to exist for the sole purpose of performing this duty to its vowel, dying without a murmur when its work is done, after the manner of certain male spiders. (In Northern English and in the Celtic dialects the "r" is more tenacious of life.) In consequence of all this, "pure" rhymes are scarce in English; but "impure" rhymes are frequent and legitimate, producing many cur-

ious melodic effects which have no parallel in the verse of pure-vowelled languages. (P. 57 n.)

Bickersteth, rather more decorously, as befitting a professor, says in effect much the same thing:

No one, surely, can seriously maintain that a language is deficient in words of like-sounding termination, which boasts of the *Faerie Queene* and *Don Juan*. For in these immensely long poems the stanza of the one requires four, and of the other three, verses to be written on the same rhyme. It is certainly true that Italian contains a vastly greater number of rhyming words than English does, and further allows of identical or "rich" rhymes (i.e., where the identity of sound is extended to the consonant immediately preceding the final stressed vowel), which English by custom does not. But, even so, the Spenserian stanza is proof positive that English possesses enough rhymes for the purposes of *terza rima*. . . . With regard to the rhymes themselves he [the translator] may allow himself the judicious use of eye-rhymes, and rhymes of open with close vowel syllables, and of breathed with unbreathed consonants, or of vowels with diphthongs of which one element is the vowel concerned: and that without apology for two reasons: first, because he has the authority of all the greatest English poets for so doing; and, second, because to employ these kinds of rhyme from time to time serves to dispose of the objection . . . that the frequency of rhyme, if always phonetically a true one, would prove trying to the English ear.[8]

Dorothy Sayers' decision to use triple rhyme was not the only ground for complaint. There were cries of dismay about her style. The most piercing shriek was emitted by the poet Peter Russell, at that time editor of a literary journal entitled *Nine*. Reviewing *Hell* himself, he berated it for lack of taste and condemned the diction as "a curious confusion of literary stock-in-trade, archaism and slang." He further expressed his extreme dislike in a sonnet, published anonymously in 1956, entitled "On First Looking into Miss Sayers' Dante":

> Oft have I paused at some cathedral door
> To hear its vaulted canopy prolong
> The murmured adoration of the throng

> Swelled by the pipes to muffle thunder's roar;
> Oft was I told of Dante, skilled to pour
> The mediaeval miracle of song
> And never dared to deem the verdict wrong
> Till Sayers rearranged the vocal score.
> Then felt I like some night-long penitent
> Who hears at dawn the minster gates flung wide
> And, hungry for the Blessed Sacrament,
> Scans the dim nave, and shrinks back horrified
> To see the madcaps of the motley season
> Capering round their Abbot of unreason.[9]

There were many who shared Russell's opinion and the Sayers translation still has its detractors today. Writing in the *Times Literary Supplement* as late as 1980, Roger Scruton referred to "Dorothy Sayers'
insufferable Penguin," giving no rationale for his dislike, evidently
assuming that everyone must share it. In the same year, C. H. Sisson,
in the introduction to his own translation of the *Commedia*, unrhymed, dismissed the Sayers version and my own continuation of it
with the utmost contempt.[10]

On balance, however, the reviews were favourable. This has been
shown by Barbara J. Dunlap in her article "Through a Dark Wood of
Criticism," published in 1979.[11] This is more comprehensive than
the relevant section in Gilbert F. Cunningham's masterly work, *The
Divine Comedy in English: A Critical Bibliography*.[12] Admiration was
expressed, for instance, by E. R. Vincent in *The Cambridge Review*, by
the anonymous critic in the *Times Literary Supplement*, who found the
translation "swift, exciting and topical," and later by Warwick
Chipman, himself a translator of Dante, who called her work "brilliant: I pay it my humble tribute." Another anonymous reviewer in
the *New Statesman*, though criticising her use of unusual words and
the retention of the antiquated "thou" to render the Italian "tu,"
acknowledged that she attained something of the grandeur of the
original. Theodore Holmes, writing in *Comparative Literature*, commended her for her use of modern idiom, though he considered that
"the admirable flow of her diction" often became clogged by rare and
antiquated words. And Gilbert F. Cunningham, who disliked the
translation on the whole, admitted that it achieved a variety which

was lacking in many others.[13] C. S. Lewis said that Dorothy Sayers' writing had a quality and temper for which she was both loved and hated. He defined it as a "cheerful energy," which irritated some readers and delighted others. Barbara J. Dunlap put the matter well, concluding, "Her translation mirrors the strong individuality of the mind that produced it, and the strength and variety of critical response evoked are testimony, often unwitting, of its great power."

Dunlap also made the suggestion that the translation would gain greatly from being read aloud. It happens that I am able to testify to the truth of this. In September 1956 I read the whole of *Hell* out loud in the space of three days. My listener was my fourteen-year-old son Adrian. My husband and daughter were away from home and we had been left with a few days of unplanned leisure. I asked Adrian if he would like me to read him the introduction to *Hell*. He was an admirer of Dorothy Sayers' writings, and not only of her detective novels. Moreover, reading out loud had long been a habit in our family. He agreed. Three days later, on 12 September, I wrote to Dorothy describing our experience. Since I set down my impressions at top speed, in the white heat of excitement, it seems better to give them verbatim, rather than paraphrase them after more than thirty years. This way of testing the translation was at least unusual, if not unique.

I have just done a thing I have wanted to do for some time: I have read right through your translation of *Inferno* from start to finish, leaving nothing out and with as little interruption as possible. In fact, I read it at three sessions and I read it out loud. What is more, I had a listener who stayed the course, namely Adrian.

I don't believe anybody who reviewed this volume did justice to the introduction, did they? I've always enjoyed it and am stirred especially by the first two paragraphs. In fact they are the key to the translation that is coming. But I hadn't ever read it to anyone before and I must say I was enthralled by its effectiveness for both of us. . . .

At the conclusion of the introduction I decided I would read just one canto; but Adrian kept saying "Go on, go on," and so I did, up to the end of canto VI, by which time it was late and I was hoarse. So we adjourned till the following evening, when we reached the end of canto XVII. And this afternoon, with a tea interval, we read from XVIII to XXXIV. I hope the speed of this doesn't horrify you. (Actually the effect was terrific.) It was too concentrated, of course, but all the same the result was more exciting than could have been achieved by reading just one canto an evening. . . .

I don't know whether reactions and impressions gathered from such a rock 'n roll performance are of any value but I thought I would set them down and see. First of all I am now quite sure that the pace and vigour (I don't mean of our reading but of your writing) are dead right; and reading canto after canto like that showed me, what I hadn't noticed before, the startling changes in pace which give the whole work an inner movement. For instance, in order to get the full effect of your treatment of canto V, you must lead up to it, and at a smart pace, with the preceding four, and follow it by at least another two. *Then* you can feel how the rhythm widens out into long, languorous circles of dizzying, weak-willed yielding. It is quite wrong to take little bits and examine them ex-context. . . . You must see canto after canto moving in broad sweeps of varying effect. I recognised quite plainly as I went through that the general panoramic variations which you achieve are those of Dante; but I must also say that getting them through the English has sharpened my observation of the original. Our relationship to a venerable ancient work is inhibiting. It has a kind of sacred quality, and we tend to brood over it and cling on to the words themselves instead of sucking the meaning out of them and moving on. . . .

I have found, as a result of this rapid reading of ours, that your words do as they will with us. If the canto is a quick, vigorous one, then the familiar English words bustle us along; if the canto is slow and meditative, the words hold us back with their slower rhythm; and, even more, that, as occasion demands, they batter us and blister and outrage and violently buffet us; and then again they call forth a gentle or laughing or shame-faced response.

She replied on 14 September:

Your letter has just arrived. Well, well, well! First of all: First Prize to Adrian for staying-power. . . . He must be a remarkably determined boy, with unusual powers of concentration. We award him the Collar of the Ancient Order of Bull-Dog, first-class, with studs. . . .

I am naturally purring like a threshing-machine; but, putting that aside for the moment—THAT IS THE RIGHT WAY TO READ DANTE.

As regards the "sharpening" effect of reading Dante in English, she remarked, "The slight shock of hearing a familiar statement re-phrased quickens one to the implications of the original: that is why *The Man Born to be King* startled quite a lot of people into realizing what the Gospels were actually saying." Twenty-three years later, Barbara J. Dunlap was to make a similar observation: "In my view, Sayers' approach to Dante was not unlike her approach to the life of Christ in *The Man Born to be King* in its emphasis on the humanness of the Divine and the determination not to obscure the poem's (or Gospels') relevance to our own spiritual condition by using received phrases or a grand style."[14]

Reviewers found fault with other features of her translation. Even her admirers were dubious about the degree of comedy she noticed in Dante. Foligno charged her with trying to graft an English sense of humour on to a mediaeval Italian poet. She replied in her letter of 25 July 1952:

> I was, as a matter of fact, rather careful *not* to say that Dante had an "English sense of humour." His humour is actually so far from being that, that most English critics say roundly that he has none. That is why the only English writer I could find to compare him with was Jane Austen, who is by no means typical of "English" humour, being malicious, witty and dry. Dante is nearer, I think, to the French sense of comedy (very alien from ours)—though he is really *sui generis*.

At this point she goes on to speak of an Italian friend "who sees absolutely eye to eye" with her in this matter: "He and I always find ourselves smiling in the same places, so I don't think it is merely that my Englishry makes me see comedy where there is none."

The Italian friend was Ruggero Orlando, who, apart from Charles Williams, arguably had the most influence on Dorothy Sayers in her translation of Dante. A writer and broadcaster, he had worked for a time in the Italian section of the BBC and later became the London correspondent of the Italian Broadcasting Corporation (RAI).[15] They first met in Cambridge in August 1947, when Orlando took part as a language instructor in the summer school of Italian Studies. Dorothy later described their meeting in a letter to C. S. Lewis, who had commented on her "metrical audacities":

Ruggero Orlando, writer and broadcaster,
who confirmed that Dante was still "alive
on men's lips."

About the metre—that does greatly interest me. As you know, I came to
Dante unprejudiced, and almost ignorant of Italian, and as I struggled
with the thing, I began to say to myself: "Unless my Italian pronunciation
is even worse than I thought it was, some of these lines scan very fluidly,
and the accent and rhythm shift about as they do in an English line and
perhaps with even more agility." But I didn't know, and couldn't find any
critic who seemed to have bothered much about it. Then I went to Cambridge in 1946, and heard a man read Dante exactly like an organ-grinder,
every line exactly like the next, and was discouraged, thinking the Italians
must scan on their fingers, without any reference to the speaking stress.
But the next year I met Ruggero Orlando (whom I mentioned when we
were talking about this at Oxford) and he immediately fell on me, talking
excitedly about the metrical effects. . . . So I said, "Oy! you're the man
I want—come and read me this stuff aloud." So he did, and it was just
what I thought it ought to be—not hurdy-gurdy at all, but very dramatic
with the stresses moving and sliding all over the place—just as you or I

would read Webster or Donne. So I rushed home and re-wrote a lot of it, determined to carry on in the way that I thought would best render for an English reader the effect of these continual stress-shifts.

In the year when she had met Orlando she wrote to E. V. Rieu:

> I have recently made great friends with an Italian gentleman . . . who is heart and soul on my side as regards my interpretation of Dante. He is being a tremendous help, especially in showing me how Dante's metre and rhythm affect the feel of the line and communicate the spirit and meaning. As a result I have made a number of improvements which will send the Penguins mad with author's corrections in galley and will probably startle the critics by the freedoms I have introduced into the English five-foot line. So from my point of view the printer's delays are a boon and a blessing, because the gain in liveliness and fidelity is tremendous, whatever the stick-in-the-muds may say.

She mentioned Orlando twice to Bickersteth, first in her letter of 15 January 1948:

> In order to get [Dante's speed, humour and flexibility] across in English, it has seemed to me necessary to depart from the syllabic rigidity of the classic five-foot line and use the full licence of English verse to vary from duple to triple rhythm, and to invert the stresses wherever the spirit of the thing seems to demand it. Dante himself does so, and indeed it was not until I heard him read aloud by an Italian friend that I realised the astonishing variations of his rhythm. . . . Some of these varieties I have tried to introduce into my own version, though not always in precisely the same places as in the original. I expect there will be a lot of trouble about it!

Then in November 1949, when Bickersteth had raised doubts about her metre, she said again:

> As regards the metre—I got an Italian friend to read the original aloud, and it did seem to me that he made a lot more variation in it than you get in Binyon or in any other of the earlier verse-translators. I noted particularly that he didn't swallow the vowels at the elision, but sort of pleated them in, like putting gathers in a piece of material.

Orlando, as well as being knowledgeable about metre in both English and Italian verse (he is himself a poet and a translator of poetry),[16] revealed a lively and humorous personality which delighted Dorothy. I was present at their first meeting, which took place at a tea party at Girton College. They talked about Dante's similes and Orlando referred to one which occurs in canto II of *Purgatorio*, where Dante compares the scattering of the souls (who had dallied to listen to Casella's singing) to the flight of pigeons startled from their feeding:

> Come quando, cogliendo biada o loglio,
>   li colombi adunati alla pastura,
>   queti, sanza mostrar l'usato orgoglio,
> se cosa appare ond'elli abbian paura,
>   subitamente lasciano star l'esca,
>   perch'assaliti son da maggior cura. . . .
>   (124–29)

In J. D. Sinclair's prose translation these lines are rendered, "As when doves collected at their feeding, picking up wheat or tares, quiet, without their usual show of pride, if something appears that frightens them suddenly leave their food lying, because they are assailed with a greater care. . . ."[17] One would never know from this how lively the original is. Orlando quoted the lines as an example of Dante's skill in drawing a picture by sound as well as meaning. Fluting and trilling his voice, especially on the words "cogliendo," "loglio" and "l'usato orgoglio," he made us *hear* the pigeons, while, at the same time, bobbing his head and strutting and puffing out his chest, he made us also *see* them vividly. There were a few scandalized glances from other members of the summer school, but this was the sort of response to Dante which Dorothy loved.

She was delighted also by the real-life instance which Orlando next gave from his own experience. In canto I of *Paradiso*, Dante compares a ray of light reflected in a V-shaped movement from a shining surface to—what? The Italian words are:

> E sì come secondo raggio suole
>   uscir del primo e risalire in suso,
>   pur come pellegrin che tornar vuole. . . .
>   (49–51)

Sinclair translates: ". . . and as a second ray will issue from the first and mount up again, like a pilgrim that would return home. . . ." This is the usual interpretation. But Orlando was certain that the term of comparison was not a pilgrim but a peregrine falcon, which the word "pellegrin" can also mean. His reason for this was that he had been out one day with a party of friends who hunted with trained falcons and he had seen a peregrine swoop and soar in the V-shaped movement of a ray of light reflected from a shining surface ("he bounced on the air"), and immediately he cried out: "Olà! olà! il pellegrin di Dante! [Look! look! Dante's peregrine!]."

It was characteristic of Dorothy that she attributed as much, if not more, importance to such living testimony as to textual corroboration. At the same time, Orlando remembers her coming to his house one day, triumphant at having recalled Dante's earlier description of the movement of a falcon in canto XXII of *Inferno*:

> non altrimenti l'anitra di botto
> quando 'l falcon s'appressa, giù s'attuffa,
> ed ei ritorna su crucciato e rotto. . . .

> [Just as the wild duck, with a falcon close
> Upon her, all of a sudden dives down quick,
> And up he skirrs again, foiled and morose. . . .]
> (130–32)

Both Bickersteth and C. S. Lewis seemed to forget that she had told them she had consulted an Italian about the variations in Dante's metre. The former, writing after her death, said in a letter to the *Times Literary Supplement* of 12 December 1958:

> Miss Sayers was, I think, too much inclined to scan Italian verse in the way that she scanned English verse, and consequently discovered in it rhythms which, as read by a native of Italy, it could not yield, owing to differences of tempo and of pronunciation (e.g., of the doubled consonant) between the two languages.

And C. S. Lewis, reviewing her posthumous volume of lectures, *The Poetry of Search and the Poetry of Statement*, suggested that she had exaggerated Dante's variations in metre by the violent rhythms by which she tried to represent them:

We English tend to read Dante to the tune of our own decasyllable. It looks as if Dorothy Sayers did. As a result, lines which will not submit to that treatment (most will) stuck out for her as they do not for the Italian reader, and the effect she tries to reproduce by her metrical extravagance does not exist. . . . Can she be right when she finds in "quando con trombe e quando con campane [now with trumpets, now with bells]" the lilt of "Diddle-diddle-dumpling, my son John"? The resemblance seems to me extremely faint. In so far as it exists at all it depends upon the fact that the English line is really two lines and that the Italian similarly breaks in two after "trombe." But don't all Dante's lines so break when read by an Italian?[18]

Evidently not.[19] "My friend," Dorothy had written to Bickersteth, "made a tremendous to-do about the 'Diddle-diddle-dumpling' rhythm" of the lines in question. One of these was the line C. S. Lewis thought she had misread, the very line which she quotes in her introduction to *Hell*, saying of it that it "rattles suddenly across the metre with a clatter as of tin trays falling down an iron staircase" (p. 59, n. 1).

It is clear that the section in her introduction in which she deals with Dante's metre (pp. 58–60) owes a great deal to her conversations with Orlando. And, it seems, to conversations with other Italian friends as well. In her letter to C. S. Lewis she mentions them, though not by name:

Other Italians to whom I have read [my translation] seem to like the shifting from iambic to anapaestic and so on—at any rate, then *they* start arguing about metre and shout lines aloud to show each other how for instance [in] the line

fino a Governol dove cade in Po[20]

the river suddenly stops flowing and tumbles into the Po with a reversed stress and a masculine ending. So I take it that my metrical flexibility does more or less bear *some* relation, in their ears, to what they find in the Italian.

Foligno had chided her for not paying enough attention to Italian Dante scholars. She acknowledged that she had been remiss in this respect, but pleaded the difficulty of obtaining Italian books in time of war and just afterwards. The truth was, however, that she did consult Italian friends and one in particular who, to her good fortune, was responsive to Dante's humour and metrical variety. The fact that he was Italian was not in itself sufficient. She had had the experience of hearing the "hurdy-gurdy" style of reading. There is also the rhetorical style, prevalent among Italian academics, in which Dante seems not only dead but embalmed. "Eppur si muove." Ruggero Orlando had confirmed for her that Dante, to quote a phrase she liked, was, even after six and a half centuries, still "alive on men's lips."[21]

9.

IN THE MIDST OF LIFE

Per correr migliori acque . . .
Purgatorio I, 1

The horrors of Hell were left behind. Dante and Virgil had emerged from the centre of the earth onto the starlit shore of the Mountain of Purgatory. At once there is a note of joy:

> Per correr migliori acque alza le vele
>   omai la navicella del mio ingegno,
>   che lascia dietro a sè mar sì crudele;
> e canterò di quel secondo regno
>   dove l'umano spirito si purga
>   e di salire al ciel diventa degno.
>
>   . . . .
>
> Lo bel pianeta che d'amar conforta
>   faceva tutto rider l'oriente,
>   velando i Pesci, ch'erano in sua scorta.

Dorothy Sayers captured the joy in the eager lift of her verse:

> For better waters heading with the wind
>   My ship of genius now shakes out her sail
>   And leaves that ocean of despair behind;
> For to the second realm I tune my tale,
>   Where human spirits purge themselves, and train
>   To leap up into joy celestial.
>
>   . . . .

> The lovely planet, love's own quickener,
> Now lit to laughter all the eastern sky,
> Veiling the Fishes that attended her.
> (I, 1–6, 19–21)

"Now lit to laughter all the eastern sky" is a happy rendering of "faceva tutto rider l'oriente."[1] Indeed her translation of *Purgatorio* has throughout a felicity in keeping with the original.

In his remarkable work *Dante the Maker*, William Anderson describes the effect of Dante's imaginative originality in placing the Mountain of Purgatory where he does:

> By removing Purgatory so completely from Hell Dante devised an environment that gave a new aim and joyfulness to the doctrine of purgation. By placing it in the unpeopled ocean of the southern hemisphere, at the antipodes of Jerusalem, then thought to be the centre of the inhabited world, he gave his audience a fuller sense of the roundedness of the Earth. . . . By attributing its creation to the mass thrown up when Lucifer hurtled from the place of the archangels and corkscrewed down to the centre of the Earth and when all the land mass of the southern hemisphere veiled itself with the sea in horror, he made the mountain part of the dynamic cosmography in which the Divine Will provides the place of healing for the consequences of the Fall. If we regard Mount Purgatory, too, as the place of the purification of the imagination, with its angel guardians, miraculous sculptures, and its cornices benevolently haunted with voices and visions, then, in rearing this prodigious mountain from below the sea-bed, he was raising the imagination of our ancestors out of the grasp of sightless rock into the light of conscious awareness. Where before they could only mine for images in their own minds and find nightmare, they could now let their visions grow and flower with new pleasure.[2]

Anderson's book was written long after Dorothy Sayers' death, but she had responded in a similar way to the image of Mount Purgatory. She considered the second *cantica* to be "the tenderest, subtlest, and most human section of the *Comedy*":

> Of the three books of the *Commedia*, the *Purgatorio* is, for English readers, the least known, the least quoted—and the most beloved. . . . The *Inferno* may fill one with only an appalled fascination, and the *Paradiso* may

daunt one at first by its intellectual severity; but if one is drawn to the *Purgatorio* at all, it is by the cords of love, which will not cease drawing till they have drawn the whole poem into the same embrace. (Introduction, p. 9)

Her pleasure in *Purgatorio* is apparent also in her letters to Scott-Giles. Abstract diagrams would of course be needed, but she wanted the mountain itself to be represented by a *drawing*, which should give some impression of its towering grandeur and awe-inspiring isolation. As early as March 1946 she was trying to visualise what she would like. All the diagrams of the mountain which she had seen so far were "hideous and preposterous . . . no beauty and no sense of height." She decided to have a shot at sketching it herself in pencil and sent Scott-Giles two attempts. "Don't laugh!" she pleaded.

To suggest the height of the mountain (three thousand miles) the drawing had to be so narrow that it was difficult to show the path taken by Dante and Virgil. Other illustrators have faked this by making it appear that the poets travelled spirally right round the mountain. But that, as the annotator of the Temple Classics edition sternly remarks, "is erroneous." The poets travel only on the northern, that is to say, the sunny, side from east to west. In her two sketches, Dorothy had dealt with this problem by twisting the rock stairways so as to bring them back a little each time, allowing room for Dante and Virgil to walk along each cornice before climbing up onto the next. She had tried, she said, to get away from "the awful factory-chimney effect" which other diagrams produce, by making Ante-Purgatory (that is, the first two terraces) tumultuous and variegated. She had also tried to indicate what the material of the rock might be like:

> I have used an aqueous rock-formation of the organpipe or Giants' Causeway variety—because it is actually in this kind of rock that you do get the towering structure and the narrow ledges. Since Purgatory "rushed up" in alarm when Lucifer fell from Heaven it ought, perhaps, to look more volcanic; but I have taken the view that these aqueous formations were already there, in the sea, and that the displacement merely brought them to the surface.[3]

She hoped that Scott-Giles would be able to produce a drawing of his own, based on one or other of her attempts: she envisaged a double-spread, with a drawing on one side and on the other a diagrammatic outline, with the two terraces and the seven cornices marked off and labelled. In the end, a drawing of the mountain was printed as a frontispiece, and in the body of the introduction a section of the mountain is shown, with areas ruled off and lettered (p. 62). The drawing, based on Dorothy's sketches, was not after all the work of Scott-Giles but of Dorothy's artist friend Norah Lambourne. It is anonymous except for one tiny detail. In the bottom right-hand corner of the mountain there is the capital letter "L," the initial which Dorothy L. Sayers and Norah Lambourne had in common.[4]

Two diagrams were also needed: one, a circular bird's-eye view, showing the progress of Dante and Virgil up the mountain during daylight, and a chart giving the signs of the zodiac, "so that people can grasp where the Sun is, and where 'Night' is, and what has become of the Moon." What she did *not* want was something like the diagrams in the Temple Classics edition, which are "filled up with such a lot of woolly-caterpillar contour work that one's eyes swivel in one's head looking at [them], and half the lettering is upside down."[5] She was pleased with Scott-Giles' diagrams when they came. Of the bird's-eye view (on p. 340 of *Purgatory*) she wrote: "The arrangement of the Purgatorial Circles looks to me as clear as anybody could possibly expect in a thing so awkwardly shaped for diagrammatising" (letter of 26 September 1952).

They had put their heads together to devise a satisfactory way of showing the signs of the zodiac and the sun's daily path at three different dates, as well as the direction of its yearly motion through the signs. The result was an excellent diagram (see p. 100 of *Purgatory*), an indispensable aid to canto IV, 61–84, where Dante, looking east, sees to his astonishment that the sun is on his left and receives from Virgil a lesson in astronomy bristling with problems for the average modern reader. It was with such difficulties in mind that Dorothy said resignedly to Scott-Giles: "I suppose we've got to have the usual clock-diagram."

Since Mount Purgatory is 180 degrees from Jerusalem, Dante is able to make great play with the relative times in the northern and southern hemispheres. Canto II, for instance, opens with a comprehensive glance at the apportionment of light over the globe:

> Già era 'l sole all'orizzonte giunto
>   lo cui meridian cerchio coverchia
>   Ierusalem col suo più alto punto;
> e la notte, che opposita a lui cerchia,
>   uscìa di Gange fuor con le Bilance,
>   che le caggion di man quando soverchia;
> sì che le bianche e le vermiglie guance,
>   là dov'ì'era, della bella Aurora
>   per troppa etate divenivan rance.
>
> [The Sun by now o'er that horizon's rim
>   Was sinking, whose meridian circle stands
>   With its mid-arch above Jerusalem,
> While Night, who wheels opposed to him, from sands
>   Of Ganges mounted with the Scales, whose weight
>   Drops in her hour of victory from her hands;
> So that, where we were, fair Aurora, late
>   Flushing from white to rose-vermilion,
>   Grew sallow with ripe age and matron state.]

In plain words, divested of mythology and astrology, these lines mean that it is sunset at Jerusalem, night in India and sunrise on Mount Purgatory. Again, in canto III, Dante, seeing only his own shadow, is afraid that he has been abandoned. Virgil reassures him, saying:

> "Vespero è già colà dov'è sepolto
>   lo corpo dentro al quale io facea ombra:
>   Napoli l'ha, e da Brandizio è tolto."
>
> [" 'Tis vesper-tide already where the tomb
>   Yet holds the body in which I once cast shade;
>   Naples received it from Brundisium."]
>   (25–27)

That is to say, it is 3 p.m. in Naples and, consequently, 6 p.m. in Jerusalem and 6 a.m. on Mount Purgatory. Readers who do not skip such passages, but take the trouble to visualise the globe and the time of day, get their reward. Canto IV, for instance, which contains the difficult lesson in astronomy, ends with a magnificent vision of the northern hemisphere veiled in darkness while the southern is flooded by the full blaze of noon:

> "Vienne omai: vedi ch'è tocco
> meridian dal sole ed alla riva
> cuopre la notte già col piè Morrocco."

> ["Forward!" said he; "look how the sun doth stand
> Meridian-high, while on the western shore
> Night sets her foot upon Morocco's strand."]
>   (137–39)

And so a clock-diagram was required. The Temple Classics edition provides one, consisting of two concentric circles. The outer one is a clock, with the twenty-four hours marked off round the rim, in two sets of twelve, from noon to midnight, and from midnight to noon. Jerusalem and Purgatory are shown opposite each other on a vertical line which bisects the inner circle. Spain and the Ganges are shown opposite each other on a horizontal line, which crosses the vertical at right angles. Italy is shown on a line between Spain and Jerusalem which springs from the horizontal at an angle of forty-five degrees. Beneath this diagram, in very small print, are the following words:

> Clock marking simultaneous hours at different regions of the earth. To indicate changes of hour, the reader may imagine the rim of the clock to revolve counter-clockwise, while the five hands remain stationary, or the hands to revolve clockwise, while the rim remains stationary.

The effect is not encouraging.

Gazing ruefully at this smudged and faint diagram and conscientiously imagining the rim of the clock, or the hands, revolving, Dorothy hit on a brilliant idea: why not make the inner circle *actually* revolve? After eager discussion with Scott-Giles, she managed to persuade Penguin to provide two pages which could be easily detached from the book. On one is a small circle showing the relative positions of Jerusalem, Mount Purgatory, the Ganges, Morocco and Rome. On the other is a larger circle, numbered like a clock, as in the Temple

Classics volume, but with an additional outer rim, showing the signs of the zodiac, with Venus in Pisces and the sun in Aries, as Dante indicates. The reader is instructed to cut out both circles, paste them onto cardboard and fasten them together at the centre with a split pin. ("I hope this isn't going to set a fashion for cutting up Penguin books," said Dr. Rieu when he dubiously agreed to this unusual arrangement.)[6] Unhappily, despite all the care that had been taken, when *Purgatory* was first published in 1955 the Ganges and Morocco were printed on the wrong sides! This was hastily put right before the first impression was sold out. Copies containing this error are now collectors' items.

By October 1947 correspondence about Dante had become well established between Dorothy and myself. I was able to lend her various books, in particular a remarkable work, *Dante and the Early Astronomers* by M. A. Orr, which she found very helpful.[7] I wrote to tell her of my attempts to interest students in Dante's time references, saying that in preparing lectures I had noticed that such allusions are essential to *Purgatorio*, being part of the very "stuff" of which that *cantica* is made—time and the alternation of day and night:

And not only that, but the events of each day are arranged along the arc of daylight, and the quality or degree of radiance from the heaven is different for each episode in the twelve hours. This has both symbolic and emotional value. In other words, the lighting arrangements of this *cantica* are fascinating to trace. For instance, Manfred, "biondo, bello e di gentile aspetto" and "sorridendo," has the full morning sun upon him; the Belacqua episode occurs in the blaze of noon-day sun. The outcry against Italy and Florence takes place in the afternoon, in shadow, and the quietude of evening follows this climax. I never realized before that we meet the blinded envious at *noon*, by which Dante seems to have anticipated Milton![8]

Dorothy replied:

It's quite true, as you say, that the "feel" of the time of day does most beautifully and subtly accompany the progress up the mountain. . . . The thing that has been striking me is the incredible cleverness with which Dante uses his "time of day" to vary and make plausible all the stuff about his shadow; and how the two things help to establish one another. For instance, when he meets the Excommunicate, and they see the shadow "run from him to the rock," you see that *long* shadow and are reminded that it is still quite early. Then, he and Virgil climb up to the second Terrace and sit looking back eastward, and he notices the sun "driving on his left hand." . . . They hear Belacqua speak, look round, and see a rock, and go and investigate. The shades are *behind* the rock, resting *in the shadow,* and are so lazy that they don't look up till Dante is standing quite close to them, *in* the shadow, so that *his* shadow is invisible. Then he goes, and they (a little more awake by this time) look after him and see his shadow on the left. Look how that places his direction again—he sits looking back east, and the *sun* is on his left: he walks on up the mountain and the *shadow* is on his left; nothing's left vague—you *see* the change of direction. (22 October 1947)

Her letters were full of such exchanges of pleasure: "Let us rejoice together over a brilliant little effect," or "Have you noticed how well Dante manages to suggest," etc., etc. *Enjoyment* was not much in vogue in academic circles then—or now. I found her letters a tonic.

Although she could bring a powerful lens to bear on the ill-doings of society, Dorothy Sayers was not by temperament inclined to despair. On the contrary: she had a Chestertonian gusto for life. She responded exuberantly to the challenge of work, to achievement, to friendship, to laughter and to fun. She was a great mixer of levels, again like Chesterton (and like her own Lord Peter Wimsey), and had no difficulty in combining intellectual pursuits with everyday life. This was one of her strengths as an interpreter of Dante to the modern reader: she could explain out-of-date concepts in terms of contemporary experience. Like many women, she was able to do more than one thing at a time. While her hands peeled vegetables at the kitchen sink, she translated Dante in her head. Pouring water into a bowl, she pondered the image at the beginning of canto XIV of *Paradiso:*

> Dal centro al cerchio, e sì dal cerchio al centro,
>   movesi l'acqua in un ritondo vaso,
>   secondo ch'è percossa fuori o dentro.

> [Water in a round bowl makes ripples glide
>   Centre to rim, or back from rim to centre,
>   As from within 'tis jarred, or from outside.]

Many of Dante's images are drawn from homely, everyday things. She was convinced that he *saw* what he wrote: it was not just a matter of words. And she was equally convinced that few translators took the trouble to *see* the picture which the words evoke. The thief in canto XXV of *Inferno* who is transformed into a snake pulls in his ears, "as a snail her horns."[9] Binyon, to her indignation, had translated this "as the snail withdraws into its shell." How, she stormed, could he fail to see the resemblance between the ear disappearing into the man's head and the tender horn of a snail being drawn in? Had he never looked a snail in the face? Possibly, but it was not often that he stepped into the back garden to bring in the washing when it rained and snails were on the path.

Her hearty sense of humour—she would laugh till the tears ran down her cheeks—saved her from ludicrous juxtapositions, which not all translators avoid. In a lecture I heard her give,[10] she made amusing play with the lapse committed by the unfortunate Neville B. Anderson, who came to grief in a passage in canto XI of *Paradiso*, where the first followers of St. Francis are described as casting off their shoes in their eagerness to hurry after him:

> . . . tanto che 'l venerabile Bernardo
> si scalzò prima, e dietro a tanta pace
> corse e, correndo, li parve esser tardo.
> O ignota ricchezza! o ben ferace!
> Scàlzasi Egidio, scàlzasi Silvestro
> dietro allo sposo, sì la sposa piace.
> (79–84)

Here is Anderson's translation. The bride is Poverty; her bridegroom is St. Francis.

> . . . whence venerable Bernard first thought meet
> to go unshod, after so great peace
> he ran, and running blamed his lagging feet.
> O wealth untold, good fruitful of increase!
> Giles bares his feet, Sylvester his, behind
> the Bridegroom, such the Bride's peculiar grace.

True, poor Anderson does put a comma after "his," but this is barely sufficient to ward off disaster, compounded as it is by the "peculiar grace" of the bride. "Let it stand," said Alice Curtayne, "as a warning against all English *terza rima* renderings of Dante."[11] Dorothy commented, "I do not know why she says that. It is the kind of accident that might happen to anybody, even in prose." She went on to show what can, after all, be done in English verse to catch the speed and rhythm of the Italian line, "scàlzasi Egidio, scàlzasi Silvestro," a sound, she said, "as of people madly shuffling off their shoes in the changing-room before rushing out on to the running-track:

> O wealth undreamed! O goods that teem and grow!
> Sylvester, Giles, they fling off their shoes, they fly,
> To follow the groom, the bride delights them so.

Although the *Purgatorio* inspired joy, she found it demanding as regards doctrine. On 26 September 1952 she wrote to Scott-Giles, "I am now really trying to get on with the notes to *Purgatory*. They are *much* harder work than the *Inferno*—so many biographies of obscure mediaeval people, and such loads and loads of clotted scholastic theology to elucidate and make palatable." A year later, on 28 September, having completed everything except the glossary of names, she wrote to Dr. Rieu:

> I am afraid you will find the *apparatus criticus* dreadfully bulky. There is so much scholastic philosophy that needs explaining; and you cannot do it briefly, or the explanation would be as incomprehensible as the text. Where the meaning of every technical term is unfamiliar, the only way is to start absolutely from scratch, and expound everything in concrete instances.

A good example of her ability to do precisely that is to be found in the notes to canto XVIII. This is a profound and difficult canto, in which Virgil holds forth to Dante on the question of free will. The thrust of his discourse is the distinction which he draws between natural impulses and rational choice. The former are implanted in us as "prime volitions" and in themselves are neither laudable nor blameworthy. Dante in reply voices a perplexity: are we not bound to pursue that which we love, that is to say, are we not victims of our temperamental urges?

To answer, Virgil draws upon the scholastic distinction between form and substance. This required skilful elucidation for modern readers. Dorothy Sayers was not content, as many translators have been and many still are, to leave her readers floundering. She knew how much help they would need and she was scrupulous in providing it. She had discussed the problem in her letter to Dr. Rieu:

> I asked an average educated person what the expression "substantial form" conveyed to him, and he replied immediately "a solid body." I then delivered a short lecture on the meaning of "substance." He was greatly interested and inquired: "But does all this come into Dante?" "Indeed it does," said I, "with how much more!" He said: "You surprise me; I always imagined Dante was a very primitive kind of person who wouldn't know much about anything of that sort." When I had partially recovered, I said, "But he lived in Florence, in the 14th century—one of the most cultured cities in the full flower of a highly sophisticated century, steeped in Aristotle and the Schools. Had you confused the First Renaissance with the Dark Ages?"

In her notes to canto XVIII she met the problem head-on. In mediaeval philosophy, she explains, the word *substance* was used to mean an individual existing being:

> Most of the beings we meet with are *material* substances, consisting of *matter* and *form*; the form being the organization of the substance, and the matter being that which is organized. At the lowest end of the scale of creation we have *inanimate* substances, in which the form is merely the shape or arrangement of the matter. (P. 211)

At this point she comes to the aid of the faint-hearted with a homely example: a card of glass buttons. Every button is a lump of matter (glass) formed into a certain (button-) shape. "It is the particular quantum of glass used in its manufacture which gives Button A its 'thisness' and distinguishes it from Button B." On the other hand, it is *form* which gives the glass its "thusness," in virtue of which it is one *kind* of thing and not another—a button, and not, for example, a wineglass or a test-tube. Here was an illustration taken from her own sewing-box.

To make plain the difference between form and substance in *ani-*

mate creatures, she took as an example the cat on her hearth-rug, or more probably a cat sitting on her shoulder as she wrote:

> Thus a cat, for example, is not merely a lump of cat-matter organized into a cat-shape: such a being exists, but it is a dead cat. The living cat has an "animal" or "sensitive" soul (*anima sensitiva*) which, animating and *informing* the cat-matter-shape, confers being upon it—makes it, that is, *substantially* the cat we know, which eats and runs and purrs and catches mice and has kittens; and this is its *substantial form*. (P. 211)

A human being has a *rational soul*: that is his or her *substantial form*; it has the power to discriminate between good and evil desires and to give or withhold assent—in other words, to choose. Thus Virgil answers Dante's question: are we not bound to pursue that which we love? In this round-about way, he has distinguished between natural love and rational love.

In her introduction to *Purgatory* Dorothy Sayers apologises to the reader, as she did in her letter to Rieu, for the "formidable bulk of the Commentaries to certain cantos":

> In commenting on the finer theological points, there appear to be only two possibilities: a brief definition, as technical as the text itself and equally unintelligible to the general reader; or a lengthy explanation, in terms of cats and cabbages and other familiar phenomena, to show what the problem or doctrine in question really means, and what its consequences are in daily experience. Of these alternatives, I have not hesitated to choose the latter. . . . (P. 54)

No apology was called for. Her ability to explain complicated doctrine in terms of "daily experience" gave her notes and commentaries their exceptional value.

She had been practising her skills of elucidation for several years in her lectures to the summer schools of Italian and elsewhere.[12] The notes and commentaries to both *Hell* and *Purgatory* benefited greatly from this preparatory work. The two lectures which she delivered in Cambridge in August 1948, "The Meaning of Heaven and Hell" and "The Meaning of Purgatory," are especially relevant. Profound and learned, they show the depth and range of her reading; but they are also clear, and they are entertaining. Already in 1948 she knew it would be necessary to include in her introduction a section explaining the Catholic doctrine of purgation. She tried this out on the summer school audience. It was a great compliment that she paid us: she did not talk down to us, but she made the subject intelligible. When the first volume of her lectures, *Introductory Papers on Dante*, was published in 1954, she invited me to write a preface. Recalling the impact of those magnificent expositions we had heard year after year, I wrote:

> Dante is not a "popular" writer and this is not a "popular" book about Dante; that is to say, neither Dante nor Miss Sayers deceives us into believing that difficult things are easy to understand. . . . Miss Sayers does not ignore or under-estimate the difficulties: what she does is to remove one by one various obstacles which prevent us from confronting the difficulties as they really are. The zest with which she performs this service is so invigorating that even the most apathetic are likely to be stirred into taking some trouble on their own account. . . . The breadth and power of her interpretation of Dante's thought and the vividness of her appreciation of his art so enlarge and enliven the mind that the reader (and the listener, as those who were privileged to hear these papers delivered as lectures can testify) finds himself scaling height after height. In her capacity for communicating mental exhilaration Miss Sayers is unequalled. (Pp. viii–ix)

The section of her introduction to *Purgatory* which deals with the doctrine (pp. 54–61) is a distilled version of the lecture which she gave in 1948, shortened, simplified, enlivened, but still theologically sound. Indeed, a Dominican priest, the late Dr. Kenelm Foster, himself an eminent Dantist, told me that he considered her statement of the doctrine of purgation to be the best he knew of for the general reader.

Her work on *Purgatory* was several times interrupted. First, there were the numerous lectures which she generously consented to give, always without remuneration. Then in 1950 her husband, who had been ailing for some years, became seriously ill. He died in June of that year. For six months at least she had been in such a state of anxiety and watchfulness that no serious work had been possible. Next came *The Emperor Constantine*, the chronicle play she wrote for the Festival of Colchester in 1951. Altogether she had lost about two years' work on Dante. Nevertheless the whole of the *Purgatory* volume, except for the glossary, was ready by September 1953.

After that came another interruption, crucial and with unforeseen consequences. Instead of proceeding with *Paradiso*, she turned aside to translate the *Chanson de Roland*. One explanation for that seemingly odd decision might be that she needed a change from Dante. But *The Emperor Constantine* had already provided a change. There is another explanation. During her frequent visits to our home in Cambridge she continued to hold lengthy conversations with my husband, Lewis Thorpe, about mediaeval French literature, this being his special field. She took a great interest in his edition of a thirteenth-century prose romance, *Le Roman de Laurin*. He talked with her about her translation of *Tristan*. I remember that he told her he preferred her own lively foreword to the introduction by George Saintsbury, which he found verbose and rambling. "Oh, but I was lucky to get him," Dorothy replied. Lewis also knew Mildred Pope, Dorothy's Oxford mentor, whom he greatly admired.

It must have been in the summer of 1953 that, reminded by such conversations of her own study of Old French at Oxford, she pulled out her early translation of *Roland*. She may even have thought of showing it to us, but now that she looked at it again she found that it was "very bad."[13] She knew she could make a better job of it now. What a temptation to try! Surely *Paradiso* could wait a while. Rieu apparently raised no objection. A contract was drawn up and by February 1954 she was well into her translation of *Roland*.

I expressed some alarm when I heard what she was doing and she looked, I remember, a little shame-faced. But she was obviously enjoying herself. She had renewed contact with her beloved Miss Pope, whose advice she sought. She also asked Lewis' opinion on a number of problems relating to the text. He offered to check the whole translation, line by line, when it was finished. She gratefully accepted. When he had done so he was much impressed. "What an outstanding Romance scholar Mildred Pope made of you!" he wrote to her, on 11 February 1957, when he returned her text. And on receiving the published volume he wrote on 24 June, "Once again I congratulate you. The text reads very smoothly and with immense force, and represents in English the effect which the *jongleur* must have produced upon a contemporary audience. The introduction is excellent." And he asked her if she would be willing to contribute an article on translating the *Chanson de Roland* for the journal *Nottingham Mediaeval Studies*, which he had recently founded. She agreed to do so.[14]

By May 1956 she had returned to Dante. On the 26th of that month she wrote to me to say, "I have been struggling with *Paradiso* I and II, which would seem to have been written with the express purpose of bedevilling the English translator and landing him in impossible rhyme schemes." By July of that year she was involved in a "grim struggle" with canto V: "Either I am growing too old for the job, or the *Paradiso* is a most damnably difficult proposition. I crawl at the rate of about three lines a day, and the horrible jig-saw of rhyme and metre goes round in my head like a squirrel in a cage, and I dream in *terza rima*. . . . One would not wish to be beaten and fall by the way." Canto V is discouragingly technical, being concerned with vows and the conditions upon which a covenant may be dissolved. She found it one of the dullest bits of *Paradiso*. She had ended it, she wrote, "with a really god-awful jingle":

> So that blest form vanished in his own blaze
> Of ever-mounting joy, and straight began,
> All close enclosed in his bright carapace,
> What next I'll sing as best my canto can.

But she need not have been so disparaging. It is a very close equivalent of Dante's own play on words:

> per più letizia sì mi si nascose
> dentro al suo raggio la figura santa;
> e *così chiusa chiusa* mi rispose
> nel modo ch'l seguente *canto canta.*

In August she was "wrestling ferociously" with canto VI. She wrote in mock exasperation about the difficulties which it presented, with its long account of Roman history and array of intractable names of persons, battles and rivers. (Yet she enjoyed the epic resonance of a catalogue of names. Auden had recently said in his inaugural lecture as Professor of Poetry at Oxford that it was the sign of a poet to respond in this way, and she was pleased to note that she passed that test at least.) "It hasn't turned out *too* badly, I think, in the end," she wrote on 15 August. A week later, driving to Colchester to visit friends, I stopped in Witham and called on her unexpectedly. She opened the door, looking tired and distracted, as though wondering, "Now, what's *this* nuisance?" I was pleased to notice that her face lit up when she saw me. "Oh, it's you, is it!" she said. "Come in and I'll read you canto VI." We went upstairs to her study and sat by her desk in the window overlooking Newland Street, the road the Romans had marched along to Colchester. And there I heard for the first time her strong, masterly rendering of the speech of the Emperor Justinian, that scroll of Roman history, both epic and romantic, from the earliest legends down to the Redemption, the fall of Jerusalem and the championship of the Church by Charlemagne. It was a stirring and memorable experience.

She enjoyed translating canto VII, which had inspired her play *The Just Vengeance*. The verse flowed easily. By November 1956 she was at work on canto XI, but five months seem to have gone by before she began on canto XII. She was not happy with either of these. By June 1957 she had reached canto XIV, "which bids fair to be one of the nastiest yet." In August she had passed the central canto and was "struggling forward to XVIII."

During this period there ran through her letters a note of discouragement and fatigue. It seemed to me that she needed some time off. I invited her to accompany me to Chichester, where I went occasionally to visit some elderly cousins. It would be an opportunity to meet Professor Bickersteth, who was living there then, having retired from his Chair of English at Aberdeen University. She accepted with enthusiasm. Accordingly, in the second week of September I called for her at Witham and we drove down to Sussex.

We were there for two days, during which we visited my relations, who gave us tea in Edwardian style, and also the Bishop of Chichester, Dr. George Bell, an old friend of Dorothy's from her Canterbury days. But the outstanding event, for both of us, was our meeting with Professor Bickersteth. I had long admired his work on Carducci and Leopardi (now regrettably out of print), which I had used in my

Geoffrey L. Bickersteth, translator of Carducci, Leopardi, and Dante.

teaching in the Italian Department at Cambridge. Dorothy had been
corresponding with him for more than ten years and they were on
excellent terms of mutual regard.

We were invited to lunch. Professor and Mrs. Bickersteth lived at
No. 2 St. Martin's Square, a beautiful house of which the founda-
tions are Roman. Mrs. Bickersteth, the daughter of a Cambridge Professor of Moral Sciences, was the sister of the war poet, Charles Sor-
ley, who was killed in 1915. With them was their daughter Ursula, a
graduate in classics of the University of Aberdeen. On the wall of the
drawing-room were almost life-size portraits of two sons, Tony and
Julian, who died in World War II, and to whose memory Professor
Bickersteth had dedicated his translation of the *Commedia*.

This had recently been published and had received an inadequate
review in the *Times Literary Supplement*. Dorothy had been most in-
dignant. On 19 August 1956 she had written to me:

I expect you saw the T.L.S. review of Bickersteth's version this week. All the stereotyped stuff about "courageously facing the challenge of *terza rima*" . . . and about "no English poet of any stature having sustained it for long, except Shelley (Morris? Browning? Bridges?—and now Mac-Neice has written an enormous poem in it, and John Wain another; they will really have to find a new gambit soon). . . . Nothing whatever about the diction, the handling of the dialogue, the attention paid to the images . . . the grasp of theology . . . nothing, in short, of the faintest interest or originality, and hardly anything that couldn't have been written without reading the book at all. It isn't fair.

Her own translation of *Purgatorio*, published at almost the same time, had fared rather better. It had received an excellent review from Colin Hardie in the *Modern Language Review*.[15] She was delighted by it, the more so as Colin Hardie "knew what he was writing about, being a Dante scholar"; he had also taken the trouble to say something about the quality of the verse. And, as she wrote to me, on 27 May 1955, "Bickersteth has, as usual, been extremely generous and kind about my *Purgatory*."

The stage was set, therefore, for a genial encounter. Conversation at lunch was extremely lively, ranging over the shortcomings of reviewers, the strange prejudice against *terza rima*, and the current state of Dante studies. "There are no great English Dante scholars left," Professor Bickersteth said. After lunch, the three of us retired into Professor Bickersteth's book-lined study and talk about Dante continued. He took Dorothy to task, I remember, about her views on Dante's humour, saying that she exaggerated it. He objected, for instance, to her admittedly ingenious but, in his opinion, inappropriate handling of *Purgatorio* II, 43–48. In this passage Dante, standing on the shore of the mountain and gazing out over the ocean, sees a boatload of souls approaching, piloted by an angel. The problem for the translator is that Dante quotes the words of a psalm which the souls are singing, and quotes it in Latin: "In exitu Israel de Aegypto [When Israel went out of Egypt]." And he rhymes *Aegypto* with *iscripto* and *scripto*:

> Da poppa stava il celestial nocchiero,
>   tal che parea beato per iscripto;
>   e più di cento spirti entro sediero.

> *"In exitu Israel de Aegypto"*
> cantavan tutti insieme ad una voce
> con quanto di quel salmo è poscia scripto.

In J. D. Sinclair's translation this reads, "On the poop stood the heavenly steersman, such that blessedness seemed written upon him, and more than a [hundred] spirits sat within. *In exitu Israel de Aegypto* they sang together with one voice, with all that is written after of that psalm." Dorothy had permitted herself the following:

> Freehold of bliss apparent in his face,
> The heavenly pilot on the poop stood tiptoe,
> And with him full an hundred souls had place.
> "In exitu Israel de Aegypto,"
> From end to end they sang their holy lay
> In unison; and so he brought his ship to.

She bowed her head in mock abashment under Professor Bickersteth's reproaches, but in reality she was unrepentant. He agreed with her that "freehold of bliss" was an excellent rendering of "beato per iscripto." Her friend Ruggero Orlando had thought so, too. They had discussed it as early as December 1947, when on the 16th of that month he wrote to her to say that "beato per iscripto" seemed to him to echo the phrase which occurs in the Gospels: "it is written," meaning "by God's will." He had suggested "a writ of bliss," but he preferred "freehold of bliss" because, he said, "it recalls and rejuvenates the original meaning of a common word, which is a great thing in poetry." Dorothy and the professor entered joyously into all these subtleties, while I sat by entranced, feeling privileged to listen to their discussion.

As we took our leave after tea, Professor Bickersteth warmly commended Dorothy's notes and commentaries in the two Penguin volumes, which far exceeded his own. He also expressed admiration for her lectures, the second volume of which, *Further Papers on Dante*, had by then been published. "Don't ever let anyone tell you those are not good," he said. "They are magnificent!"

It had been a most successful visit and Dorothy seemed in good spirits when she returned home. "I enjoyed it all amazingly," she wrote. She had by then finished translating eighteen cantos of *Paradiso.*

During the eleven years in which I had got to know Dorothy Sayers, she had become more and more like a member of our family. She felt perfectly at home with our way of life, in which academic work and domestic matters mingled and overlapped. It was rather how she lived herself. She seemed to love coming to stay with us and her letters glow with affectionate involvement in all our doings. When my son Adrian won a scholarship to his public school she wrote a long and knowledgeable letter about it. I wondered at the time that she should know so much about boys' schools. Busy as she always was, she found time to go with me to Drayton Beauchamp in Buckinghamshire to visit my father, Alfred Reynolds, the composer. They had a number of theatrical friends in common. He played her some of his songs and she sang them, sitting beside him at the piano. "Do you know," he said afterwards, "Miss Sayers has the ruins of a very pretty voice!"

With so many personal and family links, it was natural that when I made up my mind to be baptized (this ceremony having been omitted in my infancy) I should mention it to her. She expressed calm approval and asked if she might be present. I replied that witnesses would in fact be required and that I would be happy if she would consent to be one of them. She accepted, saying, "I see that the Prayer Book calls them godparents."

On the 13 December 1957 she joined our family party at the Blue Boar in Trinity Street, where we had a celebratory lunch, followed by the ceremony, which took place at the Church of the Holy Sepulchre (the "Round Church"), opposite the flat where we lived. The incumbent was Mark Ruston (later Canon Ruston), who had baptized my son and daughter. We were only a small group of about seven people who stood round the font. I remember that Dorothy alone, large and unwieldy as she was, knelt on the stone floor for a few moments to pray. Afterwards we returned to our flat for tea, and all was laughter and fun. She stayed the night at the Blue Boar and the next morning Lewis and I accompanied her to the Fitzwilliam Museum to see an exhibition of paintings by Blake. Two of them were illustrations of episodes of the *Commedia.* She then insisted on plunging with me into the crowd of Christmas shoppers in the centre of Cambridge in order herself to buy a present for Adrian—a recording of Beethoven's Fifth Symphony. By then she was looking tired and I wished she had not made that extra effort. Her chauffeur from Witham arrived soon after lunch and we said goodbye outside the Blue Boar.

The occasion had obviously meant a great deal to her, as it had to me. I had never seen her look so happy. It was as though in becoming officially a member of our family she had found a new fulfilment. We had talked of the remaining cantos of *Paradiso*: she had by then translated twenty. "The thought of the Notes and Commentaries makes me feel quite faint!" she joked. She discussed with Lewis the article on *Roland* which she had promised to write for his journal. He had just been appointed to the chair of French at Nottingham University and this too had been a reason for rejoicing that weekend. We talked also of the acres of work which still remained for me to do as general editor of the *Cambridge Italian Dictionary*, a responsibility I had taken on in 1948.[16] Altogether we were full of good resolve.

Four days later, on 18 December, I went to the University Library to work on the *Dictionary*. I had a niche on the ground floor where I was permitted to keep the piles of shoe-boxes in which thousands of cards were stored. Resuming work, I felt joyful and at peace after the momentous events of the weekend. Half-way through the morning my husband's face appeared at the window. He beckoned and spoke to me through the bars: "There's come some terrible news—it's Dorothy Sayers—she's dead."

10.

The Last Thirteen Cantos

. . . your job of torch-carrying.
Dorothy L. Sayers

When Dante died on 14 September 1321, his sons Pietro and Jacopo looked in vain for the last thirteen cantos of *Paradiso*. The manuscript did not go beyond canto XX. They were almost certain that their father had finished the work; but if so, where was the rest of it? They knew he was in the habit of sending batches of his cantos from time to time to his friend and patron, Can Grande della Scala, the ruler of Verona. But enquiries in that quarter too were of no avail. At last, yielding to the persuasions of friends, the brothers undertook to finish the poem themselves. They knew a good deal about it, having helped their father as amanuenses, and they had previously tried their hand at verse. All the same, it must have been a daunting undertaking. Fortunately, before they had gone far, Jacopo had a dream in which Dante appeared to him. He asked, "Father, did you finish the work?" Dante replied, "Yes, I finished it." Then he led his son to a house where the missing pages would be found. On waking, Jacopo went to rouse up a friend who had formerly lived in the house and together they hurried to investigate. And there, in a recess in a wall which was covered by a curtain,

they found a quantity of written sheets, all mouldy with the dampness of the wall and ready to rot away if they had been left there any longer. When they had cleaned off all the mould, they saw that the pages were numbered and, having placed them in order, they found that they had recovered, all together, the thirteen cantos that were lacking of the *Comedy*. Wherefore they copied them out rejoicing.[1]

These were the very cantos which, except for a few fragments, Dorothy Sayers left untranslated when she died. It is perhaps understandable, not only in view of her fatigue, why she made a pause where she did. The last thirteen cantos form, in a sense, a distinct entity. With the ascent of Beatrice and Dante, in canto XXI, into the Heaven of the Contemplatives, we reach a point of transition. The poem now gradually approaches its climax—the vision of God, with which the last canto ends. Dorothy knew the work well enough to realize that this final section called for a sustained effort of insight and skill. She may have decided to draw breath before rising to this culminating challenge.

In September 1956 I had gone on holiday with my husband to Arquà Petrarca, a mediaeval village in the Euganean Hills where Petrarch spent the last years of his life. Early in October I telephoned Dorothy to let her know we had returned. She wrote on the 6th, "Well, I was greatly relieved and delighted to hear your voice on the 'phone the other day. I look to you to inaugurate and sustain the new school of Humane Dantism in this country. . . . So do not, I beg you, fall into the sea or do anything tiresome before you have done your job of torch-carrying."

I wondered at the time how she imagined I would be able to perform any such exalted role. Certainly she never envisaged the task that did befall me. A year or so before her death, so I was later told, she had discussed the eventual disposition of her works with her friend Muriel St. Clare Byrne, whom she had designated her literary executrix. Muriel had said, "I shouldn't know what to do about your work on Dante." Dorothy had replied, "Oh, Barbara would see to all that." She never in fact broached the matter with me but it seems likely that she would have done so, had she not died so unexpectedly.

It is possible that she would have asked me to help her in preparing *Paradise* for the printers. Previously, as well as writing the preface to her first volume of lectures, *Introductory Papers on Dante,* I had helped her to draft the dedication and I wrote the "blurb" for the publishers. My husband, knowing how much she disliked such chores, had offered to compile the index. She accepted gratefully. He also undertook the index of the second volume, *Further Papers on Dante.* I helped with this and I read the proofs of both volumes. We enjoyed being of help to her in such ways. Since she was at that time suffering from arthritis in her hands, it was the least we could do.

If she had lived to finish *Paradise*, she might well have asked me to compile the glossary of names for her. She had found this an irksome task while working on *Purgatory*. And she would have continued to consult me, as she did from time to time, about the meaning of Italian words and phrases which seemed to her inadequately rendered by other translators or by editors of dictionaries. (She hoped for better things from the *Cambridge Italian Dictionary!*) She also discussed the problems of verse translation with me again and again, so much so that when she died it seemed as though she had left me instructions as to how to continue. But not consciously. She had no intimation that so little time was left to her. Had that been so, it is unlikely that she would have turned aside from Dante to translate the *Chanson de Roland.*

When news of her death reached Dr. Rieu he first telephoned Muriel St. Clare Byrne to ask how far Dorothy had got with *Paradise.* The last he had heard from her was that she had finished Canto VII. Muriel referred him to me and I was able to tell him that she had in fact completed twenty cantos. "Excellent!" he said. "Will you come up to London—we want to talk with you."

My visit to Dr. Rieu in his house in Highgate is still vivid in my memory. It was the first time I had met the originator of the Penguin Classics, whose translation of the *Odyssey*, the first in the series, I had long enjoyed and admired, having read it aloud twice (four times altogether) to each of my children. We spoke of the tragic interruption which had occurred. "We want you to finish *Paradise*," he said, coming straight to the point. I was horrified. Being still in a state of shock and grief, all I could do was to expostulate at some length. He let me have my say. Then, looking at me over his glasses in a shrewd but kindly way, he spoke one word: "Try."

This steadied me. I returned to Cambridge and early in January 1958 I began on canto XXI. In a few days I had hammered out a draft and sent it to Dr. Rieu. His comments were positive and constructive. I was much helped, too, by the friendly encouragement of Muriel St. Clare Byrne and Marjorie Barber, to whom I read aloud some of my early attempts. They more than anyone else were in a position to judge whether I was on the right lines, for they had listened to a number of Dorothy's cantos and were familiar with her views on verse translation. I was encouraged also by the response of Anthony Fleming, Dorothy's son, whom I now met for the first time. He gave me every facility as to unpublished articles, letters and note-books; and he proved a discerning listener.

Dr. Rieu continued to supervise my progress and I improved a number of lines under his editorship. But the most valuable and sustained help came from Professor Bickersteth. On hearing what I had undertaken, he wrote at once with his characteristic generosity to say: "If there is any way in which I can be of help, you have only to ask." I gladly took him at his word and sent him the first draft of every canto, on which he made detailed comments, drawing on his years of experience in the craft of translating *terza rima*. At a later stage I also had the benefit of being able to consult the poet John Press, who was then the British Council area officer in Cambridge and a near neighbour. He confirmed what Dorothy had said about the advantages of impure rhymes in English and encouraged me to make use of them.

Dorothy had translated a few short passages of *Paradiso* in advance; they are nearly all lines in which Dante expresses wonder and joy. In 1955 she sent me eleven renderings of the first six lines of canto XXVII, asking which I preferred. At this point in the poem Dante has triumphantly passed his examination in Faith, Hope and Love, on which in the three preceding cantos he had been questioned in turn by St. Peter, St. James and St. John. At his success all Heaven breaks out into an exultant cry of joy:

> "Al Padre, al Figlio, allo Spirito Santo"
> cominciò "gloria!" tutto il paradiso,
> sì che m'inebriava il dolce canto.
> Ciò ch'io vedeva mi sembrava un riso
> dell'universo; per che mia ebbrezza
> intrava per l'udire e per lo viso.

Dorothy's trial renderings were as follows:

> 1. "Glory to Father, Son and Holy Ghost!"
> All Paradise broke forth till every sense

Reeled with the sweetness of the singing host;
And all I saw appeared as one immense
　Smile of the whole creation, ear and eye
　Drinking at once the inebriate bliss intense.

2. "To Father, and to Son, and Holy Ghost"
　All Heaven broke forth, "be glory!" till my sense
　Reeled with the sweetness of the singing host;
　And all I saw appeared as one immense
　　Smile of the universe; through ear and eye
　　So poured that vast inebriate effluence.

3. "Glory to Father, Son and Holy Ghost"—
　So sweet, it made me drunk with bliss to hear—
　Rang out through Paradise from all the host;
　And everything I looked on seemed as 'twere,
　　One smile of all creation, such vast glee
　　Inebriate drenched at once both eye and ear.

4. "Glory to Father, Son and Holy Ghost!"
　All Paradise broke forth, and rendered me
　With sweet sound drunken to the uttermost;
　While everything I looked on seemed to be
　　One smile of all creation, ear and eye
　　So drunk at once the inebriate ecstasy.

5. "To Father and to Son and Holy Ghost,"
　All Heaven broke forth, "be glory!" till I grew
　Drunk with the sweetness of the singing host;
　And everywhere I looked I seemed to view
　　One smile of all creation, ear and eye
　　Drinking alike the inebriate rapture through.

6. "Glory to Father, Son and Holy Ghost!"
　So sweet, my sense was drunken with the sound,
　Rang out through Paradise from all the host;
　I seemed to see, spread forth from bound to bound,
　　One smile of all creation; ear and eye
　　Inebriate both, in equal rapture drowned.

7. "Glory to Father, Son and Holy Ghost!"
　So sweet, that I was drunk with melody,
　Rang out through Paradise from all the host;

> And everywhere I looked, I seemed to see
> One smile of all creation, ear and eye
> Drinking at once that huge inebriate glee.

8. "Glory to Father, Son and Holy Ghost!"
> All Heaven began, until the whole of me
> Was drunk with bliss, so sweetly sang the host;
> And everywhere I looked I seemed to see
> One smile of all creation; thus through eye
> And ear poured in the inebriate ecstasy.

9. "Glory to Father, Son and Holy Ghost!"
> All Heaven began, until the soul of me
> Was drunk for joy of that sweet-singing host;
> And everywhere I looked, I seemed to see
> One smile of all creation; so through eye
> And ear poured in the inebriate ecstasy.

10. "To Father and to Son and Holy Ghost,"
> All Heaven broke forth, "be glory!"—such sweet din
> My sense was drunken to the uttermost;
> And all I saw, meseemed to see therein
> A smile of all creation, thus through eye
> And ear I drew the inebriate rapture in.

11. "To Father and to Son and Holy Ghost,"
> All Heaven broke forth, "be glory!" Whereupon
> Drunk with sweet sound, I was in rapture lost;
> And all I saw appeared to me as one
> Smile of the whole creation, thus through eye
> And ear the huge inebriate bliss did run.

I spent about a week pondering these and then wrote as follows:

It has been most interesting examining these eleven renderings of the Glory passage. I believe if you sent out sample packets like this to all probable critics and reviewers and set them to work they would write you more intelligent reviews!

I haven't yet fixed on one as preferable to the others but I have brought it down to five. I will tell you my reasons for preferring them to the others. . . . The selected candidates are 1, 2, 5, 8 and 9. First I will tell you why I cut out the others:

3. I don't care for "as 'twere"; and "glee" worries me because of its everyday associations of mischievous and sometimes spiteful joy, although of course it has a useful association with singing.

4. This is a good one; the only thing I don't like is the archaic use of "drunk" in the last line, though it echoes the "drunken" of line 3 and together they catch the "inebriava" and "ebbrezza" echo.

6. The last three lines are too far off the original, I think.

7. "glee" again—though I like most of it. Perhaps "huge inebriate glee" is too much for "ebbrezza."

10. I don't like "meseemed to see," though I *do* like the use of the rhymes in -in, which somehow excite one and make one strain to catch the sound of far-off singing.

11. I am not sure about "huge inebriate bliss" and about "run"; and I don't like "whereupon."

Now I will say what I like about the others:

1. For the first drunkenness, "m'inebriava," I enjoy "Reeled with the sweetness of the singing host." You have let go the drunkenness and drawn forth sweetness and bliss from Dante's "inebriava" and "ebbrezza," and suggested the inebriation in the "reeled" and "drinking." It's very skilful.

2. I prefer two things about this one: I like the burst of "be glory!" coming in the second line, echoing Dante's own effect here; and I like "smile of the universe" better than "smile of the whole creation"; but I don't much care for "vast inebriate effluence." Could you not combine 1 and 2 in this way, in the last three lines:

> And all I saw appeared as one immense
> Smile of the universe, ear and eye
> Drinking at once the inebriate bliss intense.

But now I suppose I have done your metre in. How difficult it is!

5. There's nothing much wrong with this one, is there? It runs joyously and nothing spoils it.

8. and 9. These are both very taking. I like "inebriate ecstasy" and I like "poured in." "The soul of me" is exciting in English, but Dante doesn't say it. He says *he* was made drunk.

I believe after all I come back to No. 5. It is perhaps the one which most closely resembles Dante, in that it doesn't make a fuss but states simply and plainly what happened. . . . No. 10 has this same quality of direct-ness, though, as I said, I am worried about "meseemed to see therein."

Dorothy replied:

Oh dear! I didn't mean to make you work so hard! It's very good of you to have bothered. And it's very interesting to see that all the things I like *you* like, and all the things I dislike you also dislike—the trouble being that every advantage is balanced by a corresponding snag. For instance, I too like the turning-over of "be glory!"—but it means putting "Heav'n" in-stead of "Paradise" (which I really prefer); and I am particularly taken with "sweet din," but it leaves me with a poor rhyme: therein/din, and also the awkwardness in the fourth line. And so on and so on. And when you think that almost every important passage presents one with just such a set of elaborate possibilities—unless it is one of those in which there is only one conceivable set of rhymes, and the difficulty is simply to fit grammar and sense to the metre—one finds oneself falling into a kind of stupor in which ecstasy has no part. . . .

Well, I will for the moment adopt Number 5, since you feel that it is, on the whole, the best of the bunch—unless I can, by taking thought, im-prove the one with the rhymes in "-in," which I do agree has a sort of exciting quality about it.[2]

When I came to read her final version, I found that she had after all plumped for number 10, as it stood, in spite of the awkwardness of "meseemed to see." Evidently the "sweet din," which I had also liked, had won the day.

Looking back, after her death, at my comments on these lines, I saw myself as an apprentice, fumbling to come to grips with a skill under the tuition of a master craftsman. Her kindly words, "I didn't mean to make you work so hard" often came back to me with a sad irony as I laboured to complete her work. Nevertheless, this early scrutiny proved a help to me, as did the memory of our many discussions of the problems which the translation presented, and of her reasons for solving them in one way rather than another.

The circumstances in which I worked were similar to her own. She had always found it stimulating to have several pieces of work on hand at the same time. I too had a number of commitments: my lectures and tutoring ("supervisions") for the Italian Department and Colleges of Cambridge University, which sometimes totalled more than twenty hours a week; the general editorship of the *Cambridge Italian Dictionary*; and my responsibilities towards my family. My husband, who during term time commuted at weekends between Nottingham and Cambridge, gave me encouraging and sympathetic support. He helped a great deal by listening to every canto in its first draft, pointing out lines which were not clear to him and praising those which seemed to him to have an authentic Sayers touch. For that was my aim: to produce a translation which matched Dorothy's in such a way that no join was noticeable.[3] My children, too, who had liked Dorothy and enjoyed her visits, were interested and involved. My eight-year-old daughter, who collected "interesting words" to help me with the dictionary, also tried to suggest rhymes for the translation. On one occasion, when I had toiled for hours over three lines which I could not get right, my son arrived home from school and looked expectantly for supper. "While I cook you some sausages, see if you can do these lines for me," I said. "Hand it over," said the fifteen-year-old, resignedly.

The lines in question occur in canto XXIV, where Dante is asked by St. Peter, "What are your reasons for believing that the Scriptures are inspired by God?" The answer which Dante gives is that the miracles narrated in the Bible guarantee its divine authorship:

> E io: "La prova ch'l ver mi dischiude
> son l'opere seguite, a che natura
> non scaldò ferro mai nè battè ancude.
> (100–102)

Sinclair's prose translation is, "And I: 'The proof which declares the truth to me is the works that followed, for which nature never heated iron nor smote anvil.' " I had translated the three preceding lines, in which St. Peter is speaking, as:

> I heard: "These premises thou dost submit,
> The old and new, as reasons for thy creed,
> How dost thou know them to be Holy Writ?"

The author at the time of her encounter
with Dorothy L. Sayers.

The rhyme which Adrian had to pick up for the next terzain was
therefore "-eed." As I cooked, he shaped the meaning into the
following:

> And I: "The proof wherein the truth I read
> Consists in works which knew not Nature's hand,
> Nor ever from her smithy could proceed."

This seemed to me a bargain in exchange for sausages and I gladly
accepted it, picking up the rhyme in "-and" in the next terzain:

> The answer came: "Say, then, what else doth stand
> As guarantor? The same which testified
> Their truth, as witness to its own is banned."

That is to say, if the miracles prove that the Scriptures are divinely inspired, the Scriptures cannot themselves be cited as proof that the miracles occurred. The logic is irrefutable, but the lines that followed refused obstinately to go into verse.

Like Dorothy, I often sat up late into the night, wrestling with the translation. I did so that night, but I got nowhere. I wanted to keep the rhyme in "-ied," as "testified" was the important word (or, as Dorothy would have called it, "the hammer rhyme"), but the meaning of the next lines seemed not to allow it:

> "Se 'l mondo si rivolse al cristianesmo,"
> diss'io, "sanza miracoli, quest'uno
> è tal, che li altri non sono il centesmo". . .

In Sinclair's prose translation this reads, " 'If the world was converted to Christianity without miracles,' I said, 'that one is such that the rest are not a hundredth part of it.' " That is to say, the spread of Christianity is itself proof that the miracles occurred (an argument in support of the Faith said to have originated with St. Augustine).

The next morning, exhausted and defeated, having got the children off to school, I took our dog for a walk. We went up Castle Hill and, entering a grassy enclosure, climbed to the top of the mound where the castle originally was. My mind a complete blank, I stood for a few moments gazing out over the Cambridge roof-tops. Suddenly I felt a soft sensation on the right side of my brow, as though a finger were touching it, and one word slid into my mind: "bide." It was not in the context of the lines I had been struggling with, nor did their meaning suggest it. However, I took it as a hint and, picking up the dog's lead, I addressed her: "Come on, Sally, we'll go home and see what 'bide' will do." On arriving home, I took up my tormented scribbles and wrote:

> If without miracles the world did bide
> By Christ, then all the miracles I know
> Are by this one a hundredfold outvied.

Not perfect, but at least I was out of that dark wood. The rest of the canto was somewhat easier but even so I had to sit up late over it for several more days. At last, at about 2 a.m. one morning I finished it.

Dante has done so well in his examination in Faith that the light of St. Peter whirls round him three times:

> As when a Lord has heard his page relate
>   Tidings so pleasing he doth kiss his cheek,
>   Embracing him, his joy to celebrate,
> So, singing blessings then for my soul's sake,
>   As I was silent, round me thrice did go
>   The apostolic light which bade me speak.

I knew that I should go to bed, but I could not resist just glancing at the beginning of canto XXV, to remind myself what I would have to deal with the next morning. And at once, without the slightest effort, nine lines floated into my head, complete with rhymes:

> If it should chance that e'er the sacred song
>   To which both Heaven and Earth have set their hand
>   Whence I am lean with labouring so long,
> Should touch the cruel hearts by which I'm banned
>   From my fair fold where as a lamb I lay,
>   Foe to the wolves which leagued against it stand,
> With altered voice, with altered fleece today
>   I shall return, a poet, at my font
>   Of baptism, to take the crown of bay.

Both these experiences of an unconscious "yielding up" of words were new to me and seemed to provide a glimpse into the processes of creativity. I was to experience such moments again, in later years, when I came to translate Ariosto's romantic epic *Orlando Furioso* into rhymed octaves.

Working in the midst of life, rather than in an ivory tower, brings certain advantages. It enables one to see beyond words to the reality which they evoke and from which they arose. I will give one example. In canto XXX Dante sees a river of light, in which he eagerly bathes his eyes; and immediately he beholds the saints in Heaven seated on thrones rising in tiers which form the petals of a white rose. He compares himself, in the rapid movement he makes as he bends over the stream, to a hungry infant:

Non è fantin che sì subito rua
   col volto verso il latte, se si svegli
   molto tardato dall'usanza sua,
come fec'io. . . .

           (82–85)

Sinclair's translation is, "No infant, waking long after its hour, throws itself so instantly with its face to the milk, as I. . . ." True, Dante does say "il latte," which, translated literally, means "the milk," but the picture he is seeing and wants the reader to see is of an infant at its mother's *breast*. This is a baby who has slept past the usual hour of its feed and has awakened extra hungry. When this happens, the baby, on being put to the breast, opens its mouth very wide and makes a sudden, darting movement with his head ("subito rua"). I had often seen this happen and knew exactly what Dante was describing. Not so Sinclair, nor any of these other gentlemen:

Bickersteth:

> No infant ever turned his face with more
>   of a rush toward the milk, if wakened late
>   from slumbering long past his wonted hour. . . .

Mackenzie:

> No babe that wakes much later than its wont
>   So quickly thrusts its face towards the milk. . . .

Wicksteed:

> Never doth child so sudden rush with face turned to
>   the milk, if he awake far later than his wont. . . .

Sisson:

> No child ever makes so sudden a rush
>   To where it sees the milk, if it wakes up
>   A long time after its usual hour. . . .

All these renderings convey the sense of a sudden movement, but "the milk" suggests a feeding-bottle or a cup rather than a mother's breast; while in Sisson's version the "fantin" has become a little boy running to meet the milkman. Dante has *watched* a baby at the breast and has *remembered*. I translated:

> No little infant mouths as readily
>   Towards his mother's breast, if he awake
>   Much later than his hour is wont to be. . . .

Dante, like the baby, had been asleep—in a dark wood—and had awakened late.

I translated the last three cantos, not in the midst of University work and family clamour, but on holiday. In the autumn of 1958 my husband and I returned to our little village in the Euganean hills. We went for long walks over the hills and through the woods. Each day I took with me a copy of part of a canto and tried out English words for it as we strode along. Sometimes we rested in the shade of a vineyard, looking out over the landscape. Once a farmer and his little daughter passed by and looked back, I thought suspiciously; but no, he evidently trusted us, for the little girl came running back, bringing a beautiful bunch of grapes on a vine-leaf. Such surroundings were an inspiration and some part of the beauty of the scenery, I like to think, has entered the following lines:

> I looked above and, as the orient scene
>   At dawn exceeds the beauty of the west,
>   Where the declining sun has lately been,
> So, mounting as from vale to mountain-crest,
>   These eyes beheld at the remotest rim
>   A radiance surpassing all the rest.
>   (XXXI, 118–23)

On another occasion an extraordinary coincidence occurred. I had been puzzling over a passage in the same canto, in which Dante compares his wonder on seeing St. Bernard to the amazement of a traveller from Croatia who looks at the veil of St. Veronica in Rome:

> Qual è colui che forse di Croazia
>   viene a veder la Veronica nostra
>   e per l'antica fama non sen sazia. . . .
> (103–5)

The meaning of these lines is: Like someone who perhaps comes from Croatia to look at our veil of St. Veronica and gazes unsated, held by its ancient fame. . . .[4] Why, I wondered, does Dante mention Croatia? And how am I to render the harsh sound of *Croazia*, when Croatia is such a mild-sounding word in English? We stopped at a little wayside tavern in a valley, where foreigners seldom came, it seemed, for the landlord was astonished to learn that we were from England. As we sat eating bread and salame and drinking the dark red local wine ("vino nero"), there entered a wild-looking, dusty peasant, his legs wrapped round with narrow strips of cloth, like puttees. He told us, in his rough dialect, that he had been guarding flocks up in the hills and that often he had to strangle snakes with his bare hands. He was not a native of these parts, he said, but had immigrated. "Io venni da Croazia," he said, [I came from Croatia]. I could hardly believe my ears. Here was a living example of what Dante must have meant—a wild, uncouth man from a far-off, outlandish place. Even so, I failed to get the harshness of the Italian lines:

> Like one who, haply, from Croatia came
>   To see the veil of St. Veronica
>   And, held unsated by its ancient fame,
> Looks all he may, musing the while with awe:
>   "Lord Jesus, Christ, true God, this likeness of
>   "Your face is, then, the form your features bore?"

The most delicate and daunting part of my work was the task of joining my translation to the fragments left by Dorothy. No doubt I often failed, but I think my most successful attempt is the joining passage I supplied in canto XXXIII, between lines 57 and 82. The rhyme which I had to pick up was "-ind"; the rhyme I had to meet was "-umed":

As from a dream one may awake to find
   Its passion yet imprinted on the heart
   Although all else is cancelled from the mind,
So of my vision now but little part
   Remains, yet in my inmost soul I know
   The sweet instilling which it did impart.
So the sun melts the imprint on the snow,
   Even so the Sibyl's wisdom that was penned
   On light leaves vanished on the winds that blow.
O Light supreme, by mortal thought unscanned,
   Grant that Thy former aspect may return,
   Once more a little of Thyself relend.
Make strong my tongue that in its words may burn
   One single spark of all Thy glory's light
   For future generations to discern.
For if my memory but glimpse the sight
   Whereof these lines would now a little say,
   Men may the better estimate Thy might.
The piercing brightness of the living ray
   Which I endured, my vision had undone,
   I think, if I had turned my eyes away.
And I recall this further led me on,
   Wherefore my gaze more boldness yet assumed
   Till to the Infinite Good it last had won.

And here Dorothy's translation joined on:

O grace abounding, whereby I presumed
   So deep the eternal light to search and sound
   That my whole vision was therein consumed!

I like to think that she would have been pleased with her apprentice.

The first draft of my translation had taken nine months, from January to the end of September 1958. Then came revision. And there remained the notes and commentaries, the glossary of names, and, most difficult of all, the introduction. Penguins had asked for completion by 30 June 1960. I met the obligation. The foreword is dated 13 June, a birthday which, as it happens, I share with Dorothy Sayers.

In *The Zeal of Thy House*, the first play which Dorothy Sayers wrote for Canterbury Cathedral, the architect William of Sens, who is re-building the quire after it had been destroyed by fire in 1174, is badly injured by a fall when he is attempting to put the keystone of an arch into position. After a long struggle with himself, having tried vainly to continue directing procedures from a sick-bed, he hands over his work to another architect, to William the Englishman:

> He will respect my work as I do his
> And build a harmony of his and mine.

Twenty years after the first performance of this play, Dorothy Sayers was to die suddenly of a heart attack. I have often wondered: when the agonizing pain seized her in the chest, was there a moment, before she fell, when she knew she was leaving her work unfinished? When news of her death reached me, the first thing I said was "Oh! and she hasn't finished translating the *Paradiso!*" I knew well the importance she attached to her last, perhaps her greatest, work.

When I had finished my attempt to "build a harmony of hers and mine," her friend Muriel St. Clare Byrne, writing to express her pleasure in what I had done, quoted the words of William of Sens:

> Let my work, all that was good in me,
> All that was God, stand up and live and grow . . .
> The perfect work, finished, though not by me.

It was a solemn tribute, and one which I greatly value.

II.

THE BURNING BUSH

. . . and, behold, the bush burned with fire, and the bush was not consumed.

Exodus 3:2

The creative energy which Dante generated in the mind of Dorothy Sayers carried her far beyond the translation of the *Commedia*. From an early stage she had set herself not only to translate the poem but also to expound it in relation to present-day concerns, highlighting its timeless relevance. If she had lived to finish *Paradise* her encounter with Dante would have inspired still further works. Indeed, this was already happening. One of her projects was to have been a book entitled "The Burning Bush." She mentioned it to me in several of her letters, and jottings in her Dante notebooks show that she was collecting material for it.

Some of this material was used in a lecture which I heard her give at the University of Nottingham on 7 June 1957. Entitled "The Beatrician Vision in Dante and Other Poets,"[1] it examines the nature of Dante's experience of love and shows that it has been shared by writers, whether of poetry or prose, of many different periods. Beginning with the author of Exodus, from which the title of her book was to have been taken, she goes on to quote from St. Matthew's account of the Transfiguration, from Traherne, Blake, Wordsworth, Browning, Tennyson and Aldous Huxley.[2] All the passages chosen convey a vision of reality transfigured, a glimpse of an eternal reality. The most familiar instance in English poetry occurs in Wordsworth's *Intimations of Immortality*:

There was a time when meadow, grove, and stream,
    The earth, and every common sight,
        To me did seem
    Apparelled in celestial light,
The glory and the freshness of a dream.

(I, 1–5)

She defines such an experience "in the proper and technical sense mystical." It is not an imaginary vision, but has a basis in the world of physical phenomena. A statement in prose of a similar experience is found in Thomas Traherne's *Centuries of Meditations:* "The corn was orient and immortal wheat, which never should be reaped, nor was ever sown. I thought it had stood from everlasting to everlasting. . . . Boys and girls, tumbling in the street and playing, were moving jewels. . . . The city seemed to stand in Eden." Aldous Huxley induced a comparable vision by taking mescalin, as he described in *The Doors of Perception:*

> [Plato] would never have seen (as I was seeing) a bunch of flowers shining with their own inner light . . . could never have perceived that what rose and iris and carnation so intensely signified was nothing more, and nothing less, than what they were—a transience that was yet eternal life. . . . Words like Grace and Transfiguration come into my mind, and that of course was what, among other things, they stood for. (P. 12)

It is not necessary to take drugs in order to experience such a vision. It can occur in normal circumstances. For example, a passage from Pamela Hansford Johnson's autobiography, *Important to Me*, published in 1974, sketches a similar other-worldly experience:

> Then, on the little slow train between Marks Tey and Cambridge, it happened. We were just passing through the charming small town of Bures. It was . . . a radiant late afternoon in Spring. I was looking, lacklustre, out of the train windows.
> Then the glory opened.
> I can only weakly describe it. The trees sprang to three times their normal height and burst out in blossom. . . . All was a golden enormity, beyond everything I had ever seen or ever can conceive. Size and gold. A

sky golden all over. Familiar and yet unfamiliar, something of almost insufferable beauty.[3]

Dorothy Sayers never read this passage, but had it been written during her lifetime it would have joined others like it in her Dante notebooks. She called such moments "the Beatrician vision," not because they are always—as they manifestly are not—inspired by a man's love for a woman, "but in honour of Dante, who was the first, and is perhaps still the only, writer to have systematically charted the mystical way which leads from the Vision of Beatrice to the Beatific Vision."

There are echoes here of Charles Williams, as anyone who knows his works will recognize. It is appropriate at this point to consider the extent to which Dorothy was in fact influenced by him in her interpretation of Dante. Undoubtedly she was deeply impressed by *The Figure of Beatrice* when she read it in 1943; after all, it made her resolve to read the *Divine Comedy*. As she did so, she became more and more convinced that Williams had grasped the essential nature of Dante's allegory. That is why she was so eager that he should provide the introduction and notes to her translation. He had agreed to do so but death intervened. It is significant that, reluctant as she had been to undertake that part of the work herself, she did not ask anyone else to do it. Instead, she incorporated into her commentary a number of Williams' ideas. The most important of these, as regards her translation, was his concept of the image.

In his introduction to *The Figure of Beatrice*, Williams explains what he means by the term "image." It is close to what Coleridge required of a symbol: it exists in itself, it derives from something greater than itself, and it represents in itself the greatness from which it derives:

> I have preferred the word image to the word symbol, because it seems to me doubtful if the word symbol nowadays sufficiently expresses the vivid individual existence of the lesser thing. Beatrice was, in her degree, an image of nobility, of virtue, of the Redeemed Life, and in some sense of Almighty God himself. But she also remained Beatrice right to the end; her derivation was not to obscure her identity any more than her identity should hide her derivation. (Pp. 7–8)

Here is the key to those sections of Dorothy Sayers' commentary which appear at the end of every canto under the heading of "The Images." They are separated from the factual notes because they serve a deeper and more comprehensive purpose. They are heralded in an introductory section in the first volume, *Hell*, under the heading "The Greater Images." Seven major symbols are fundamental to the entire poem: Dante, Virgil, Beatrice, Hell, Purgatory, Paradise, and the Empire or City. This organization is an important feature of the Sayers Dante. It represents something new, not because the interpretation is unorthodox (on the whole, it is traditional), but because the images are shown clearly to be both themselves and what they signify. In Williams' words, their derivation does not obscure their identity, not does their identity hide their derivation. The reader is free to give undivided attention to the story, while the allegorical meanings emerge in parallel without blurring or diminishing the literal.

Dorothy Sayers may have thought that Williams himself would have organized the commentary in this way. This is implied in her introduction when she writes, "I must not . . . fail to acknowledge my debt to Charles Williams' study *The Figure of Beatrice*, which lays down the lines along which, I believe, the allegory can be most fruitfully interpreted to present-day readers" (p. 66). It is doubtful, however, whether he would have been as intelligible to the general reader as she was. Indeed, to those who find *The Figure of Beatrice* obscure, it may seem surprising that she found it so illuminating. One explanation may be that she first read the *Commedia* in the Temple Classics edition, in which the notes are exceedingly crabbed, as well as arbitrary. Here, for instance, is what that edition offers on the three wild beasts of *Inferno*, canto I:

lonza [leopard]: Worldly Pleasure: *politically*: Florence.
leone [lion]: Ambition; *politically*: the Royal House of France.
lupa [she-wolf]: Avarice; *politically*: the Papal See.

Obviously, something more clarifying than this was needed for Penguin readers—and was provided.

Dorothy Sayers did more than acknowledge her debt to Williams in her introduction. She dedicated both *Hell* and *Purgatory* to him and would undoubtedly have dedicated *Paradise* to him also. The wording of the dedication is significant:

TO THE DEAD MASTER
OF THE AFFIRMATIONS
CHARLES WILLIAMS

There follows in each case a quotation, one from *Inferno* and one from *Purgatorio*, recalling a tender exchange between Dante and two people whom he looked on as his masters: Brunetto Latini and Guido Guinicelli.[4] The phrase "the dead Master of the Affirmations" needs to be interpreted in terms of Christian mysticism.

Within this tradition, there are two journeys which a contemplative can take towards apprehension of the Divine. One is known as the Negative Way, or the Way of the Negation of Images. This has been followed by such great mystics as St. Theresa of Avila, St. John of the Cross and the author of *The Cloud of Unknowing*.[5] This way proceeds through darkness and solitude as, one by one, the finite images of the infinite are rejected. The other journey is known as the Affirmative Way, or the Way of the Affirmation of Images. This proceeds by the recognition of the infinite in the finite, the eternal in the temporal, the heavenly in the terrestrial. Of the two ways, the affirmative, the more typically incarnational, was central to Catholic teaching in the Middle Ages.[6]

Williams had himself experienced intimations in his personal life of the Affirmative Way. When he came to read Dante he found the Way confirmed.[7] In Dante's vision of the Divine in the person who was Beatrice, Williams saw an image of the Incarnation.

Dorothy Sayers was much taken with Williams' definition of Dante as a poet of the Affirmative Way. Why did it appeal to her so powerfully? First, because it was congenial to her understanding of the writer as creator, shown in *The Mind of the Maker* as an analogue of the Divine Creator, made in this sense "in His image." Second, because, as a Christian rooted in the Catholic tradition, she was at home with the sacramental concept of reality. This concept is connected with the doctrine of the Trinity and of the true Manhood of God in Christ. Her belief in, and I would venture to say, her experience of, the Nicene Creed had been deepened and clarified by writing *The Man Born to be King*. Focusing in these plays on the human nature of Christ in his earthly life, she had, at the same time, to keep in mind his divine nature and devise ways, in terms of drama, of communicating it. This dual vision, sharpened by her task as a playwright, made her alert to Williams' ideas concerning Dante's use of images. And third, because she responded as an individual artist. This can be sensed in the following passages, taken from her lecture, "The Fourfold Interpretation of the *Comedy*," delivered in 1948 and published in *Introductory Papers on Dante*:

> [The Way of the Affirmation of Images] is essentially the way of the artist and the poet—of all those to whom the rejection of images would be the rejection of their very means to intellectual and emotional experience; and it would seem to follow from this that the great Masters of the Affirmative Way will tend to be secular, and that they will be more concerned to record their experience than to analyse it in the manner of the regular theologian. (P. 122)

To someone of her temperament, with her hearty enjoyment of life, of all that writers and artists create, of the marvel and make-believe of the theatre, of the delights of the passionate intellect, the Way of the Affirmation of Images must have seemed a liberating sanction. No wonder she embraced it so joyously and gave her mind to it with such vigour. In another revealing passage in the same lecture she distinguished between two methods of meditation:

> In the ordinary method of meditation on, let us say, the kingship of God, we might form in our *imagination* a picture of God seated on a throne like a king; and we might think about the attributes of kingship, such as power and authority and splendour and so forth; and we might perhaps further meditate how all earthly kingship is derived from God. But if we were following in Dante's steps, we should do almost the direct opposite. We should look, perhaps in imagination, or more likely with our bodily eyes, upon an actual king—it might be our late King George VI—in some ordinary, perhaps trivial situation, at a football match or a garden-party; and we should suddenly see, burning and shining through the mortal body and the modern clothing and all the solemn absurdities of Court ceremonial, the glory and authority of all kings, and of the King of Kings, made known in His fleshly Image, focused in that point and diffused upon

the whole City. The scriptural type of the former kind of image is the Vision of Isaiah: "I saw the Lord sitting upon a throne, high and lifted up, and His train filled the temple." But the scriptural type of the second kind is Our Lord's Transfiguration: "He was transfigured before them: and His face did shine as the sun, and His raiment was white as the light." The bodily presence is not withdrawn—it remains planted where it was in earthly time and space; but it is known for an instant as it is known in Heaven, in its awful and immortal dignity. (P. 125)

This is Dorothy Sayers at her most characteristic, translating an unfamiliar concept into an everyday, recognizable picture. She does this as much for her own sake as for her readers. For her, all the images remain planted where they are in earthly time and space. In a letter to Bickersteth, dated 12 June 1957, she wrote:

I can enter into Charles' type of mind to some extent, by imagination, and look through its windows, as it were, into places where I cannot myself walk. He was, up to a certain point, I think, a practising mystic; from that point of view I am a complete moron, being almost wholly without intuitions of any kind. I can only apprehend intellectually what the mystics grasp directly.

She knew her limitations, but she knew also how to turn them to good account. Her creative imagination, as well as her intellect, was attracted by Williams' doctrine of love.

He himself called his doctrine "romantic theology," a phrase which even in his lifetime gave rise to misunderstanding. C. S. Lewis tried to clarify it by saying that a romantic theologian was not romantic about theology but theological about romance. The late Patrick McLaughlin, who knew Williams well, wrote to me as follows:

We pleaded with him to find a different title. We knew that for him "romantic" meant the mediaeval "roman," the Courts of Love, etc.; but we argued that today the word is generally taken as referring to the Lake School and Keats and Shelley and even Swinburne. Charles agreed, and undertook to find another word—but never did. I've never found another epithet to put with "theology" and still to mean what Charles meant. . . . I prefer not to speak of Charles' "theology" at all, but rather of his "doctrine" of the Way of Affirmation (of Images). This seems to me far safer ground.

R. J. Reilly includes a chapter on Williams in his book *Romantic Religion*. He defines Williams' writing as a "religio-literary phenomenon." He is less concerned with its validity than with the cast of mind that produced it: "It is surely clear that this cast of mind can hardly be called anything but romantic." But he sees Williams as

> more the poetic romantic than the analytical romantic, more concerned with Wordsworth's vision than with Coleridge's glossings of the workings of the human mind. What we find in Williams' work is emphasis on the union of the intellect and the imagination as the highest means of reaching religious truth. We find him time and again insisting on this union in terms for which he has to resort to Wordsworth: this union results in "the feeling intellect" or "absolute power" or "reason in her most exalted mood."[8]

The "union of the intellect and the imagination as the highest means of reaching religious truth"—this, above all, is what Dorothy Sayers appreciated in Williams. It confirmed and reinforced in her an ideal to which she herself already aspired, and which she eagerly proclaimed as existing in Dante.

She developed this ideal in a lecture which she gave in 1952 to the Chelmsford Arts Association, entitled "The Poetry of the Image in Dante and Charles Williams."[9] In that lecture she explains that by "poetry of the Image" she means poems written in a certain philosophical or mystical tradition in which all images of reality, within their limits, are valid for the apprehension of the ultimate reality, which is God—in other words, poetry which is itself an affirmation of images. She takes as an example the appearance of Beatrice at the climax of the procession on the summit of Mount Purgatory. Following the Dante scholar J. D. Sinclair, she sees Beatrice at this moment as an image of the Host, the sacrament of the Eucharist, the pageant itself being an image of the Corpus Christi procession. Whether or not this interpretation is valid (and it is by no means generally accepted), her comments show how she perceived the function of an image:

> There is not—or at any rate there need not be—any overt, rationalised *statement* about the reality which the image is put there to convey. There is simply the showing of a picture, or the telling of a story, in which the truth

is shown in action, and the universal structure of reality is laid bare. Because it is an image, and not an argument, it speaks directly to the senses and the intuition of those to whom it is shown; and because it springs out of personal—if you like, out of existential—experience, it appeals to the personal and historical experience of men, and gathers into itself all the experience which they themselves are able to bring to it. And because it is rooted in the fleshly and the visible, it remains an expression of the *whole* of human experience. . . . (P. 193)

There was another strand in Williams' doctrine which was new to her. It was also, she suggested, subsequent to Dante. This was Williams' concept of the hierarchy of love, a system of relationships for which he adopted or renewed the term "co-inherence." It is a principle of divine community, involving substitution and exchange. To the lover, beholding the glory of the Divine in his beloved, the moment of revelation is unique; but it is also universal. The revelation can be experienced by anyone at any time. What is more, the beholder, as it might be Dante, may in turn be a vehicle of glory for someone else. Such reciprocity was imaged for Williams in the City. The concept was original but it was also orthodox. In a lecture delivered in 1986 at the Charles Williams Conference in Duisburg, the Reverend Dr. Brian Horne said, "The transfiguration of all human life into the life of God is, for Charles Williams, the true meaning of salvation. In this he stands centrally in the tradition of the doctors of the early Church." Already in 1944, in her letter of 18 October, Dorothy had asked Williams to clarify his concept of reciprocity: "Suppose, say, Dante himself had been to some other person the revealing image—possibly, let us say, to the Lady of the Window— then in *her* 'Commedia' would *he* have been seen in just that heavenly place?" Williams had replied, "Beatrice is, for her proper moment, and not only for Dante, but for all heaven, in the glorious function of revelation, [close] to the B.V.M. . . . but so, in the continually changing glory, is everyone else."[10] Dante had said something similar but, living as he did in an age of fixed hierarchies, he conceived of the glory flowing from above downward. In her Chelmsford lecture Dorothy describes the process: "Throughout the great ladder of creation, each rank draws up the one below it by the cords of love; every being looks up in love (*eros*) to the one above it and downward in charity (*agape*) to the one below it . . ." (P. 193). Or, as Dante says of the heavenly hierarchy:

> Questi ordini di su tutti s'ammirano
> e di giù vincon sì che verso Dio
> tutti tirati sono, e tutti tirano.

> [And all these orders upwards gaze with awe,
> As downwards each prevails upon the rest
> Whence all are drawn to God and to Him draw.]
> (*Paradiso* XXVIII, 128–30)

"To this noble conception," she said, "Charles Williams . . . brings the further conception of the exchange of hierarchies. . . . Not wholly abandoning the conception of [fixed] hierarchy, not wholly accepting an absolutism of equality . . . [Williams] sees a humanity in which the relation of higher to lower is fluid" (pp. 193–94).

In his novels, Williams works out an exchange of hierarchies, moving from man to woman, and from woman to man, from present to past and back again. In *Descent into Hell*, Pauline Anstruther sees Peter Stanhope as Dante saw Beatrice: he is to her the vision of glory incarnate. But she herself possesses a glorified "other self," which she actually sees and of which she is afraid. Stanhope, in the vicarious bearing of burdens ("substitution"), carries her fear for her, as she, in her turn, carries a burden of fear for an ancestor. In all this, Dorothy Sayers observes:

> We see what one original poetic mind can do with the image implanted in it by another. Dante sees Beatrice's body transfigured; Charles Williams' Pauline sees her own. The concept of the vicarious endurance of suffering, derived from the archetype of Christ's Passion, is not in Dante's poem very explicit, except in its Archetype. It is found in the great seventh canto of the *Paradiso*, which is perhaps the finest poetic exposition of Atonement theology ever written. Here, Williams blends it with Dante's own imagery, in a new apprehension of the exchanged hierarchies.[11]

She never wearied of saying how much she owed to Williams. Her lecture "The City of Dis" opens with these words: "I shall never cease to be grateful that my first introduction to Dante came through the late Charles Williams, himself, like Dante, a poet, and, like Dante, a theologian of a very original and creative turn of mind." She expressed gratitude also in a letter to Williams' son, Michael: "I am so glad [Charles] was my guide to Dante. . . . He had the great gift of making every author he touched alive and relevant, so that the great dead were never pushed back into a historical past but remained in his writing quick and vibrating with their own vitality and meaning." She had this great gift herself. On this matter she did not so much learn from Williams as agree with him. Too little had been done, she considered, "to rescue Dante from the exalted isolation in which reverential awe has placed him, and to compare him with other poets writing on similar themes." That is why she intended to write a book entitled "The Burning Bush," in which she would show how poets "do not merely pass on the torch in a relay race; they toss the ball to one another, to and fro, across the centuries."[12]

Ralph E. Hone, in *Dorothy L. Sayers: A Literary Biography*, writes of Williams' influence on her: "She had met a master-spirit whose words were her lifeblood." That is well said. She knew already that the bush burned and was not consumed. When she read *The Figure of Beatrice* the bush burned for her with an even brighter flame.[13]

12.

THE FIGURE OF DANTE

Dante is everyman. But he is also the individual Dante.
Dorothy L. Sayers

Dorothy Sayers' response to Dante went beyond delight in his poetic skills, beyond a feeling of kinship with his moral convictions and religious belief, beyond even the inspiration she drew from him for her own work. He became a familiar presence in her life. It is not surprising, therefore, that she should wonder what he was like as a person, above all, how it would have been to hold conversations with him.

She indulged her imagination in that direction more than once, when the novelist in her got the upper hand. Intellectually, too, it fascinated her to explore the terrain which a fourteenth-century and a twentieth-century mind would have in common. Indeed, in her lectures, as well as in her notes on the *Commedia*, she encouraged readers to explore such a terrain for themselves. She herself enjoyed imagining how Dante would have responded to twentieth-century concepts if he had been made aware of them. She experimented twice with this idea.

The first attempt took the form of a short story, untitled and unfinished, probably written early in 1945. Late in the previous year Ravenna had been captured from the Germans, who had withdrawn "to previously prepared positions," as the military euphemism has it. In the story, two British officers who are off duty have been for a swim in a river, not far from the region "dove 'l Po discende/per aver pace co' seguaci sui [Where Po with all his streams comes down to rest]."[1]

Did the officers, one wonders, remember these lines? One of them perhaps did, for, as they are discussing a broadcast they had heard from London about post-war planning, he says: "They remind me of the damned souls in *Inferno*—they know everything about the future and nothing about present reality." The other officer, the narrator, agrees: "Completely out of touch," he says. At that moment a bomb explodes, dropped as a final gesture by the retreating Luftwaffe on the outskirts of Ravenna.

The narrator is knocked unconscious and the blast of the explosion tears off what scanty clothing he had begun to put on after his swim. When he comes to himself, it is dark and he finds he is being carried along a narrow street between high walls. People walk beside him holding torches, "not the electric kind, but the real thing—flaring and smoky, with a strong resinous smell." The narrator's rescuers have found him lying naked by the river and assume he has been stripped and robbed. They take him to a large house belonging, they tell him, to Guido Novello, the lord of Ravenna, and lay him on a bed. After another spell of unconsciousness, he wakes to see people in the room, dressed as though for a mediaeval play but wearing their clothes, he notices, with a more natural ease than actors. They begin to question him. He replies by asking for a cigarette and they stare at him, uncomprehendingly. Though he knows some Italian, their words make little sense to him, while they, for their part, think he must be mad or possessed. At last they decide to send for someone who may be able to unravel the mystery. There enters an elderly man, whose face seems familiar to the Englishman, though he can't put a name to him. The reader has no such difficulty.

In this, her first attempt at a portrait of Dante, Dorothy Sayers adheres to the traditional iconography: "He was dressed in a straight, dark gown and a hood to match, with a little white coif under it. He moved rather slowly, stooping and peering a little, as though he were either short-sighted or absent-minded—or perhaps reluctant." His eyes are very dark and bright, his nose strong and beaklike, his face thin and heavily lined. All these features are to be expected, but two touches already anticipate the way in which the figure of Dante was to develop in what she called "the workshop" of her mind: his voice, though agreeable, "had an edge to it, as though it had acquired a habit of irony"; and his eyes, in contrast with his face, "were as lively and brilliant as those of a young man." Later we notice that he has a habit of rueful self-mockery and, more important, an insatiable curiosity and eagerness to understand ideas that are new to him.

At first neither character understands what has happened and they talk at cross-purposes. When the Englishman asks if he is in Heaven "or the other place," Dante suspects that he is being mocked and bursts out in anger. He is pacified only when the other kisses a crucifix in sign of his good faith. Then the narrator asks what date it is. Dante replies, "Since the Incarnation of our Blessed Lord, the sun has returned to the sign of the Ram one thousand, three hundred and [one] score times, all but two years." After puzzling for a moment, the Englishman works this out as A.D. 1318. He is horror-stricken: "I have lost the whole of my world!" he exclaims. On being urged to explain, he reveals that his name is John Richardson, that he was born in Richmond, near London, in 1916 and that he was educated at Eton and Oxford. "There is a University at Oxford," Dante interrupts. "Yes," replies John, "but my College [Wadham] was not founded in your time. I mean, from your point of view, it isn't there yet."

From here on in the manuscript there are two versions of the story, in which some of the details vary. In one, John has taken a degree in history at Oxford and has become a schoolmaster; in the other, he has read "Greats" (classics) and explains to Dante the syllabus of *Litterae Humaniores*. As John explains, Dante

> was greatly excited, and began to catechise me on the *Ethics*, which he seemed to know inside out, which was more than I did. But I got my own back by quoting a passage, which I luckily remembered, of the original text.
> "What language is that?"
> "Greek."
> "You read those books in Greek?"
> "Naturally."

This astonishes Dante, who is at a loss to understand how such texts can have been obtained. John tells him about the Revival of Learning and the invention of the printing press: "The idea of such a multiplication of texts seemed to intoxicate him."

All such details, the "small change" of astonishment, are predictable enough. More interesting is the main point of the conversation: however much the specifics of life have altered in 627 years, Dante's grasp of general principles remains unshaken. He is interested to hear of our scientific inventions but not in the least surprised to learn that so many of them have been turned to evil ends. He asks: "How should a man love God and his neighbour more for being able to move very fast from one place to another? Even to know all the mysteries of the heavens will avail nothing unless the heart is filled with wonder before the All-Mover's glory." He questions John about the war in which he is involved. First the German Reich has to be disentangled from the Holy Roman Empire, to which Dante seems to think Hitler is asserting a claim. "It is not the Empire," says John, "it is the corruption and perverted image of the Empire." The position of the Pope causes further confusion. Dante is saddened, though not surprised, by what he learns of the Reformation: "I keep on telling them," he says, "that they should not meddle with the temporal power. They will wreck both Church and Empire."

He is distressed to learn that in six hundred years the world will still be full of faction, irreligion and armed conflict. John notices, however, that he is less shocked and startled "than an elderly Liberal politician of our own day" would be by stories of barbarities, persecutions and concentration camps, "seeming, indeed, to accept them as part of the inevitable wickedness of mankind. I realized that he had hoped for the conversion of the world, but not for any steady growth towards perfection." John recognizes here the great divide, the fundamental difference between Dante and the modern world: "the dazzling mirage of Progress had never shimmered on his mental horizon."

Such statements are persuasive evidence that the character of John Richardson is a thinly veiled persona of Dorothy Sayers herself. These are the very matters she would have liked to discuss with Dante, and which, in a sense, she *did* discuss with him in her own mind and went on discussing. In 1951 came another product of this imagined dialogue, this time in the form of a confrontation between Dante and a modern physicist and astronomer, Sir Arthur Eddington. It occurs at the beginning of her lecture entitled "Dante's Cosmos.''[2] She had been invited to address an august scientific body, the Royal Institution. Eddington had recently died, or, as Dorothy puts it, was "now, to the regret of his colleagues and readers, released from the limitations of the space-time continuum." She asks her audience to imagine that "clothed in that aerial body with which (as Dante has told us) spirits are endued between death and the Last Judgment . . . he has hastened, at a speed exceeding that of light, into the fourteenth century." This is the situation of John Richardson over again: a modern mind is transported to the time of Dante and, as in the unfinished short story, the point of interest is the way in which Dante's mind is shown to respond to twentieth-century concepts, which he relates to his own mental universe.

In this imaginary conversation Eddington is in the house in Ravenna where Dante lies dying of malaria. He is reading to the poet from his own book, *The Nature of the Physical World*.[3] Though hovering between life and death, Dante, "his insatiable curiosity still unquenched," follows the argument with close attention. Eddington has begun with the description of two tables: one, the familiar object of everyday environment, and two, what he calls a "scientific" table. There arises at once a discussion as to the meaning of the word "substance." The first table, Eddington reads, "has extension; it is comparatively permanent; it is coloured; above all, it is *substantial*. By substantial I do not merely mean that it does not collapse when I lean upon it—." Dante interrupts: "I should think not indeed! Why do you have to warn your audience against an error so ridiculous?" Eddington explains that in the twentieth century the word has come to be used as a synonym of "solid." "How lamentable a corruption," exclaims Dante, "when its proper meaning is almost the direct opposite!" As Eddington continues reading, it appears that by "substantial" he means that the table is constituted of "substance":

"It is a *thing*; not like space, which is a mere negation, not like time, which is—Heaven knows what! But that will not help you to my meaning because it is the distinctive characteristic of a 'thing' to have this substantiality and I do not think substantiality can be described better than by saying that it is the kind of nature exemplified by an ordinary table. And so we go round in circles."

Dante interrupts a second time: "Forgive me; but in *my* day we were taught not to argue in circles." And he objects that a substance is not necessarily a thing like a table. The word means only an individual subject, as distinct from a universal or a quality. "That is more or less what I mean when I say it is 'a thing,' " says Eddington. He then moves to his description of the "scientific" table. This, he explains, "does not belong to the world previously mentioned—that world which spontaneously appears round me."

Dante: In short, it is not sensible.

Eddington: Quite—though if I used that word many people would think I mean that it was not rational or prudent—that, in short, it was lacking in common sense.

Dante: But the common sense has no connection with prudence. It means—

Eddington: (*hurriedly*) I am afraid a great many philosophical terms have changed their meaning since your day. . . . "My scientific table is mostly emptiness. Sparsely scattered in that emptiness are numerous electric charges rushing about with great speed; but their combined bulk amounts to less than a billionth of the bulk of the table itself. . . ."

Then he breaks off to say, "I fear, Messer Dante, the nature of an electric charge is unfamiliar to you." Dante replies that it is, and Eddington attempts an explanation:

Eddington: It supports my writing-paper as satisfactorily as Table No. 1, for when I lay the paper on it the little electric particles keep on hitting the underside, so that the paper is maintained . . . at a nearly steady level. . . . If I lean upon this table I shall not go through—"

Dante: One moment. Are you not illegitimately confusing two different orders of things—your phenomenal paper and phenomenal body with your scientific table?

Eddington: I am coming to that; [he reads] "or, to be strictly accurate, the chance of my scientific elbow going through my scientific table is so excessively small that it can be neglected in practical life."

Dante: You mean that your paper and your elbow are also composed of the sparsely distributed electric particles whose nature is still to be disclosed?

Eddington: That is the whole point. Does that surprise you?

Dante: Of course not. That was to be expected. . . . Your audience is familiar with electric particles?

Eddington: They all know how to use electricity in practical affairs, though they have not all a thorough understanding of its scientific composition.

This does not surprise Dante, either. "They know it in its effects," he replies, "though not in its nature. That is likely enough." He asks to hear more about electric charges, for "I believe you can satisfy a curiosity that has tormented me half my life." Eddington reads on until he has concluded the passage in which the structure of the atom is made clear. Dante, filled with excitement and grateful beyond measure, exclaims:

It appears as though you had come very close to perceiving the first form of the prime matter, out of which the whole visible universe is shaped. Further than that first form you cannot go, for matter without form is unintelligible. . . . It is all most wonderful. . . . Wonderful, too, is what you tell me about the Heavens and the multiplicity of universes—though I am almost glad I did not know it earlier.

Eddington: Would it have disturbed your faith?

Dante: Why should it? No, but I should have had to re-write my poem. . . .

Eddington: Does not our modern cosmology overthrow your notions about the location of Heaven and Hell?

Dante: It seems I shall have written in vain. Did I not make it sufficiently clear that Heaven has no location?[4]

In this dialogue it is Dante's mind, rather than his character, that is displayed, though in the outburst of joy at understanding something of the first form of prime matter the two become fused. Whether the members of the Royal Institution realized it or not, Dorothy Sayers had offered them a glimpse of the figure of Dante she had herself created. By now he was as familiar to her, and as well loved, as an intimate friend.

These two literary imaginings were not her first musings on the subject. Already in 1944 she had amused herself by speculating, in her second letter to Williams, what sort of house guest Dante would make and how he would compare in this respect with Milton:

> Either of them, I fancy, would have been gey ill to live with, but if I *had* to take one of them as an evacuee, I think I would choose Dante, in spite of the warning that he would find the bread salt and the stairs discouraging. Of course, it would be rather trying to sit night after night listening to his grievances about Florence and the iniquities of Pope Boniface—but probably no worse than Milton on divorce and the freedom of the press and the iniquities of the bishops.

She expands on the idea the following morning, continuing in the same letter:

> I had an alarming vision just now in my bath. I had *both* Dante and Milton as evacuees. After a long wet day, which they had whiled away by reading each other's works, they sat one on either side of the fire, Dante like a mournful eagle in captivity, and Milton like a bull in the arena, whose eyes were beginning to roll dangerously. I said nervously, "Well, well, it's been wretched weather, hasn't it?" Whereat Milton, ignoring me, suddenly opened his mouth and told Dante exactly what he thought of young women who gave their boy-friends lectures in theology. When he had finished, Dante rose to his feet, slowly unfolding to his full height until, like a black pillar, his form obscured the light of the fire, and then he spoke—but, like the *grido* of the sphere of Jupiter, the sound was so terrible that the sense escaped me.

This frivolous scenario had in it the seeds of a serious comparison of Dante and Milton as poets and as men. As we saw in chapter 2, Dorothy Sayers' first reaction to the *Commedia* was partly influenced by the fact that she had just been rereading *Paradise Lost*. She continued to reflect on the differences and resemblances between the two poets, especially in their experience of love. Her thoughts on these matters were ripe for expression when in 1952 she was once again invited to lecture at a summer school of Italian Studies, held that year at Magdalene College, Cambridge. The paper she gave was entitled "Dante and Milton."[5]

It begins with a brilliant pastiche of "an entry from a popular encyclopaedia of literature," so ingeniously devised and phrased that it could stand in every detail either for Dante or for Milton. Indeed, their two lives, despite the three hundred years between them, do show a striking parallelism. So convincing was this prelude to the lecture that she was asked afterwards to which of the two poets it really referred and from which encyclopaedia she had taken it. She replied, in some astonishment, "I wrote it myself!"

Her interest in Dante's physical experience of love had been aroused, as we saw in chapter 3, when she first read the ode beginning "Così nel mio parlar vogl'esser aspro." She had indignantly rejected Papini's view that it betrays a streak of cruelty in the poet's nature. With equal scorn she now rejected the view put forward by George Santayana that Dante as a lover was not "natural or manly." The offending passage occurs in that critic's *Three Philosophical Poets:*

> Love, as Dante feels and renders it, is not normal or healthy love. It was doubtless real enough, but too much restrained and expressed too much in fancy; so that when it is extended Platonically and identified so easily with the grace of God and revealed wisdom, we feel the suspicion that if the love in question had been natural and manly, it would have offered more resistance to so mystical a transformation. The poet who wishes to pass convincingly from love to philosophy should accordingly be a hearty and complete lover—a lover like Goethe and his Faust—rather than like Plato and Dante. (P. 129)

In this, Dorothy Sayers remarked, Santayana "has brought the misunderstanding of Dante to a fine art." It was true, she argued, that Dante's love for Beatrice was a mystical experience, "having no connection either with the violent possessiveness of passion or the mutual comfort of marriage." That was to be expected. In his period, three types of relationship between the sexes were distinguished and, for the most part, kept distinct: married love, sexual passion and courtly love. The Church, holding marriage to be a sacrament, tended to discourage passion, whether in marriage or out of it. Courtly love, the theme and possibly the invention of the Provençal poets, was taken up in Italy, notably by Guido Guinicelli and his followers, who enhanced the spiritual aspects of the cult. Dante went still further and finally achieved a synthesis between love of a woman and love of God: that is mainly what the *Commedia* is about. It is also his great originality, for the Church, trusting more to the Negative than to the Affirmative Way, had seen the dangers, rather than the possibilities, of courtly love.

This is not to say that Dante had no experience of other kinds of love; on the contrary, as a young man he was reputed by his contemporaries to be "much given to sensuality."[6] From the age of about twenty until his exile at the age of thirty-seven, he lived as a married man. His wife, Gemma Donati, bore him at least four, some say five, children. Poems of his later years seem to have been inspired by love affairs, especially the poems concerning the "Donna Pietra," of which the ode mentioned above is one.[7] This, Dorothy asserted, "was written by a man of considerable experience," by someone who knew "that bodily desire is, and should be, mutual . . . ," who recognized "that it is the man's duty to bestow pleasure and to content desire—not exclusively the other way round." Though the poem is "ferocious, fleshly, and only too aphrodisiac . . . it is full of a kind of plangent beauty and a blazing generosity." This quality she did not find in the poetry of Milton.

In the three hundred years which separate the two poets, and the two men, important cultural changes had occurred, her lecture explained, which affected the concept and, consequently, the experience of love. Dante's synthesis of love-and-worship had been replaced by a Platonic idealism. Marriage had come to be expected to accommodate not only the domestic affections but also passion and romantic love. Milton the Puritan's high ideals of marriage and his bitter disillusionment are well known. She commented as follows:

The bridegroom [Milton] was a male virgin of thirty-three; the bride a totally inexperienced girl of seventeen. We hear of no difficulty on the physical side, though it is likely enough that the inexperienced husband may have been clumsy, exacting, and inconsiderate through no fault of his own. Mutual love and affinity of mind could easily have got over that; or, on the other hand, a deep and mutual physical delight might have smoothed the way to love and understanding. But on Milton's side there was a strong and religiously rooted conviction of the natural inferiority of woman, combined (perhaps inconsistently) with very high expectations of companionship in marriage. Courtly love might have saved him—but courtly love had gone. (P. 157)

In other words, "Milton was a Dante deprived of Beatrice—of Beatrice, that is, in the whole range of her significance, literal and allegorical":

What did the man who was to write "he for God only, she for God in him," and to insist so strongly upon the divinely-ordered subjection of woman to man as to make it the key and turning-point of the loss of Paradise—what did he make . . . of the exaltation of Beatrice? One would expect it to appear to him not merely unnatural but blasphemous. (P. 158)

The factor of sexual experience, she maintained, operated to nourish Dante's poetic development, but to stunt and distort Milton's. "Dante's whole nature was integral with, and fully expressed in, his faith, as Milton's was not." What Milton lacked was "the sacramental mystery, and the taking up of all love into the one Love." E. M. W. Tillyard had spoken of Milton's "mature, one may say middle-aged philosophy of life."[8] Dante, as Dorothy Sayers perceived him, "was never middle-aged—not even at forty-six when he was writing the *Convivio*; at fifty-six he is as young as he was at eighteen, only more mature. . . . He does not fundamentally change. . . . His exultation is not in the past nor in the world to come, but here and now, and he feels it as he writes, and that very exultation is to him the assurance of beatitude":

> credo ch'io vidi, perchè più di largo,
>   dicendo questo, mi sento ch'io godo.

> [Yea, of this complex I believe mine eyes
>   Beheld the universal form—I feel,
>   Even as I speak, such springs of rapture rise.]
>   (*Paradiso* XXXIII, 92–93)

With Dante, but not with Milton, "the strong flight into felicity is maintained to the very end, with increasing vigour and certainty." As in his own simile of the lark ascending, "the higher he goes, the sweeter and louder he sings; his adoration is drunken with delight." This is the same poet who at the age of eighteen, on meeting Beatrice and receiving her greeting, was transported to the uttermost bounds of bliss: "me parve allora vedere tutti li termini de la beatitudine."[9] This is the same man who, she believes, was "sexually centralized, as Milton was not . . . and had no doubts of himself":

> Whether or not he and Gemma got along comfortably or otherwise, we may believe him to have been a satisfactory bed-fellow. The legend that his marriage was unhappy rests on Boccaccio's splenetic outburst against wives in general, and the statement that Gemma and he never came together again after his exile. If that is true, there may have been other reasons for it. (P. 162)

The audience who listened to this lecture in 1952 were not accustomed to such frank speaking in public. Some of them were embarrassed and disturbed. The professor of Italian said solemnly to me that he was dismayed to see "such a fine mind obsessed with sex" and he regretted the line she had taken, considering it unsuitable for a summer school organized by the Society for Italian Studies. We were then some way from the liberated sixties. I thought it interesting at the time, and significant, that another colleague, the late Kenelm Foster, a Dominican priest—the same who thought so highly of Dorothy's introduction to *Purgatory*—should thank her warmly for saying of Dante what he had often wished to say himself but had felt inhibited from saying by his cloth.

Like the members of the Royal Institution, the summer school audience of a year later had no means of knowing that the figure of Dante presented to them came from long-term imaginings that had by now taken the form of a full-scale portrait. For some time Dorothy Sayers had been engaged in a work quite unlike anything else she had ever written: a novel about Dante during his last years at Ravenna.

13.

DANTE AND HIS DAUGHTER

And when we put completeness on afresh,
All the more gracious shall our person be,
Reclothèd in the holy and glorious flesh.
Paradiso XIV, 43–45

On 17 September 1949 Dorothy wrote to me to say, "I have
. . . undertaken to read some essays on Dante by Barbara Barclay
Carter who, a good many years ago, wrote an unsuccessful romantic
and very learned novel about Dante, called *Ship Without Sails*. She
really does know her facts and historical stuff, inside out." She wondered if some publisher might not be persuaded to bring out a new
life of Dante, since all the biographies we had were so out of date: "I
think Miss Barclay Carter would be the person to do one; there is an
article in this typescript on Dante's friends which is full of stuff that
doesn't appear in the standard lives."

Barbara Barclay Carter, an American by birth, was adopted as a
child and brought up in Wales. Educated at the Sorbonne and at the
University of Florence, she knew Italy and Italian well. She was a
young woman of twenty-one when Mussolini came to power, and her
sympathies were ranged instantly on the side of those who opposed
him. Among them was a Sicilian priest, Don Luigi Sturzo, who
founded the Partito Popolare, a Catholic party. When the Vatican
withdrew support, Don Sturzo resigned his leadership and in 1924
went into exile. Barbara Barclay Carter, who had become a friend,
offered him a home in England. Her historical novel, *Ship Without
Sails: A Telling of Dante in Exile*, was published by Constable in 1931.
The outcome of wide reading and research, it is a remarkable
achievement for a young author.[1]

I do not know whether Dorothy read *Ship Without Sails* before 1949, but I think it unlikely. I suspect that when Miss Barclay Carter sent her the typescript of her articles she also provided a copy of her novel and that Dorothy read it then for the first time. Sad to say, Miss Barclay Carter, who had been ill for some time, returned soon afterwards to her home in Bordighera, where she died in 1951, aged fifty. But her novel remained alive in Dorothy's imagination, so much so that she wrote what is, in effect, a sequel to it.

Ship Without Sails begins in the year 1304. It is over two years since Dante was banished from Florence. He has joined other exiles in Arezzo, where his step-brother Francesco has been to visit him. At home in Florence the family are eagerly awaiting news of him. Their feelings are mixed. Some, like Francesco's wife, are resentful: Dante's misfortunes have involved them all in financial loss and insecurity. Why must he be so obdurate and unconciliating? Dante's own wife, Gemma Donati, is dependent for maintenance and protection upon her kinsfolk, of whom the most powerful is the notorious Corso Donati, leader of the Black Guelfs, the faction who sentenced Dante. She adds to her small income by doing needlework, for she has five children to rear: Giovanni, Pietro, Jacopo, Antonia and Beatrice.[2]

As the story proceeds we see Dante in the midst of political strife, involved in the machinations of White Guelfs and Ghibellines who, making common cause, plan to return to Florence by force. At last, disillusioned, he breaks away from them. We follow him from Verona to Padua, where he finds his friend Giotto at work on the frescoes of the Scrovegni Chapel, and on to Moroello Malaspina's castle in the Lunigiana; through region after region he is, as he says in the *Convivio*, "a wanderer, a beggar . . . a ship without sails."

His final refuge is Ravenna, where the ruler of the city, Guido Novello da Polenta (bearing Dante no grudge for putting his aunt, Francesca da Rimini, in Hell), offers him a house. Here the poet's sons Pietro and Jacopo, who have also been exiled, can visit him. He can earn his livelihood by teaching rhetoric at the university and by taking private pupils. By jealously defending precious hours he is able to finish *Purgatorio* and to proceed with *Paradiso*. Here, too, he finds congenial friends. First among them is Guido Novello, who himself takes lessons from Dante in the art of poetry.[3] Others include Piero

Giardini, a notary and also a poet, and young Dino Perini, who has followed him from Florence and endures privation for his sake.[4]

The Barclay Carter description of the poet is similar in several ways to the picture which Dorothy herself had formed of a man "grey-haired before his time, yet whose eyes, darkly burning in the pallor of his face, held the wisdom of age and yet were as clear as the eyes of a child." His intellectual curiosity, too, is described as being insatiable. At Padua, Giotto, hearing that Dante is frequenting the laboratory of Pietro of Abano, a learned doctor at the university, teases him, saying: "You hunger and thirst for knowledge. Why, in this at least you are a glutton and a drunkard, Dante." A further similarity can be found in Barbara Barclay Carter's realistic depiction of Dante as a lover. Like Dorothy Sayers, she believed that the poems concerning the Donna Pietra were inspired by an actual love affair.

It must have been fascinating, even perhaps something of a shock, for Dorothy to find her visualisation of Dante anticipated in so many details. She obviously read the book with close attention, probably more than once, for she carries much of it over into her own novel. Her imagination seized on one incident in particular, to creative effect. At a point towards the end of the novel, Giotto is invited to Ravenna to decorate Guido Novello's castle.[5] He and his wife arrive from Florence and Dante goes to greet them. They have brought him a gift. "At least," says Giotto, "the bringing is ours, for the gift is Gemma's. The best, she said, that she could find to give." The gift is Dante's daughter, Beatrice.

This is the point at which Dorothy begins her novel. How, she must have wondered, would Dante react to the arrival of a seventeen-year-old daughter who bore the name of his great love? How would the girl react to him? What would it be like to keep house for a father she did not know? And such a father! And why had her mother not come with her? What were Dante's feelings about this after fifteen years of separation? Disappointment—or relief?

Dorothy's story explores these questions. It is not a historical novel in the strict sense; political events play little part in it. It is instead an imaginative reconstruction of daily life in a small household in fourteenth-century Ravenna. A plan of the house, such as Dorothy often drew for her detective stories, is provided, and rooms

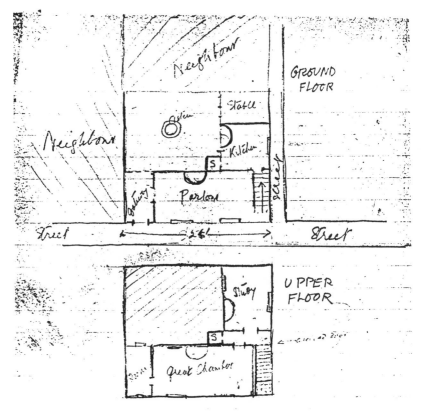

A rough sketch of Dante's house in Ravenna as imagined and drawn by
Dorothy L. Sayers.

and furnishings are described in detail. Off one of the bedrooms is a
sanctum where Dante writes his great poem. We see the parlour
where meals are served and where friends are received. We see the
kitchen where Martha, an old servant, bustles about preparing food.
Outside is a mews where hawks are kept. Friends come to talk of
philosophy and art, or to make music. We meet Pietro and Jacopo
and are shown something of their attitude to their father and of his to
them. Guido Novello and his wife Caterina hover in the background,
a kindly couple, ever mindful of Dante's comfort and welfare. (They
have been taken over from Barbara Barclay Carter's novel, but without their children and having acquired a strong-minded, elderly aunt,

Donna Margherita, who plays an important role as a confidante.) We learn about Dante's lectures at the university and meet one of his private pupils, a brilliant but uncouth lad from Calabria, whose Latin is more intelligible than his Italian. There is a hawking party and we see Dante on horseback, an expert and vigorous rider. (Why not? Dorothy knew that he had fought in the ranks of the cavalry at the Battle of Campaldino.) There is an attack on his life, but no murder, though we sense one trembling on the tip of the pen. It is all good Sayers fun—engaging dialogue, intellectual debate, varied narrative, vivid detail, especially in the description of how things *worked:* how hawks were manned, what it was like to take a bath sitting knees to nose in a small tub covered with a canvas tent to keep in the steam, how hose were tailored and fitted onto the body. But contained in those pages is something more, something new, which makes this novel the most personally revealing of anything she ever wrote.

In 1944 Dorothy had asked Williams to clarify for her a point relating to his doctrine of the exchange of hierarchies. Did he mean, she wanted to know, that Dante himself could have been for someone else a vehicle of divine glory, as Beatrice had been for him? Could he have been seen in this light by, for instance, the Lady at the Window? For readers unfamiliar with the *Vita Nuova* it may be useful to explain that the "Lady at the Window" is the Donna Gentile (Gracious Lady) with whom Dante fell in love after the death of Beatrice. He relates that he first saw her gazing compassionately at him from her window. Before long he is stirred by love for her and feels guilt at his infidelity to the memory of Beatrice. After a struggle within himself he overcomes his new passion and is rewarded by a vision of Beatrice in Paradise.[6] In a later work, *Il Convivio,* he seems to deny that there ever was such a lady; she was a symbol of philosophy, in the study of which he had found consolation for the loss of Beatrice. The figure is a subject of controversy among Dante scholars: did she, or did she not, exist in real life?[7]

Dorothy believed that she did. She gave cogent reasons for her belief in her lecture "The Paradoxes of the *Comedy*," delivered in 1949 at the summer school of Italian studies, held that year at Magdalen College, Oxford ("a broad-minded saint, however spelt," Dorothy said in a letter to me, jocularly referring to Cambridge's insis-

tence on spelling its college of the same name with a final "e.")[8]
Reading now between the lines, I can see that the possibility raised in
her letter to Williams had continued to intrigue her: how did the
Donna Gentile regard Dante? The following scenario which she
sketched for us at Oxford could almost be taken as the outline of a
novel or a short story:

> What actually happened is anybody's guess, and mine is this. I think the
> account in the *Vita Nuova* can be taken at its face-value: it wears an air of
> candour which is convincing. I think there was a real lady, that for a time
> he was attracted to her and desired her as a man desires a woman, and that
> he eventually conquered that desire, exactly as he says he did. But I think
> he went on seeing the lady, and that he came somehow in his mind to
> identify her calm and soothing personality with the philosophy that he
> was studying at the time, and in particular with that Lady Philosophy who
> appears in the *Consolations* of Boethius. He told himself—and perhaps he
> told her—that she was a kind of Muse or Egeria to him; possibly, God
> help him! he sat in her parlour and explained to her with much eloquence
> how beautiful this kind of Platonic friendship was, with no foolish non-
> sense about sex. Young men do say these things. What the lady's reactions
> may have been is matter for illimitable fancy. She may have been secretly
> disappointed, she may have been what a later generation would have
> called a blue-stocking and thought it all very spiritual and uplifting.
> (P. 197)

This lecture was delivered in August. A month later she mentioned
Barbara Barclay Carter's novel in a letter to me. According to my
conjecture she read it then for the first time, with the result that her
idea that the Donna Gentile might have seen Dante as a vehicle of
glory was transferred to his daughter Beatrice.

The next few years were busy ones. Dorothy was translating *Purgatorio*, writing lectures and caring for her invalid husband. After his
death, her energies were next absorbed in writing *The Emperor Constantine* for the festival of Colchester and in coping with the difficulties which arose in the course of the production. That over, she resumed work on *Purgatory*. But all the time, in the workshop of her
imagination, Dante and his daughter were living their life together in
the house in Ravenna. She even thought of going there.[9] But on 8
May 1952 she wrote to Norah Lambourne:

I have abandoned the notion of Italy—there is far too much to do, and if I went away I should only end by being devil-driven for the rest of the year. . . . Though I really must go *sometime* to Ravenna, having become suddenly obsessed (as if I hadn't enough to cope with already) by a novel about Dante and his daughter, which has been simmering for some time at the back of my mind.

She went on to say that the BBC had asked her to write two items on Dante for the Schools Programme: "I rashly undertook to write them a little scene between Dante and the daughter (by way of introducing 'biographical detail' and 'atmospheric background')." This, she said, had jerked the novel into life "and the harm was done." But the "harm," if harm it was, had been done long before. The seed was sown in 1944 by Williams' doctrine of the exchange of hierarchies. Then, from 1949, the seed was nurtured by Barbara Barclay Carter's novel.

The first of the intervening "items" for the BBC consists of a dialogue between Dante's daughter Bice (short for Beatrice), a young man named Gino who is making a fair copy of the *Purgatorio*, and Dante himself. James Brabazon calls it "a somewhat embarrassing little playlet," the chief interest of which is the fact that Richard Burton was cast as the young man but failed to turn up. In fact, all three of the actors had to be replaced at the last moment: Stephen Murray, who was to have played Dante, was ill, and Ruth Trouncer, cast as Bice, had developed German measles. They were replaced by Frank Duncan, John Wise and Diana Maddox. Brabazon says that the broadcast was live, but Dorothy, writing to Norah, says it was recorded. After a somewhat protracted rehearsal, which she insisted on attending, "as though it were a proper play," it went over, she says, "surprisingly well."

The second item was an enactment of the episode of Francesca da Rimini from canto V of *Inferno*. Hermione Hannen "read Francesca da Rimini beautifully," Dorothy reported to Norah, and John Slater played Paolo. Dorothy herself read the part of the narrator.

Both items had been commissioned for the "Schools Religion and Philosophy Programme." The two twenty-minute dialogues were therefore not intended to be plays in their own right, but classroom lessons about Dante, and as such they are very skilful. The pupils listening were told a good deal in a short time about the reasons for Dante's exile and about his hopes for peace. The dialogues also provide an attractive introduction to the Divine Comedy. In the first, Gino has just finished copying canto XXX of Purgatorio and reads aloud to Bice the passage where Dante (in the poem) sees Beatrice on a chariot in the midst of a cloud of flowers cast by the hands of angels. He knows instantly who she is, looks back to Virgil for guidance at this crucial moment—and finds him gone. As Bice and Gino lament the sadness of Virgil's departure, Dante enters unnoticed and continues the quotation:

> "Dante, weep not for Virgil's going; keep
> As yet from weeping, weep not yet, for soon
> Another sword shall give thee cause to weep."

In the dialogue which follows it emerges that Gino is in love with Bice. Dante feels compassion for him, for he knows that Bice does not reciprocate his love. Gino leaves and Dante asks his daughter to treat the young man kindly. This leads to a conversation about Dante's own love for Beatrice Portinari and about the nature of that love.

At this point the dialogue takes on a surprising dimension: it becomes, no less, a description of the Beatrician vision, which may be what Brabazon found embarrassing about the play. Yet in a programme devoted to religion and philosophy it was not inappropriate. Dante explains to his daughter that he had been privileged to see Beatrice "as God sees her, with the beauty that is not of this earth."

Bice:　I don't think I quite understand.

Dante:　When our Lord was transfigured upon Mount Tabor, those three disciples saw the glory of His divine reality shine through the veil of His created flesh. That reality was always there, though they could not always see it. He was not changed, but for a little while He changed them. And we all bear about in our bodies the splendour with which we shall be raised at the last day.

He reads to her from his Vita Nuova the description of the effect which Beatrice's greeting had on him:

Such a simple experience too—just an ordinary young woman, as it might be you, and an ordinary, shy, awkward young man, as it might be Gino, or anybody; and yet listen:

"I say that when she appeared from any direction, then, in the hope of her wondrous salutation, there was no enemy left to me; rather there smote into me a flame of charity which made me forgive any person who had ever injured me; and if at that moment anybody had put a question to me about anything whatsoever, my answer would have been simply *Love*, with a countenance clothed in humility."[10]

Bice recognizes this as something she has herself experienced, though not for any person:

Sometimes when I have been praying before the Blessed Sacrament, I have seemed to see the glory flow out from the Tabernacle and touch the whole world, so that for a time the trees seemed greener, and the sky bluer, and the streets of Florence like those of the New Jerusalem, with the happy souls walking up and down in them.

This is said by a young woman who after her father's death will take the veil.

The play is closely related to the novel with which at this period Dorothy said she was "obsessed." In the novel there is also a young man who is in love with Bice, but his name is Dino Perini; he has been taken over from *Ship Without Sails*, where he plays the same role. As in the play, Bice does not return his love, being aware of her religious vocation. But her capacity to experience the Beatrician vision, only suggested in the play, is explored in the novel to the full, until it becomes the main theme of this remarkable work.

Brabazon is dismissive, and somewhat scornful, of the novel's mystical content:

The notion behind the story is that it belatedly occurs to Dante, after he has written the *Commedia*, that the experience that meant so much to him might have been less significant to Beatrice—indeed that she might have found it amusing, if not mildly ridiculous. This causes an emotional crisis in Dante. The story is written in Dorothy's most impassioned style, harking back to her Musketeer days. . . .[11]

This is an unfair summary of the work. It is true to say that it has a number of defects. It is unfinished; some of the chapters are rough drafts only; it is not even certain in what order Dorothy intended to arrange them; and the quality of the writing is uneven. Nevertheless, the novel has certain features which merit serious consideration.

The first is the characterization of Dante's daughter, whose origins can be traced to Barbara Barclay Carter's *Ship Without Sails*. In that novel the moment when Bice first arrives in Ravenna is fraught with tension:

> A tall, dark girl slipped through [the curtains] and stood tense, as though, but for a resolute will, like a shy wild thing she would have fled.
>
> Dante took a step forward, and his eyes met hers—dark as his own—and it was as though he saw in a pool his own youth. "Are you mine?" he asked huskily. "Is it—Bice? O Bice, Beatrice, am I not dreaming?"
>
> She laughed at that, a little clear laugh that was half a sob.
>
> "Oh, father," she said, and hid her head on his shoulder, "then I did right to come."[12]

It is significant that Beatrice is uncertain of her welcome. By contrast, a more forceful Bice appears in Dorothy's novel. Dante, out of a sense of duty, has written to his wife to invite her to join him in Ravenna, now that he has at last a settled home to offer her. He has sent his two sons to fetch her at a confine where she is to wait, having travelled there from Florence. On a dark, wet evening in October in the year 1316 he is looking out of his chamber window, awaiting their arrival:

> As though through a silver curtain he saw a small draggled party plodding slowly along the street—Jacopo on his bony roan; Pietro on his ambling plump-bellied, ecclesiastical grey; behind Pietro, on the pillion, a shapeless female form huddled in a thick hooded cloak. . . .
>
> As he set his foot on the stair, he heard the horses turn in under the arched and narrow entrance. He gave them time to file through, and then, passing across the parlour, opened the door of the house and went out after them into the rain. . . . Pietro was helping the woman from her cramped perch. She extricated herself with an ease and lightness which rather surprised him, and with three quick, running steps, dropped smoothly to her knees on the wet cobbles before him.

"Sir, pray give me your blessing. I am Beatrice."
His heart turned over.

The sound of the name still has power to move him and he is angry
with himself for being moved. Nevertheless, he answers: "God
bless you, my daughter; you are very welcome."

The Sayers novel explores the intricacies of the father-daughter
relationship from the first moments the two are united. When Beatrice goes upstairs she realizes that the matrimonial chamber had been
prepared for her mother. This she is now to occupy and she is
troubled, thinking that she ought not to have come. In a tender and
delicate scene of courteous and subtle dialogue, father and daughter
come to an understanding: he is to send her home if he finds her
troublesome, she is to return if she feels homesick.

Left to herself, Beatrice examines her reasons for coming. Her
mother had been reluctant to leave Florence and to risk the damp,
marshy region of Ravenna; also, an elder sister, Antonia, was about
to have a baby and had need of her mother. Jacopo and Pietro had
written to the family, persuading them that their father was ailing and
required someone to look after him. So Beatrice had volunteered to
come. Now she feels that she has been meddling and officious. Moreover, she is afraid to tell her father her real reason for coming: that all
through her childhood she has idealized him.

Here again, Barbara Barclay Carter's novel has provided a starting
point. Describing the life of Dante's children, she relates that Ma-
rietto Portinari, the brother of Beatrice and a close friend of Dante (as
he himself describes him in the *Vita Nuova*), used to tell them stories
about their father, so embroidering his image that he became a leg-
endary figure to them:

Sometimes, when they begged him, he would retell some of the tales the
Jongleurs sang in the market-places and banquet halls, of how Charlemagne had come to Florence with his Twelve Peers, and how he had rebuilt the city, of how Roland and Oliver and Archbishop Turpin died at
Roncesvalles, or else the legends of the Round Table and the Knights of
Arthur, Tristan and Lancelot, Galahad and Perceval, till the whole
blended into that second life of dream that is the real living of imaginative

children, to form a world in which Dante himself appeared a figure of legend, finding his peers among the old heroes.[13]

This is very similar to the scene in Dorothy's novel in which Dante questions his daughter as to her reasons for coming to Ravenna. Was she seeking a husband? Was she unhappy at home? At last she confesses to him what the figure of her famous, absent father has meant to her all her life:

> As far back as she could remember, his name had held for his children a secret promise. It had stood for mystery, and also for spaciousness, largesse, and *leggiadrìa*; for Paradise Lost and the Golden Age to come. . . . The girls had envied the boys, destined as everybody knew to join their father as soon as they reached the age of manhood. . . .
>
> "And you, I suppose, stayed at home and read romances."
>
> "Yes, I'm afraid so," she agreed meekly. Stumbling over phrases which seemed to become more and more awkward and inappropriate, she tried to explain. How he had got mixed up with the romances, how Lancelot the great lover and Tristram the peerless singer rode in his person through the enchanted woodland of Brocéliande; Guinevere looked down from a high tower as he passed through the streets of Camelot. . . . There were other stories too: he was Charlemagne, summoned by the note of Oliphant, hurrying through the pass too late.

Such fostering of romantic illusions in her childhood serves as a preparation for what eventually takes place: the substitution of the false by the true image.

In the meantime, what are Dante's feelings at this entry into his life of a daughter he did not know? He was relieved, rather than disappointed, that his wife had not come: he was now freed from the past. But fate had given him something in exchange—for a wife, a daughter and a discovery. "With indefatigable curiosity he advanced eagerly upon the uncharted," a territory that is unmarked for father and daughter both. While the novel is the exploration of this unusual relationship, it is also an exploration of the forms and faces of love.

It was an exploration which required courage. At the entrance to Hell, Virgil had said to Dante, "Qui si convien lasciar ogni sospetto [Here must all cowardice be left behind]." Dante's daughter quotes the line to him and asks, "You would not say *only* at the gates of

Dante as Dorothy L. Sayers imagined him.

Hell?'' Her father replies, ''No, at the gates of every adventure, and the beginning of every journey, and the exploration of all the secret places.''

This conversation takes place at the end of a chapter in which Dante has searched his heart in an attempt to define and distinguish his experiences of love. He looks back over his life and meditates on four women: Beatrice Portinari, the Donna Gentile, the Donna

Pietra, and his wife, Gemma. His love for Beatrice was something apart, beyond and above all else; he had received by grace ineffable bounty, from a word, a smile, a glance, a gesture. "This love had never had to bear the strain of intimacy, the frets of time and change. Death and distance had fixed it in an eternal youth." He is at peace with himself when he thinks of her.

But not when his thoughts turn to the Lady at the Window. He knows that here he was lacking in grace and generosity. His recollection of the episode is an expansion of the scenario which Dorothy sketched in 1949 and tried out on her audience at Oxford. It is an attempt to answer the question, Did the lady really exist, and if so, how and why did Dante later on identify her with the Lady Philosophy? Dorothy's treatment of Dante's musings on the subject is so entertaining as fiction that it is worth quoting at some length:

> Her compassion had drawn her to him. In his despair at the death of Beatrice, she had looked pityingly upon him, and for that he was grateful, and thought to see in her a new image of love. She was older than he, but a beautiful woman and very well educated; he had liked going to see her. He had poured out to her his love and his grief; and she had sympathised, and lent him Boethius on *The Consolations of Philosophy*. . . . Their conversation was on a very lofty plane; . . . he called her playfully "my Lady Philosophy," and the elusive charms of Philosophy presented themselves to him in an image of dark eyes gravely smiling in a pale face. . . . When he saw desire beckon to him from those balconies of the soul whence Philosophy had been wont to deliver her demonstrations, he was appalled. . . . In a fit of self-righteousness, he fled the field, like the young prig that he was.

This is what Dorothy's "illimitable fancy" about the Lady of the Window had produced in the space of three years! She produces next an equally seductive scenario for the Donna Pietra, to whom Dante's thoughts also turn:

> The Lady Pietra! . . . A cold young devil, if ever there was one, beautiful as a larch in spring, slender and green and golden; hard as a stone, frigid as a stone—widowed at eighteen, having tormented and mocked into his grave the doting old man who had wedded and thought to bed her; going about looking for new cruelties to practise, casting her brilliant eyes on

Dante Alighieri, poor and a poet and hardly worth the bird-lime, but a poet all the same and therefore entertainingly vocal upon the rack.

Then Dante comes to considering his married life with Gemma. We know very little about this, apart from Boccaccio's statement that it was unhappy. Dorothy, as she had done in her lecture "Dante and Milton," here supposes that they got along comfortably enough:

> And if from time to time trouble occurred, he could always do away with it by the simplest of all conjugal remedies. He knew how to give pleasure with his body—readily, considerately, satisfyingly; and she brought to the game a simple enjoyment, too lazy to be called passion, too cheerfully animal to be called love, too purely physical for it to matter if he bestowed his embraces with his mind elsewhere—and perhaps on somebody else.

Thus Dante ransacks his memory, and in the light shed by his ruminations over the women in his life, he finally sees clearly what his current problem is: "He must learn, and at one-and-fifty years old, to dwell harmoniously with this girl of seventeen. . . . In the ordinary way, of course, this situation would never arise. One did not, as a rule, find one's self faced with a ready-made, fully adult daughter."

The crisis of that particular relationship is a mystical vision experienced by Bice. She does not at first tell her father about it, but confides in the elderly aunt of the Polenta family, Donna Margherita, who questions her about her love for him. She replies that she thinks it must be something not wholly of this earth, "because I have seen him in another body, and that vision is always with me; . . . for me, love is in him, as Our Lord is in the Host, and the cup of his blessing is the cup of salvation." Donna Margherita tells Dante of his daughter's vision and he rejects it, having no desire to be seen in such a light. She rebukes him and suggests that his lady Beatrice may have found *his* devotion unwelcome. This brings about a crisis in Dante's confidence. Has his poem, then, been founded on a lie? The vision which he had of Beatrice was true, of that he is certain; but if she rejected him, she could not truly be someone whose greeting was his salvation (*salute*). After struggling with his pride, he finds his dilemma solved. He comes to believe in the validity of his daughter's vision and consequently accepts his spiritual function towards her. This helps him to regain faith in the spiritual role towards *him* of his lady Beatrice. He asks his daughter to describe her vision. She tells him,

> I was happy in Ravenna, and happy with you as I had never been before. But I did not know why the sky was so blue and the trees and all the colours enchanted, till that morning when I saw you standing with your hand on the rope of the rail. . . . And the stair was golden and it ran up behind you into a great light.

Dante recognizes that she possesses "the double vision," as he does. Father and daughter talk together about the nature of such mystical experiences. Dante asks her to describe what she called "the body of glory." She says, "It is difficult to put into words. It is not light and it is not colour, though it gives light and colour to everything else." She asks, "Is it spirit itself made visible? Or is it that aery body which you attribute to the souls after death?" Dante replies,

> I believe it is of the flesh, and that your name for it is the right one. It is the body of glory. For it lies, does it not, in the flesh, and has the same features; yet though it is distinct from the natural body it does not cover it, nor hover upon it, nor separate from it, but indwells it, other than it, but occupying the same space.

And he compares it with the body of Christ's Transfiguration, identifying it with the body of our resurrection: "The holy and glorious flesh—which we bear about with us, unknown to ourselves. That is what God sees always, and love sees sometimes, and in the Last Day all the blessed will see each other so."

This is the spiritual core of the book. It is also the nearest Dorothy Sayers ever came to exploring the full implications of the Beatrician vision.

14.

SEARCH OR STATEMENT?

It requires moral courage to grieve;
it requires religious courage to rejoice.
Kierkegaard

One of Dorothy Sayers' last lectures on Dante, which she wrote specially for the Cambridge University Italian Society and gave on 8 May 1956, was entitled "Dante Faber."[1] It was published, after her death, in a volume called *The Poetry of Search and the Poetry of Statement,* a distinction which had been the theme of the lecture. This grappling with the nature of the poet as poet was part of a further and, as it turned out, a final extension of her long journey with Dante, a journey which was leading her on a spiritual exploration of her own.

In a letter dated 3 April 1956, Dorothy had asked me what I thought would interest the undergraduates:

I have a lecture which I have just delivered at Manchester to the University Dante Society; it is definitely along the line I want to open up—viz: bringing Dante into relation with other poets. He seems so often to be treated as a kind of lonely monument. It is called "The Beatrician Vision." . . . But perhaps it is a little too religious in tone.

Alternatively, she had another in mind:

I think of calling it "Dante Faber," with perhaps a sub-title about "Structure in the Poetry of Statement." It will start off with a few words about the two kinds of poet—those who write to find out what they feel and those who write to tell what they know—and will go on to examine two or three examples of large-scale and small-scale structure in (chiefly) the *Paradiso.* . . . Let me know what you think.

I chose "Dante Faber."

The distinction between poets of search and poets of statement was, of course, too categorical, as Dorothy herself acknowledged. Some poets are both, at different times. In defining Dante as a poet of statement, in contrast, for instance, to Keats and Tennyson, whom she regarded primarily as poets of search, she was focusing on and trying to account for the precision and clarity of the *Commedia*, that very "lucidity" which C. S. Lewis had called into question.[2] She wrote, "The poet can be lucid and precise because he knows what he intends to say; his structure can be massive in outline and intimately related in all its parts because it is planned, and he knows, while writing, exactly what [relationship] every word and line bears to the whole poem. . . ."[3] She recognized in Dante a *maker*, one who fashioned into narrative and allegorical form materials already chosen. In this respect he resembles a *playwright*, who does not so much *write* a play as work it into dramatic shape, as a cartwright makes a cart or a wheelwright a wheel. It is significant that William Anderson chose to call his book *Dante the Maker*, for he believes that Dante matured the content of his poem in his mind for many years, even committing long portions of it to memory before he wrote it down.[4]

It should be said that, while it is true that the *Commedia* shows the hand of a maker, Dante was not always "a poet of statement." In his early love poems, and later, in the first years of his exile when he was writing his philosophic treatise *Il Convivio* (which he left unfinished), he was more "a poet of search." Unsure of his direction, sometimes unsure even of his meaning, he made discoveries as he went along, and he himself acknowledged as much.[5] As a reader, too, he awoke gradually to implications in other poets' works. This occurred particularly when he reread the *Aeneid* in his exile.[6] In the first canto of *Inferno*, at the magical moment when he meets Virgil, he appeals to him in the famous words:

> . . . vaglianmi il lungo studio e il grande amore
> che m'ha fatto *cercar* il tuo volume.

[. . . let plead for me the years of zeal and the great love which have made me *search* thy volume.]

Now, creating his own poem, he will *state* what he has learnt, not only from Virgil but also from other poets, as well as from life.

To which of these two categories did Dorothy Sayers herself belong? In 1944, when she first began to read Dante, she would no doubt have regarded herself, if she had then formulated the distinction, as a writer of statement. She knew her own mind on a number of matters. She had mastered the technique of several literary forms: detective fiction, drama, polemical writing, Christian apologetics and poetry. All this expertise, as I have shown, she brought to bear on her reading and translation of the *Commedia*: from her novel-writing, the habit of visualising a narrative in three dimensions and the ability to handle structure, characterization and dialogue; from her experience as a playwright, a heightened awareness of the interplay of character and plot; from her polemics, skill in the marshalling of facts and in presenting a case with logic and cogency; from her Christian apologetics, a grasp of doctrine and a capacity to expound unfamiliar concepts in present-day terms; from her poetry (which she wrote all her life), skill in verse-form, metre and rhyme.

And yet her mind, she had said, was "unprepared" for what she found in Dante. I have considered what she meant by this: the narrative power of the poem took her by surprise, as did the directness of the style, the homeliness of the similes, the humour and the joy. But that is not the whole story. In another sense, reading, interpreting and translating the *Commedia* was for her, and continued to be, a journey into the unknown. In this, her last literary adventure, Dorothy Sayers became a poet of search, in quest of spiritual truth.

As we have seen, when William Temple, archbishop of Canterbury, asked if he might confer on her a Lambeth Doctorate in Divinity, she declined on grounds of professional integrity.[7] But there was also a deeper, more personal reason: she had doubts about herself as a Christian. In her first reply to the archbishop, dated 7 September 1943, she wrote:

Thank you very much for the great honour you do me. I find it very difficult to reply as I ought, because I am extremely conscious that I don't deserve it. . . . A Degree in Divinity is not, I suppose, intended as a certificate of sanctity, exactly; but I should feel better about it if I were a more convincing kind of Christian. I am never quite sure whether I really am one, or whether I have only fallen in love with an intellectual pattern. And when one is able to handle language it is sometimes hard to know how far one is under the spell of one's own words.

It is significant that only a month before writing this she had been corresponding with Charles Williams about the intellectual pleasure she took in the pattern of the Christian doctrine. He had replied:

Moved by a sentence in your letter which you will remember, I permit myself to say again that I feel that this matter which we were discussing is very serious indeed. There is a point at which you and I will no longer be able to get away with an explanation of how admirable we think the pattern is, and I think that point is very near for both of us. I know as well as you do of the byways of the literary mind, but I do not feel they are going to be much use. There are awful moments when I think that perhaps it is precisely people like us, who are enthralled by the idea and stop there, who are really responsible for a great deal of the incapacity and the harm.[8]

A year after this she began reading Dante.

In 1954, on Maundy Thursday, in the vestry of St. Thomas' Church, Regent Street, she was challenged in similar but more forthright terms by John Wren-Lewis, a young scientist who was deputy director of research at Imperial Chemical Industries and a writer and broadcaster on religious and philosophical subjects. The conversation led to a correspondence from which it appears that Wren-Lewis accused Dorothy and other Christians like her of being interested only in the dogmatic pattern. On Good Friday she replied to his charges in a letter of seventeen pages.[9] She admitted that she was not by temperament an evangelist and that she was incapable of religious emotion, though she had a moral sense and a strong conviction of the reality of sin. Since she could not, as she put it, come at God through intuition or "inner light," there was only the intellect left:

You said that I . . . gave people the impression of caring only for a dogmatic pattern. That is quite true. I remember once saying to Charles Williams: "I do not know whether I believe in Christ or whether I am only in love with the pattern." And Charles said, with his usual prompt understanding, that he had exactly the same doubts about himself. But *this* you must try to accept: when we say "in love with the pattern," we mean *in love*. (Though Charles was different, he did love people, and he was capable of romantic love and I think of a personal love for God in a way that I am not, though he recognized that there were others who could love Christ more personally and intimately than he could.) The thing is, however, that where the intellect is dominant it becomes the channel of all the other feelings. The "passionate intellect" is *really* passionate. It is the only point at which ecstasy can enter. I do not know whether we can be saved by the intellect, but I do know that I can be saved by nothing else. I know that, if there is judgment, I shall have to be able to say: "This alone, Lord, in Thee and in me, have I never betrayed, and may it suffice to know and love and choose Thee after this manner, for I have no other love, or knowledge, or choice in me."

The Reverend Dr. E. L. Mascall has discussed this letter in an article entitled "What Happened to Dorothy L. Sayers that Good Friday?"[10] As a writer on Christianity she was, he wrote,

intensely anxious to avoid any kind of apologetic that was not radically rational and intellectual, any offer of Christianity as providing emotional satisfaction, personal fulfilment or any other motive for acceptance than the conviction of its truth. . . . Her central concern is clear and it is supported by almost everything that she ever wrote about religion. It is that, when all is said and done, the only really relevant reason for accepting Christianity is that you are convinced that it is *true*; not that it is comfortable or uncomfortable, interesting or uninteresting, profitable or unprofitable, or what-have-you, but simply that it is *true*.

This does not mean that her own experience of religion was detached and objective. On the contrary. Dr. Mascall considers her correct in insisting that the intellect can be passionate, that through it we can be in love and that it can be the point at which ecstasy enters: "This can be true on the purely natural level, as every pure mathematician knows; it can be true on the supernatural level as well."

In the same letter to Wren-Lewis, as Dr. Mascall points out, Dorothy says that her contact with Dante is through "the passionate intellect": "It is by that contact that I can accept and interpret his other side—the 'Beatrician' side, which, by itself, would be meaningless to me. Because he knows beatitude as 'luce intellettual,' I can believe him when he adds 'pien d'amore.' "[11] When she wrote those words she had been reading Dante for almost ten years. For a year or more she had been working on her novel about Dante and his daughter.

In her lecture "The Meaning of Purgatory," delivered in 1948, Dorothy had said, "To understand Dante it is not of course, necessary to believe what he believed, but it is, I think, necessary to *understand* what he believed, and to realise that it is a belief which a mature mind can take seriously."[12] Both this and the lecture which preceded it, "The Meaning of Heaven and Hell," are magnificent expositions of all three concepts and of the imagery by which Dante conveys them. But in 1948, though she clarified Dante for us, she did not commit *herself*. Four years later, in her lecture "Dante and Milton," she proclaimed her spiritual kinship:

> The sin which besets all makers of critical comparisons is, of course, the sin of partiality. . . . I shall not be exempt from this failing. Due discount must be made for the fact that I can be at home in the universe of Dante's mind as I cannot be in Milton's, *because Dante and I share the same faith*; on that side, therefore, my sympathy is likely to overweigh my judgment. On the other hand, my judgment tells me this: that if (as the world on the whole seems to think) Dante's achievement is more satisfying, intellectually and aesthetically, than Milton's it is largely because Dante's whole nature was integral with, and fully expressed in, his faith, as Milton's was not. (My italics)[13]

Some members of the summer school audience were startled when they heard her say this and wondered if she had "gone over to Rome." But it was not so. Her friend Patrick McLaughlin (of Irish extraction, born in England, initially an Anglican, albeit of the most "Anglo-Catholic" kind, and later a Roman Catholic when he migrated to live in Rome) wrote to me as follows:

> I am quite sure that she did not merely *understand* Dante's faith, but that she *shared* it to the full. How not? It was the faith in which she had grown up. . . . For us children of the Oxford Movement the schism from Rome was essentially a juridical one. . . . Divergence in doctrine came later, as a rationalisation of circumstances. . . . Protestantism certainly infiltrated the Church of England . . . but *not* to the extent of extinguishing its essential catholicity. So Dorothy never felt any impulse (so far as I

know) to become a Papist, because the whole catholic faith was there all the time in the Church of England.

For anyone born and formed in the catholic tradition, as Dorothy had been, the apprehension of divine truth by the intellect was paramount.[14] But, as McLaughlin also pointed out, Christianity is not primarily a religion but a faith, the acknowledgment that Jesus is Lord and Saviour.

At a Sayers Festival organized at Wheaton College, Illinois, in 1978, Kay M. Baxter, author of *Contemporary Theatre and the Christian Faith*,[15] contributed a lecture entitled "Theatrical Values in the Work of Dorothy L. Sayers." Though she found the Sayers plays too generally wordy and too intellectual to be theatrically effective, she made an exception in the case of *The Man Born to be King* concerning which she also said:

> I suspect that by reading the Testament in Greek . . . and slogging many hours a day at compiling the four gospels into one continuous narrative divisible into sections, and having to write directions to producers and actors, clarifying the resultant text . . . that she actually suffered a *conversion* . . . "surprised by joy" perhaps, but certainly caught up in the astounding story she had to tell. . . . In spite of the fact that she said dogma was the most exciting study in the world, I think in *The Man Born to be King* she found something even more exciting, and looked with a steady and resolute and simplified gaze at Jesus Christ.[16]

This may be so. But I am inclined to think that Dorothy's faith, in its entirety, was deepened and strengthened still further by her reading of the *Commedia*. When she had first read right through *Paradiso* she wrote, as we saw, to Charles Williams, "Was there ever a heaven so full of nods and becks and wreathèd smiles, so gay and dancing? or where the most abstract and intellectual kind of beatitude was so merrily expressed? Surely nobody ever so passionately *wanted* a place where everybody was kind, courteous, or carried happiness so lightly." She had underlined the word "wanted." Is Dante's heaven the kind of heaven in which *she* wanted to believe?

> luce intellettual, pien d'amore,
> amore di vero ben, pien di letizia;
> letizia che trascende ogni dolzore.

[Pure intellectual light, fulfilled with love,
　Love of the true Good, filled with all delight,
　Transcending sweet delight, all sweets above.]
(XXX, 40–42)

Perhaps she longed to be, as Dante was, astonished and overjoyed by understanding God's justice and love, to share in the contentment of the souls. Did her will assent to the image?

In this connection it is significant that the fragments of *Paradiso* which she chose to translate in advance are nearly all passages expressing wonder and joy. Her imagination responds to them, her pulses quicken and the quality of her writing is heightened. This energy and intensity can also be seen in her lectures wherever she interprets the meaning of Dante's Heaven. An ecstatic passage, for instance, in "The Fourfold Interpretation of the *Comedy*," proclaims:

> In the sphere of Jupiter, the whole hierarchy of the Active Life is included under the Eagle, the sign of the perfect Empire. Where those who say "I" mean "We", *there* is Justice, *there,* here and now. . . . So that, if anyone asks, "Where, in the *Commedia*, has Dante found room for that perfection of the Active Life, and the Perfect Universal State of which his earlier writings are so full?" the answer is: Here; not in the Earthly Paradise, but in the Heavenly, where all perfection is. Here, with its law-makers and lovers and poets, its scholars and warriors; here, with its civic decencies and family affections; here, with its order and empire and justice. This is the picture of the world as it might be; as, if the Kingdom come, please God it will be; as, in so far as the Kingdom is already here and at work, it already is. Here, not hereafter; though it shall be hereafter, and in the Heaven which knows neither before nor after, here it eternally is.[17]

It is not possible—perhaps it is impertinent to try—to assess what the *Commedia*, in particular the *Paradiso*, meant to Dorothy as a Christian. It may have helped her in moments of "spiritual dryness," if indeed she suffered any. Patrick McLaughlin doubted that she did: "Her mind was a river in full spate, often overflowing its banks. It irrigated multitudes of other souls; and her own soul always seemed to be fully irrigated itself." Among those "multitudes" were readers of the Penguin Dante.

In the preface which Dorothy asked me to write to her first volume of lectures, *Introductory Papers on Dante*, I said, "This book on Dante by Dorothy L. Sayers makes possible a new relationship between Dante and the modern reader." In my foreword to *Paradise* I referred as follows to what I had said eight years before:

> I still think this is true. The most valuable and original service she per-
> formed for readers of Dante was to redirect attention to the literal mean-
> ing of the *Comedy.* This she did by commenting, in a stimulating and
> readable manner, on the story. . . . In interpreting the allegory, Dor-
> othy Sayers continually drew the reader's attention to the relevance of the
> *Comedy* to life. By her masterly and observant handling of both these
> aspects, in her lectures, in her introductions and commentaries on *Hell*
> and *Purgatory* and in her translation itself, she brought Dante within reach
> of thousands of readers for whom he would otherwise have remained
> unintelligible.

And now, thirty years after her death, what do I think?

I still consider that she made possible a new relationship between Dante and the modern reader; but the "thousands of readers" for whom she made him intelligible have by now become millions. It is possible that they nowadays take for granted what was once new and startling. Has her presentation become outdated? It may have, as re-gards some aspects of the translation. The use of "thou" and "thee" and "thy" for "you" and "your" in the singular, with which present-day readers have become unfamiliar, may make the poem seem more remote than it did in 1949, when *Hell* was first published, and even then objections were raised. Some of the vocabulary is unusual, the word-order is occasionally antiquated and the colloquialisms, by contrast, tend to be disconcerting, or even by now old-fashioned. Dorothy herself was dissatisfied with her translation of *Inferno*; there are things in it which she would have altered. She was better pleased with her translation of *Purgatorio.* Had she lived to complete *Paradise* she would no doubt have revised the first twenty cantos before finally committing them to print.

And yet her translation stands up well to its recent competitors. It is still the most lively and varied version available. It is never dull. In the didactic passages, some of them very difficult, it is technically accurate and extremely lucid. And in her notes and commentaries she is supreme. Her two volumes of lectures on Dante, now out of print, deserve to be republished. When I reread them now I experience anew something of the impact which they made on me when I first heard them. I was exhilarated by their amazing blend of imaginative and intellectual power, by their triumphant clarity, above all by the delight and eager joy which they communicate.

Since Oxford was Dorothy's *alma mater* ("I that am twice thy child," she wrote of herself),[18] it is appropriate to let two Oxford voices be heard. The first, Colin Hardie, said of her *Purgatory:* "The translation as a whole is more than an accomplished tour-de-force: it conveys a great deal of Dante's poetry and style, and for long stretches such a marriage of two minds and two languages as no longer to seem a translation."[19] This is high praise, coming as it does from a fastidious and discerning scholar who elsewhere took her to task on a number of learned points. In his review of *Further Papers on Dante,* published in *Italian Studies* after her death, he uttered a note of warning: "There is a danger that her trenchant and self-confident, even peremptory, views may be accepted without demur and combat. The inexperienced reader will not be led by her into the real state of 'Dantologia,' nor introduced to the Italian masters." He acknowledged, however, that Italian Dantists had tended to be untheological and perhaps anti-clerical, "and one of Miss Sayers' strong points is her theological understanding." In a recent correspondence with me Mr. Hardie writes: "I have a slightly uneasy feeling that I did not sufficiently appreciate the novelty in Britain of her work on Dante, with its emphasis on theology . . . though I welcomed her break with the narrow, blinkered Italian tradition (except for Nardi) and insistence on the *Comedy* as a great orthodox religious poem." And in his review of *Purgatory* he commented, "When the novelist and the theologian are uppermost, she is at her best."

This was also the view of Cesare Foligno, who had been professor of Italian at Oxford. After Dorothy's death he published in *Il Mattino* an obituary article in which he surveyed the whole range of her writings. I give below in translation what he there said about her work on Dante.

Italians, who rarely read Dante's work in its entirety and even more rarely reread it, need to be reminded that English translations of the *Comedy* are almost without number. . . . New ones appear from time to time, precisely because the non-Italian reader who believes he has understood the *Comedy* responds almost inevitably to the challenge to conquer the work by means of a new translation. At her death Dorothy L. Sayers had already published her translation of the *Inferno* and of the *Purgatorio* and was two thirds of the way through the third Cantica. . . . In accordance with the editorial policy of the Penguin series of translations, she rendered Dante's *Divine Comedy* in terms of modern English with the aim of making him comprehensible, with the help of a few essential notes, to the common reader. And although in her *Inferno* the choice of modern diction appears excessive here and there, in her *Purgatory* a balance is achieved, and this version is one of the best of all the many English versions which exist. . . .

Her ever deepening study of Dante resulted further in two volumes of essays. Perhaps because professional Dantists are prejudiced against the attempt of an author of detective novels to rank herself among them, or because they are naturally touchy and hostile towards all intruders, these essays have not yet had the attention they deserve. Some of her ideas may in the end prove unacceptable, but her essays, with their clarity, perspicacity, boldness of comparison and fluency in exposition (qualities usually conspicuously absent from writings of the kind) are in many respects outstanding. An expert in narrative herself, she lays particular emphasis, for instance, upon Dante's most remarkable gifts as a narrator, his ability to arouse interest, and to hold it by means of suspense, surprise and variety. We had all perhaps sensed or presumed this quality in Dante, but had anyone previously undertaken to set it in evidence with such striking clarity?

Particularly admirable is her discussion of Dante's allegory. The supra-senses of the *Comedy* constitute the most vexing problem of Dante scholarship, not to say the principal embarrassment of commentators. This is because the allegorical habit of mind does not belong to our time and we tend to see the supra-senses as so many *superstructures,* varying in their effectiveness, while in fact they derive from a particular way of feeling and thinking, as a result of which the narrative is rendered almost transparent by its multiple significance. This of course is no new discovery, but it is difficult to expound and to exemplify consistently and coherently. It is often forgotten that Dante was writing for readers who were well prepared and well equipped to understand the many meanings of his work. Few people have succeeded in elucidating this complexity with such clarity and accuracy as Dorothy L. Sayers.

A great deal of praise has been given to a somewhat superficial little

Dorothy L. Sayers in the last year of her life (1957). From a portrait by Fritz Kraemer.

essay on Dante by T. S. Eliot, mainly because T. S. Eliot wrote it. Dorothy Sayers' essays on Dante are unquestionably of far greater importance. Byron liked to say he was a poet among lords and a lord among poets; might one not perhaps say that Dorothy L. Sayers was a Dantist among detective novelists and a detective novelist among Dantists? In both activities she achieved distinction.[20]

Both Colin Hardie and Cesare Foligno have focused on the creative dynamism which resulted from the union of her intellect and her imagination. I would add a third ingredient: the joy she found in creativity.

One must not make the mistake of attributing to her a personal belief in everything her intellect took pleasure in clarifying or her imagination delighted in contemplating. It would be bordering on "the personal heresy," for instance, to regard her unfinished novel about Dante as a confession of her faith. It is more probably an exploration, a testing, of the Beatrician vision. How would it work out in everyday life? Could it be made believable in the medium of a novel? She may have written it as an experiment, having in mind the book she one day hoped to write on the theme of the Burning Bush.

She also wrote it for her own pleasure, and for fun. She *enjoyed* creating the character of Dante, imaginary but based on his writings and on traditional descriptions of him. She had been conversing with him in her mind for years. Now she imagined what it would be like to live in the same house, to walk about Ravenna with him, to meet his friends, and to hear him talk. He is in his fifties, grey-haired, but still unquenchably young in spirit. Intellectually curious, he is interested in the causes of things and in new experiences. He delights in discussion. He is touchy and irascible but quick to repent an angry outburst. His manners are formal and charming. He is elegant in his person. He is a competent horseman and enjoys hunting with trained falcons. He has been a vigorous and expert lover and is still attractive to women. Above all, both as a poet and as a man, he is still capable, as he was when he first fell in love with Beatrice, of ecstasy.

Many critics echo each other in saying that Dorothy Sayers fell in love with her detective hero, Lord Peter Wimsey. But she was content to give that experience to Harriet Vane. Despite all the qualities with which he is endowed, it is doubtful if Lord Peter could ever have met all the requirements of his creator as an ideal companion. I think, rather, that she fell in love with Dante, not only with his poetry, but with the man as she imagined he might have been. At the same time, the character she creates has more than a touch of Lord Peter about him, the serious and intellectual Lord Peter of *Gaudy Night*, the ecstatic Lord Peter of *Busman's Honeymoon*. And the delicate sketch of Dante's profile which she drew to accompany her novel bears some resemblance to her most famous brain-child.

This may be mere fantasy. What is certain is that Dorothy Sayers' encounter with Dante the poet was an affair of the heart, or, as she would have preferred, of the passionate intellect.

APPENDIX

CHRISTMAS 1946

THE HEART OF STONE
DANTE ALIGHIERI

THE HEART OF STONE

BEING THE FOUR *CANZONI*
OF THE "PIETRA" GROUP,
DONE INTO ENGLISH BY
DOROTHY L. SAYERS
FROM THE ITALIAN OF
DANTE ALIGHIERI
(1265–1321)

WOOD ENGRAVING BY
NORAH LAMBOURNE

These four *canzoni* make up what is known as the "Pietra" group, because they all play upon the meanings of the word "pietra" (stone). The same imagery runs through all of them, and indeed the last three are, to all intents and purposes, one poem in three different versions. All of them are obviously addressed to the same lady, of whom we know nothing except what may be deduced from the poems themselves. We do not know her name; and seeing that Dante says himself (in the third stanza of the first *canzone*) that he is anxious not to betray the object of his passion—since to do so would have been considered extremely shocking by all canons of courtly love—we may be fairly sure that it was not "Pietra," though this word may possibly contain a play upon her real name. We may infer that she had curly golden hair, that she looked well in green, that she was very young and did not return Dante's love, and (perhaps) that his own passion was as short-lived as it was violent. The poems bear all the marks of having been written within a comparatively brief period; he has wooed the lady, he says, in a meadow whose green grass breathed out love, and by mid-winter he feels his position to be pretty well hopeless; perhaps six months may have covered the episode from start to finish.

Precise dates are lacking, but in any case the poems were all written before 1308, for Dante proposed to include them in his *Convivio*, a philosophic commentary upon his own *canzoni*, which he was writing about that time, but never finished. Presumably he intended to interpret them allegorically, though he might have had some difficulty in persuading his readers that the first of them (at any rate) was originally meant to be a Hymn to the Lady Philosophy. It appears more likely that the stony-hearted lady (whoever she was) represents one of those mundane distractions for which, through the mouth of Beatrice, Dante reproached himself when, having left the Dark Wood and passed through the vision of Hell, he arrived at the Earthly Paradise on the summit of Mount Purgatory.

The poems are here presented in the order which appears to be the logical one, and in which it is thought that Dante intended them to be included in the *Convivio*. The original metre and rhyme-scheme are followed in the translation, and a note on the construction of *canzoni* is appended for the benefit of those who are curious in such matters.

1

Così nel mio parlar voglio esser aspro

Now would I fain speak daggers; now I want
   Fit words to match the ways of that fair stone
   Daily and hourly grown
To cruel hardness still more petrified.

She is so cased in coat of adamant
   That through weak joint, or weakness of her own,
   Arrow was never none
From quiver shot could find her naked side.

She slays at will; no harness can abide,
   No foot can flee her deadly strokes at all,
   For like winged bolts they fall
Cleaving her victims through the mail that fenced them,
And I've nor wit nor power to stand against them.

I find no shield she knows not how to break,
   I find no cover from her dazzling ray;
   Like blossom on the spray
Topping my thoughts she sits and sways me so;

Me and my misery she seems to take
   As easy as a ship on a calm day
   Takes the smooth sea. How weigh
With these light rhymes my leaden load of woe?

O ruthless rasp of pain, whose rough teeth go
   Through rind and core, killing my heart with care,
   Why wilt thou not forbear
Thus like a hidden canker to gnaw through it,
As I to tell who gave thee power to do it?

This, more than death, my soul feels terror of:
    Lest, when I think of her in any place
    Where men may scan my face,
My thought peer through, and they should read the
    thought;

For death already with the teeth of love
    Mangles my wits; so crazy is their case,
    Their operant powers apace
Flare up in dreams and crumble away to naught.

He beats me flat, and with the sword that wrought
    Elissa's death stands o'er me as I lie—
    Love, upon whom I cry,
Humbly beseeching grace; but he'll afford me
None, seeming set in hainous mood toward me.

Again he lifts his hand, and yet again,
    Threatening my feeble life; intransigent
    He holds me pinned, too spent
Even to quiver, vanquished and outstretched.

Each wincing nerve shrieks out; from every vein
    The scattered blood, responsive to the drum
    And thud that calls it home,
Flees backward to the heart and leaves me bleached.

He pounds me under the left rib; he's fetched
    Me such sore buffets that my whole heart rings
    With pain; "And if he swings
The sword once more," I think, " 'twill all be ended;
I shall be dead before the stroke's descended."

Might I but see him drive his dreadful blade,
    Splitting her heart that splits my heart in three,
    Less dark the death would be
I haste to at her hand, the fair and dire;

But she smites hard in sunshine as in shade,
   Robber and murderess! Woe's me! why should she
   Not lie and howl for me,
As I for her, gulfed in the pit of fire?

"Me to the rescue!" with a most entire
   Delight I'd cry, loosed hotfoot to the hair
   That Love for my despair
Gilded and crisped, and on the glittering treasure
Would set my hand, and then would do her pleasure.

Once let me grasp the golden braids entwined
   To be my scourge and lash, those locks of hers.
   I'd cling them close from terce
Till vesper bell and evening bell had tolled;

Clement I would not be, nor courteous-kind,
   But like a bear at play; and though Love's fierce
   Hand lay his whips on worse
I'd be revenged for all a thousandfold.

Yet for a while would I withhold, and hold
   Locked fast with mine the sparkling eyes which dart
   The flame that kills my heart—
So stern a treaty of amends I'd draft her;
And then with love would yield her peace thereafter.

Song, make thy way straightway to that proud lady
   Who smites and slays me, and denies the draught
   I thirst for. Speed thy shaft
Clean through her breast and do me right upon her,
For fair revenge is an affair of honour.

(CONVIVIO 6)

2

Al poco giorno ed al gran cerchio d'ombra

To the short day and the great circle of shadow
I've come, alack! when winter on the hills
Falls white, and all the colour leaves the grass;
And yet my longing changes not its green,
It is so barbed in that inclement stone
Which hears and speaks as though it were a woman.

And in like manner this unnatural woman
Stands frozen, like the snow beneath the shadow,
Wholly unmoved, as she were made of stone,
By the sweet season that re-warms the hills
And changes back their whiteness into green
By decking them with flowers and springing grass.

When she goes coronalled with leaves of grass,
Thought has no room for any other woman;
So fair the crisped gold mingles with the green
That Love comes there to sojourn in the shadow,
And holds me limed between the little hills
Faster by far than any calcined stone.

Her beauty's power yields to no jewel-stone,
Her wound nor herb nor medicinable grass
Can cure; for I have fled o'er plains and hills
Seeking for some escape from such a woman;
But from her scorching ray naught gives me shadow,
Mountain, nor ever wall, nor leafy green.

Some time have I beheld her clad in green,
Such fashion as would put into a stone
The love I bear unto her very shadow;

Wooing her so in a fair mead, whose grass
Seemed breathing love like any amorous woman,
A place enclosed, set round with loftiest hills.

Yet rivers shall run backward to the hills
Before this tender wood, sappy and green,
Shall e'er take fire, after the wont of woman,
From me, that would lie naked on hard stone
All my life long, and like a brute eat grass,
Only to glimpse her garments' passing shadow.

If, where the hills have thrown the gloomiest shadow,
She pass in her green gown, half-girl, half-woman,
Gloom vanishes, like a stone dropped in the grass.

(CONVIVIO 7)

3

Amor, tu vedi ben che questa donna

Love, thou perceivest well how that this lady
Heeds not the power, at any tide or time,
Of thee, the wonted lord of every lady.
Nay, when she knew herself for my liege-lady,
Seeing my glowing face reflect thy light,
She studied to become a tyrant-lady,
Seeming to have no heart of womanly lady,
But of whatever beast love leaves most cold;
For whether in warm season or in cold
She shows me but the semblance of a lady
Sculptured in beauty from the marble stone
By the skilled hand of some great worker in stone.

And I, who am constant as a rock of stone
To obey thee for the beauty of a lady,
Bear hid in me the wound of the sharp stone
Shot from thy sling, as at a stumbling-stone
That had offended thee this long, long time,
Piercing my heart and turning it to stone.
Nor ever yet was found the jewel-stone
That, whether of the sun's or planets' light,
Contained enough of virtue or of light
To break the power of this magnetic stone
That leads me with the lure of beauty cold
Thither where I shall soon lie dead and cold.

Lord, thou dost know how by the freezing cold
Water is changed to a crystalline stone
Under the North Star in the mighty cold,
Till, air being all transmuted to the cold
Element, water reigns as sovereign lady
In all those parts, by reason of the cold.
Even so, beneath her aspect's deadly cold,
My blood is frozen, winter and summer-time,
And heart's desire, which wears away my time,
Transmutes itself into salt water cold
Down-dripping from my eyes, whereon lit light
The first clear beam of that dispiteous light.

In her is gathered up all beauty's light,
Even as all cruelty's relentless cold
Runs to her heart, no ray of thine can light;
Wherefore her beauty is the very light
Of my eyes—I see her image in a stone,
Yea, everything whereon my glances light.
Forth of her eyes streams such a dazzling light
As makes me blind to every other lady;
O that she were a kind and merciful lady
To me, who, whether in darkness or in light,
Seek for her service but the place and time,
Nor for aught else desire to live long time.

Wherefore, O Power that art the elder of time,
Elder than motion or than sense-felt light,
Pity me that endure so evil a time.
Enter her heart—indeed it is high time—
And drive away from it the frost and cold
That will not suffer me to enjoy my time;
Love hath its season; but should thy strong spring-time
Catch me as I am, that well-bred mask of stone
Will see me laid beneath my narrow stone,
Never to rise until the end of time;
Then shall I see if ever was fair lady
In all the world like this most bitter lady.

Song, in my heart abideth such a lady
That, though to me she bear her like a stone,
My courage makes all other men seem cold;
Therefore I dare to sing against the cold
Things new; and through thy form there breaks a light
Undreamed-of yet in all the years of time.

(CONVIVIO 8)

4

Io son venuto al punto della rota

Now have I reached that point upon the wheel
    When the horizon, at the fall of day,
Brings forth the Twins and shows them to the night,

And love's own star, following at Phoebus' heel,
    Is sundered from us by the brilliant ray
That straddles her and folds her up in light;

When the chill planet that is most of might
    To aid the frost, on the great circle rides
Whence all the seven of them cast shortest shade;—
Yet is my heart not made
    By one thought lighter of the love that bides
Heavy on it; for it is hard as stone
Still to retain the image of a stone.

Up from the sand of Ethiopia leaps
    The alien wind, and troubles all the air;
For the sun's disc has scorched it to a blast

That whirls across the sea, and drives and heaps
    Such cloud as, if no cross-wind meet it there,
Locks our whole hemisphere, and seals it fast,

Till it resolves, and falls to earth at last
    In white-flaked snow, or noisome rainy sleet
Poured down from weeping skies mournful and black;—
Yet Love, though he draw back
    His nets on high, for all the winds that beat
Will never set me free, so fair the lady,
So fair and cruel, dealt me for sovereign lady.

Now every summer-seeking bird has flown
    Those European climes that never lose
The seven cold stars upon the turning Wain;

And all the others, save to make their moan,
    Have bound their tender voices under truce
To speak no note till spring-time come again;

All nature's merry wantons now refrain
    Their courtship, and cast off the yoke of love,
Made dull of spirit by the winter frore;—
Yet I love all the more,
    Whose sweet desires no season can remove,
Nor are they given to me by tide or time
But by a lady still untouched of time.

The springing leaves, called forth on every bough
  Once, by the vigorous Ram, to deck the year,
Have had their day and gone; the grass is dead;

No branches wear their verdant mantle now,
  Only the laurel and the pine and fir,
Whose melancholy green is never shed;

O 'tis a murderous hard winter—sped
  Are all the flowers that made the meadows fine,
Being too tender to abide the flaw;—
Yet Love will not withdraw
  His piercing thorn from out this heart of mine,
And I must bear the smart my whole life long—
Even for ever, could I live so long.

Forth of the deep earth's moist and concave womb
  Through every vein the reeking waters teem,
Sucked from stored vapours in the abysmal vault,

So that the path by which I loved to roam
  In summer, now rolls down a rushing stream,
And shall, while Winter holds his grand assault;

The ground's one rigid pavement, set like smalt;
  The stagnant pools, locked in the icy grip
That bars them from without, are turned to glass;—
Yet I, in this great pass
  Of arms, have yielded not one single step—
Nor would not, since, if torment is so sweet,
Death, of all sweets, must be surpassing sweet.

O Song, what will become of me when spring
  Brings in its sweet renewals, every part
Of heaven down-raining love on all the earth,
If, in this frozen dearth,
  Love, that spares all the rest, still wrings my heart?—
Nothing—the image of a man in marble,
If girl so young can have a breast of marble.

                              (CONVIVIO 9)

OF THE CANZONE

Each of the four poems here translated is a *canzone*—one of the most beautiful and flexible of the mediaeval "fixed forms." The rules for its construction are given at some length by Dante himself in the *De Vulgari Eloquentia*, and may be summarised as follows:—

The *canzone* is a series of stanzas upon a single subject, written in the elevated style, without refrain, and suitable for setting to music. It may have any number of stanzas, all alike in metre and rhyme-scheme; and is usually, though not invariably, concluded by a *tornata* which (again usually though not invariably) repeats the metrical scheme of the second part of the stanza.

The form of the *canzone* is governed by that of the tune to which it is set, and is of two principal kinds:—

1. Where the tune is continuous, without repetition or division, from beginning to end of the stanza.

2. Where the tune is divided into two melodic sections, known as the *odi*; in this case one of the sections *must* be, and both *may* be, repeated. The transition from the first to the second *ode* is called the *diesis* or *volta*.

If the repetition occurs in the first *ode* (i.e., before the *diesis*), the stanza is said to have two *piedi*, followed by a *sirma*, or *coda*.

If the repetition occurs in the second *ode* (i.e., after the *diesis*) the stanza is said to have a *fronte*, followed by two *versi*.

If the repetition occurs in both *odi*, the stanza is said to have both *piedi* and *versi*. (In the only specimen of Dante's *canzoni* which displays this variation, there is an extra transitional line linking the two *odi* at the *diesis*, and rhyming with the last line of the *piedi*.)

The two *piedi*, or *versi*, of each stanza must correspond to each other exactly in rhyme-scheme as well as in metre.

Any rhyme-scheme may be used, provided that it remains uniform throughout the poem. Sometimes the second *ode* takes up and weaves in the rhyme-sounds from the first *ode*; sometimes it has a totally new set of its own; sometimes the first line of the *sirma* picks up the last rhyme-sound of the *piedi* and so links the two *odi* together. (Dante mentions, but does not use, other variations, in which lines may be left unrhymed, to be picked up and rhymed in the succeeding stanzas. Otherwise, a rhyme-sound, once used, is not repeated in any succeeding stanza; Dante does not lay this down as a rule, but it is common practice among the exponents of fixed form.)

Lines of any number of syllables may be used in the *canzone*, but the "heroic" line should preponderate.

Of the four *canzoni* of the "Pietra" group, the first and the fourth show the division of the stanza into *odi*, each stanza consisting of two *piedi* and a *sirma*, rhyme-linked at the *diesis*.

The other two *canzoni* are without division. Of these, Number 2 ("To the short day and the great circle of shadow") is a *sestina*. In this form there are no rhymes; it consists of six stanzas of six lines apiece, and the same six end-*words* are repeated throughout the poem, the order of repetition in each stanza being that of lines 6, 1, 5, 2, 4, 3 of the stanza before. In the *tornata* of three lines, the same words reappear, three at the end, and three in the interior of the line.

Number 3 ("Love, thou perceivest well how that this lady") is an elaboration of the *sestina*, invented by the poet (as he explains in the *tornata*) in order to celebrate his devotion by a suitably illustrious offering.

In the *sestina* and its derived forms, it was held to be a mark of superior skill and taste in the poet to play as ingeniously as possible upon the various meanings of the end-words: e.g., "light" may appear as verb, noun, or adjective, and with the meanings "bright," "weightless," "to alight," etc.; "stone" may signify a rock, a sling-stone, a jewel, and so forth.

Each of the four *canzoni* is followed by a *tornata*, addressed in three instances to the poem itself, after the manner of an *envoi*.

NOTES

CHAPTER 1.

1. On 22 January 1921 Dorothy Sayers wrote to her mother, "I have chosen this moment to be visited with ideas for a detective story and a Grand Guignol play. . . . My detective story begins brightly, with a fat lady found dead in her bath, with nothing on but her pince-nez." Nothing seems to have come of the idea for a Grand Guignol play, but the detective story turned into *Whose Body?*. (Dorothy Sayers said later that the idea of a dead body in a bath originated in a party game which she played at Oxford.) On 16 July she wrote to her parents, "Novels seem the thing to write nowadays. . . . Unfortunately, novels seldom interest me, even to read, and the thought of grinding one out is fearful." Yet on 17 October she wrote again, saying, "Lord Peter is almost ready to be typed." James Brabazon (*Dorothy L. Sayers: The Life of a Courageous Woman*, Gollancz, 1981, pp. 1–2, 82, 87) takes this to mean that between July and mid-October she had changed her mind and written a novel at top speed. But this conflicts with the letter of 22 January. The contradiction is resolved if we distinguish, as Dorothy Sayers seems to have done at this time, between a novel and a detective story. Even if she was not reading novels at this period she was certainly a voracious reader of detective stories and had even tried to persuade Eric Whelpton to collaborate with her in writing some. (See Ralph E. Hone, *Dorothy L. Sayers: A Literary Biography*, Kent State University Press, 1979, p. 32.)

2. *Whose Body?* (Gollancz, 1935), chapter 1, p. 21. This footnote dates from the first edition of 1923. A page from a copy of the folio Dante which Bunter acquired for Lord Peter is reproduced herein (see p. 4). It shows lines 37–51 of canto XXIX of *Inferno*. The pen-and-ink drawing in the margin is attributed to Giuliano da Sangallo. We do not know which part of the *Commedia* Lord Peter had reached when, "communing with Dante," he made up his mind to convey a warning to Sir Julian

Freke, but this passage would have been appropriate, as it refers to a hospital. The falsifiers and impersonators (also appropriate to the crime committed by Sir Julian) are compared to people lying stricken with disease. Dorothy Sayers was later to translate these lines as follows:

> Thus we talked up the cliff, till presently
> The next moat's bottom came in sight, or would
> Have come in sight had there been light to see.
> There, from the crossing-span's high altitude,
> Malbowges' final cloister all appears
> Thrown open, with its sad lay-brotherhood;
> And there, such arrowy shrieks, such lancing spears
> Of anguish, barbed with pity, pierced me through,
> I had to clamp my hands upon my ears.
> Could all disease, all dog-day plagues that stew
> In Valdichiana's spitals, all fever-drench
> Drained from Maremma and Sardinia, spew
> Their horrors all together in one trench—
> Like that, so this: suffering, and running sore
> Of gangrened limbs, and putrefying stench.

3. The exhibition was opened on 30 April by the historian H. A. L. Fisher. The catalogue shows that it included four copies of the 1481 Florentine edition and one of the Aldine edition of 1502, but no copy of the 1477 Naples folio. The exhibition closed on 14 May. There was also an exhibition of Dante editions which opened on 2 May in the Reading Room of the British Museum.

4. *Dante: Essays in Commemoration: 1321–1921* (University of London Press, 1921).

5. *Whose Body?* chapter 12, pp. 257–58.

6. P. 105.

7. Chap. 8, p. 194.

8. P. 243.

9. The mention of Sir Julian Freke's earlier book on crime makes clear what his views are. Entitled *Criminal Lunacy*, it was published in 1914. (See *Whose Body?*, chapter 8, p. 197.) The reader is given another nudge in chapter 10, when the ingenuous medical student, Mr. Piggott, invited to Lord Peter's flat, notices "a great folio Dante which was lying on the table."

10. Chap. 11, p. 245. The conversation with the Russian mother immediately follows the reference to Lord Peter's perusal of Dante. It is intriguing to find that the Dante supplement published by the *Times* contained an advertisement panel appealing on behalf of Russian children, victims in 1921 of famine and pestilence. If Dorothy Sayers saw the supplement and was prompted by it to introduce the incident at this point, it would have been a late addition, for the date of the supplement is 14 September 1921.

11. "For the *Divine Comedy* is precisely the drama of the soul's choice" ("Introduction," *Hell*, Penguin Classics, p. 11).

12. "Dorothy L. Sayers as a Translator," in *As Her Whimsey Took Her*, edited by Margaret P. Hannay (Kent State University Press, 1979), p. 110.

13. *Gaudy Night* (Gollancz, 1935), chapter 3, p. 44. The official title of Miss Lydgate's book is *A History of Prosody* (see chapters 12 and 22).

14. From an unpublished ms.

15. "The Translation of Verse," in *The Poetry of Search and the Poetry of Statement* (Gollancz, 1963), p. 127. This earlier translation of *Roland* is unpublished.

16. *The Song of Roland: A New Translation* (Penguin Classics, 1957) p. 45.

17. *Op. 1* (Blackwell, Oxford, 1916).

18. See *Modern Languages* 1, no. 5 (June 1920): 142–47; no. 6 (August 1920): 180–82. It was later published in its entirety by Ernest Benn, who in the same year (1929) brought out an edition of *Whose Body?* in Benn's Library Series.

19. Pp. xxx–xxxi.

20. Eustache Deschamps (ca. 1338–1407) was an authority on fixed form. His *Art de Dictier* (1382) is the earliest treatise in French on the composition of poetry. His rules for the structure of *laiz* are quoted by Dorothy Sayers at the heading of her own *Lay* (*Op. 1*, pp. 20–31). The translation is as follows:

As for the lay, it is a long affair and difficult to compose, for there must be 12 stanzas, each divided into 2, making 24 in all. The stanzas can consist of 8, 9, 10 or 12 lines (totalling 16, 18, 20 or 24 for the pair); and the lines may be of full length or short. The rhymes of each pair must be different, except for the last, the twelfth (which brings the total up to 24 divisions), which is and must be the conclusion of the lay. This must have the same rhyme and the same number of rhymes as the first pair, without a refrain.

21. "The Translation of Verse," p. 127 (see note 15).

22. From a letter to John Cournos, dated 18 October 1925, quoted by Barbara Reynolds, "G. K. Chesterton and Dorothy L. Sayers," *The Chesterton Review* 9, no. 2, (May 1984): 136–57.

23. "Authors' Note," *Busman's Honeymoon: A Detective Comedy in Three Acts* (Gollancz, 1953), p. 7.

24. In *Catholic Tales and Christian Songs* (Blackwell, Oxford, 1918), pp. 43–53.

25. The writer Harold Child had already asked Muriel St. Clare Byrne to approach Dorothy Sayers on the question. (See Brabazon, p. 160.)

26. "Introduction," *The Man Born to be King* (Gollancz, 1943), p. 24.

27. P. 19.

28. The series, accepted by Methuen, was planned in the spring of 1940. The editors were to be Dorothy L. Sayers, Muriel St. Clare Byrne and Helen Simpson. *The Mind of the Maker* was published in January 1941. Six more titles were announced: Denis Browne (who was the husband of Helen Simpson), *A New Charter in Medicine*; U. Ellis-Fermor, *Masters of Reality*; Muriel St. Clare Byrne, *Privilege and*

Responsibility; A. P. Herbert, *The Point of Parliament;* and Helmut Kuhn, *Encounter with Nothingness.* Of these, U. Ellis-Fermor's *Masters of Reality* was published in 1942. In part a descant on *The Mind of the Maker,* it deserves to be better known than it now is. A. P. Herbert's *The Point of Parliament,* most of which had already appeared in *Punch,* came out in 1946. Helmut Kuhn's *Encounter with Nothingness* was published by Methuen in 1951, but not as part of *Bridgeheads,* which had been discontinued. The other works do not appear to have been published, if indeed they were ever written or completed. A copy of the "Statement of Aims for the Proposed *Bridgehead* series of Books" is published by Brabazon as an appendix, pp. 278-82.

29. For the three levels of allegory in the *Commedia* see *Paradise,* Penguin Classics, translation by Dorothy L. Sayers and Barbara Reynolds, "Introduction," pp. 44-49.

30. *Begin Here,* published by Gollancz, went through seven impressions between January 1940 and May 1941. The quotations are from pp. 35-37.

31. In *Il Convivio* Dante speaks of the natural laws ("love") which govern all things. Heavy objects tend downwards towards the centre of the earth, fire leaps upwards, certain plants thrive best in certain environments. Similarly, the human or rational soul aspires towards truth and virtue. (See Tractate III, chapter ii and iii.) In canto I of *Paradiso* Dante asks Beatrice how it is that he, in his mortal body, is ascending to Heaven. She explains that the natural law by which fire burns upwards, heavy bodies are drawn earthwards and brute creatures are impelled by instinct is the same force by which creatures endowed with love and understanding (angels and humans) are drawn upwards to their appointed site, the abode of God.

32. ". . . And Telling You a Story," *Essays Presented to Charles Williams* (Oxford University Press, 1947), p. 2.

CHAPTER 2.

1. Among recent books on Charles Williams are Alice Mary Hadfield, *Charles Williams: An Exploration of his Life and Work* (Oxford University Press, 1983); Glen Cavaliero, *Charles Williams, Poet of Theology* (Macmillan Press, 1983); Agnes Sibley, *Charles Williams* (Twayne Publishers, 1982); Thomas T. Howard, *The Novels of Charles Williams* (Oxford University Press, 1983).

2. "He spoke from the briefest notes, often beginning before he had reached the desk, fast, excitingly, throwing out original ideas like sparks in seeming asides, opening unexpected fresh glimpses upon old thoughts" (Hadfield, p. 40).

3. 29 August 1943, p. 3.

4. ". . . And Telling You a Story," *Essays Presented to Charles Williams* (Oxford University Press, 1947), p. 1.

5. ". . . And Telling You a Story," p. 2. Hitler's guided missiles were nicknamed "doodle-bugs" by Londoners.

6. The Temple Classics edition of *Inferno* was first published in 1900. The *Purgatorio* appeared in 1901. They had been preceded by *Paradiso* in 1899. The translation

of *Inferno* is by John Aitken Carlyle (younger brother of Thomas), edited and revised by H. Oelsner. The translation of *Purgatorio* is by Thomas Okey, also edited by Oelsner. The translation of *Paradiso* is by Philip H. Wicksteed.

7. From an unpublished letter to her parents, dated 17 November [1912].

8. Letter dated 6 October 1944. The phrase "lamenting with their legs" is a reference to *Inferno* XIX, 45: "quei che sì piangeva con la zanca [. . . he who made/Such woeful play with his shanks]." The sinner in question is Pope Nicholas III.

9. *Paradiso* III, 85. The line is quoted in *The Mind of the Maker* (Methuen, 1941, p. 33). It seems that at that date Dorothy Sayers was content to quote at second hand. She did not in any event turn up her copy of the Temple Classics edition of *Paradiso*, in which the line is given as "e la sua volontate è nostra pace [and His will is our peace]." When she came to translate it she preferred the Temple Classics reading (accepted also by Edward Moore, editor of the Oxford Dante). Her reasons for doing so were communicated in a letter to me. Briefly, she considered that the line echoed the words "Ipse enim est pax nostra [For He is our peace]" (*Epistle to the Ephesians* 2, 14).

10. Letter dated 16 August 1944. In *Inferno* the Hypocrites, bowed down by gilded cloaks of lead, walk slowly round the sixth *bolgia* (ditch) of the eighth circle.

11. ". . . And Telling You a Story," p. 1.

12. Letter undated but probably 25–26 August 1944, in reply to one from Charles Williams dated 24 August. The context of the "lithe proboscis" is:

> th'unwieldy elephant
> To make them mirth us'd all his might, and wreathed
> His lithe proboscis.
> *Paradise Lost* IV, 345–47

13. Dorothy Sayers had visited Venice and Yugoslavia with her friend Marjorie Barber in 1937. They returned to Venice in 1938.

14. For Charles Williams' warnings about "Francesca-like lingerings," see *The Figure of Beatrice*, pp. 150–51.

15. "Dante's Virgil," *Further Papers on Dante* (Methuen, 1957, p. 59).

16. Letter of [?]25–26 August 1944. The mention of Lancelot is a reference to the Arthurian romance, *La Charrete*, by Chrétien de Troyes. (See Lewis Thorpe, *The "Lancelot" in the Arthurian Prose Vulgate*, Monograph Series, no. 1, published by Wheaton College, Ill., 1980.)

17. Letter of [?]25–26 August 1944. The pageant occurs in *Purgatorio* XXIX, 16–154. The transformations of the chariot occur in canto XXXII, 109–60. Reference to the notes to Dorothy Sayers' translation of these passages in *Purgatory* will show that she later changed her mind about them.

18. *Paradiso* XXVIII, 87.

19. Letter dated 31 August 1944. See *Paradiso* II, 49–105.

20. See n. 9.

21. Letter of [?]25-26 August 1944. She is beginning to think she could improve on the Temple Classics translation!
22. Letter dated 10 October 1944.
23. Ibid.
24. The lecture was later published in *Introductory Papers on Dante* (Methuen, 1954), pp. 151-78. On the comic spirit in Dante, see also Barbara Reynolds, "Humour in the *Divina Commedia*," *The Poetry Review* (April-May 1948): 167-77.
25. ". . . And Telling You a Story," p. 20.
26. "Introduction," *Commedia*, trans. Geoffrey L. Bickersteth (Blackwell, Oxford, 1981), p. xxxi.
27. *Paradise Lost* IV, 799-800.
28. *Inferno* XXXIV, 53-54.
29. Letter dated 26 September 1944.
30. Letter of various dates up to 6 October 1944.

CHAPTER 3.

1. Williams' other books were: *The Descent of the Dove, Witchcraft, The Forgiveness of Sins, The Region of the Summer Stars* and *The House of the Octopus.* He also wrote a long essay, *What the Cross Means to Me,* as well as articles, reviews and poems.
2. See Humphrey Carpenter, *The Inklings* (George Allen and Unwin, 1978).
3. Pound's criticisms of Milton appeared in the *Criterion* in January and April 1934.
4. See *Essays and Studies,* The English Association (Oxford University Press, 1936); reprinted as "Milton I" in *On Poetry and Poets* (Faber and Faber, 1957), pp. 138-45.
5. *Revaluation,* chapter 2, "Milton's Verse."
6. Alice Mary Hadfield, *An Introduction to Charles Williams* (Robert Hale, 1959), pp. 98-99.
7. Quoted by Hadfield, pp. 101-2.
8. See Brabazon, pp. 24-26.
9. Published in *The Wimsey Family,* edited by C. W. Scott-Giles (Gollancz, 1977). See also chapter 5 of the present work.
10. E. M. W. Tillyard and C. S. Lewis, *The Personal Heresy: A Controversy* (Oxford University Press, 1939).
11. Strange to say, Charles Williams had himself referred to Topsy in an earlier letter, dated 7 September: "I will venture to remark that there was a good deal to be said for Topsy, even as a critic." Dorothy Sayers must either have overlooked the reference or registered it subconsciously, for her own mention of Topsy is phrased as though the matter had not arisen before.
12. See "Introduction," *La Vita Nuova [Poems of Youth],* translated by Barbara Reynolds, (Penguin Classics, 1969), pp. 11-12.

13. Giovanni Papini's *Dante Vivo* was published in 1933 (Libreria Editrice Fiorentina). The passage quoted comes from "Dante Crudele," chapter 28, p. 251. The original is: "non credo che in tutta la lirica amorosa del mondo, anche in quella di sdegno, s'incontrino desideri così atroci come nella canzone famosa."

14. *The Heart of Stone*, printed privately, Christmas 1946, with wood engravings by Norah Lambourne. See appendix, pp. 223–35.

15. The "Lady at the Window" (or the "Donna Gentile") is someone with whom Dante fell in love after the death of Beatrice. See *La Vita Nuova*, Penguin Classics, sections 35–39, pp. 89–96.

CHAPTER 4.

1. Marjorie Barber is the friend quoted at the beginning of the article ". . . And Telling You a Story."

2. Letter dated 8 April 1945. The contract was not signed until 16 April 1946, but Dorothy Sayers had agreed before then to continue on her own.

3. ". . . And Telling You a Story," in *Essays Presented to Charles Williams* (Oxford University Press, 1947), pp. 1–37. The article was reprinted in *Further Papers on Dante* (Methuen, 1957), pp. 1–37.

4. Humphrey Carpenter in *The Inklings*, p. 224, quotes C. S. Lewis as saying that he considered the article "a trifle vulgar in places." There is no sign in the correspondence with Dorothy Sayers that he thought so and Carpenter gives no source, but the comment occurs in a letter to Owen Barfield dated 16 December 1947: "Your essay is magnificent and I don't know why you are disappointed with it. Tolkien thinks the same and has read it twice. His is *v*. good too. Mine *thin*. D. Sayers perhaps a trifle vulgar in places." (I am indebted to the Reverend Walter Hooper for this information, as well as for the amusing correspondence concerning the misunderstanding with Sir Humphrey Milford.)

5. Letter dated 24 May 1945. The phrase "deus fortior me" comes from Dante's *Vita Nuova*, section II: "Ecce deus fortior me, qui veniens dominabitur mihi [Behold a god more powerful than I who comes to rule over me]," i.e., Love.

6. Letter dated 24 December 1945. *Taliessin Through Logres* is an Arthurian poem by Charles Williams. The quotation from T. S. Eliot is taken from his essay *Dante* (Faber and Faber, 1965), p. 10.

7. ". . . the poem, like the pilgrim, is crowned and mitred over itself": these words refer to Virgil's farewell to Dante: "io te sovra te corono e mitrio [I crown and mitre thee over thyself]," *Purgatorio* XXVII, 142.

8. The original lines are: "largior hic campos aether et lumine vestit / purpureo, solemque suum, sua sidera norunt. / pars in gramineis exercent membra palestris, / contendunt ludo et fulva luctantur harena; / pars pedibus plaudunt choreas et carmina dicunt . . . / stant terra defixae hastae, passimque soluti / per campos pascuntur equi . . ." (*Aeneid* VI, 640–44; 652–53).

9. P. 33. The quotation from Charles Williams is taken from *The Figure of Beatrice*, p. 117. See also pp. 111–12.

10. "Milton," in *Critical and Historical Essays Contributed to "The Edinburgh Review"* (London, 1954), vol. 1, pp. 9–10.

11. These words are spoken by Virgil to Charon, *Inferno* III, 95–96. They are spoken again to Minos in canto V, 23–24.

12. Originally published in 1895. English translation, *Vergil in the Middle Ages* by E. F. M. Benecke (Allen and Unwin, n.d.).

CHAPTER 5.

1. Published in *Introductory Papers on Dante*, pp. 1–43.

2. *Gaudy Night*, chapter 11. The context and exact quotation are as follows. Harriet Vane is expecting a telegram from Lord Peter. Her secretary enters with a telegram in her hand: "Wordy and unnecessary cable from American magazine representative to say she was shortly arriving in England and very anxious to talk to Miss Harriet Vane about a story for their publication. Cordially. What on earth did these people want to talk about? You did not write stories by talking about them."

3. See Brabazon, pp. 44–45.

4. Marjorie Barber had helped Dorothy Sayers with criticism and suggestions concerning *The Man Born to be King* (see introduction, Gollancz edition, p. 39). South Hampstead High School, where she taught English for 35 years, is one of the independent grammar schools founded over a hundred years ago by the Girls' Public Day School Trust. Muriel St. Clare Byrne had been a pupil at one of them and herself taught for a time at South Hampstead. In 1954, the year of Miss Barber's retirement, Dorothy Sayers attended the end-of-term ceremony and gave away the prizes. I am indebted to the present Headmistress, Mrs. Averil Burgess, for these details.

5. Related to me by Dorothy Sayers.

6. "Betty Radice Remembers E. V. Rieu," *Times Higher Education Supplement*, 19 October 1984, p. 17.

7. C. W. Scott-Giles (1893–1982), a graduate in history of Cambridge University and a member, later a Fellow Commoner, of Sidney Sussex College, of which he wrote a history, was secretary to a professional institution. In his leisure time he wrote over ten books, many of them on heraldry, on which he became a recognized authority. In 1957 he was appointed one of Her Majesty's Officers of Arms, with the title Fitzalan Pursuivant of Arms Extraordinary. In this capacity he attended the Queen at the State Opening of Parliament and other ceremonial occasions. Among his best-known works are: *The Romance of Heraldry* (London, J. M. Dent, 1929), *Civic Heraldry of England and Wales* (Dent, 1933, revised edition 1953), *The Road Goes On: A Literary and Historical Account of the Highways, Byways and Bridges of Great Britain* (London, Epworth Press, 1946, rep. 1948), *Shakespeare's Heraldry* (Dent, 1950), *Heraldry in Westminster Abbey* (London: The Heraldry Society, 1954).

8. Privately printed "for the family" by Humphrey Milford, "edited by Matthew Wimsey," n.d.

9. *The Wimsey Family: A Fragmentary History Compiled from Correspondence with Dorothy L. Sayers* (Gollancz, 1977; paperback, New English Library/Times Mirror, 1977 and New York, Avon Books, 1979). The Confraternitas Historica was founded in 1910 by Jack Reynolds, the first historian to be elected to a fellowship at Sidney Sussex College. He was succeeded in 1919 by James Passant, under whom Scott-Giles studied. By courtesy of the late Dr. R. C. Smail, who was present at the meeting, I give the following excerpt from the minutes book of the society:

(1937) The 182nd meeting of the Confraternitas was held in the College Hall on Sunday March 7th, being the occasion of the Visitors' meeting.

Lengthy correspondence during the Michaelmas and Lent Terms had at last borne fruit and for this unusual and highly entertaining evening the Confraternity's thanks go to Fr. Passant.

The guests of honour were Miss Dorothy L. Sayers, Miss Helen Simpson, Miss M. St. Clare Byrne, C. W. Scott-Giles Esq.

After post-prandial refreshment in Fr. Passant's rooms, the Society and its guests migrated to the Hall, there to hear some sidelights upon the history of a little-known noble house from the earliest times. It is said by those who knew him that the late J. H. Round was contemplating a history of the Wimsey family at the time of his death. The world at large has been robbed of this, but there are some advantages, for the Confraternity was able to hear the history of the Wimsey family with the knowledge that its members were privileged in sharing in knowledge not yet known to the generality of men.

Mr. Scott-Giles told of the stirring history of the Wimsey family in the Middle Ages, of the family's life under the Angevin kings, contributing no small part to that glorious tradition of Liberalism, which has made England what it is— (Cheers! but gestures of disapproval from an Anglo-Indian in the front row). By the Liberal tradition is meant *of course* the great services of the English aristocracy to the cause of freedom, tolerance and the Empire.

But Mr. Scott-Giles devoted the major part of his time to the problems of heraldry raised by the Wimsey arms. The fact that these included 3 mice was of importance in a rather different connection. It has long been a major heresy to suppose that the plays of Shakespeare were written by an uneducated actor of that name. Bacon and the Earl of Oxford have both been proposed as the true authors but Shakespearean students must now revise their views, for Miss St. Clare Byrne has proved convincingly that the bulk at least of the plays were written by no less a person than that shy statesman Peregrine, 5th Earl of Denver. Mice were shown to play a large and perplexing part in the Shakespearean imagery, a part which can only be explained by the fact that the mouse had a special significance to those who knew.

Miss Helen Simpson dealt with the domestic life of the Wimseys in the 17th century. She was fortunate to have in her possession a household book containing recipes for all manner of dishes and cures for most diseases.

Miss Dorothy Sayers read a pamphlet, written by a clergyman of the established church and dedicated to the 2nd Duke of Denver. This gives an account of an obscure member of the Wimsey family who lived in the late 18th century. He was indeed a most remarkable man: after running through the whole gamut of dissipation and heterodox opinion, he retired to live as a hermit in a lonely part of the east coast. He read only the Bible, dressed, for the most part, in the scales of fishes, and was never known to speak. By the locals he was considered the chief wonder in that part of the world.

Altogether a very pleasant evening and a fine display of scholarly fooling: conducted chiefly in the spirit of intelligent parody, it was in this eminently successful.

A. B. Simpson (Magister Rotulorum)

Princeps.

10. *The Road Goes On: A Literary and Historical Account of the Highways, Byways and Bridges of Great Britain*; see n. 7.

11. Michelangelo Caetani, Duke of Sermoneta (1804–82), *La Materia della "Divina Commedia" dichiarata con sei tavole* (1865).

12. Letter dated 5 March, 1946.

13. From an undated letter.

14. P. 237. The point, as Dorothy Sayers said, is subtle. It has not been made by other commentators. The distinction can be seen at once to be valid as regards Guido da Montefeltro, the sinner who tells his tale in canto XXVII. Pope Boniface sent for him to ask his advice: how could he defeat his enemies, the Colonna family, who had withdrawn into their fortress at Palestrina? Promise them amnesty, advised Guido, and when they have surrendered destroy them. The plot succeeded, but for giving this advice Guido is in the eighth ditch of the Circle of Fraud, deceived in his turn by the Pope, who had guaranteed absolution in advance. In the case of Ulysses the point requires further consideration. He certainly deceives his crew with his *orazion picciola* (little speech). He also deceived a number of readers, including Tennyson, as is shown. The point in question is: can Dante's Ulysses be seen as a giver of fraudulent counsel or as one who counselled others how to deceive? If the latter, it would follow that Dante has devised for Ulysses a speech which is a supreme example of how to deceive: "That's the way to do it—it didn't take long—just a few words—*orazion picciola*." Guido da Montefeltro's tale could then be seen as a more explicit example, which throws light retrospectively upon the figure of Ulysses. Her reference to "the men who counselled fraud" can be found in "The Eighth Bolgia," in *Further Papers on Dante*, p. 108.

CHAPTER 6.

1. ". . . the living justice which inspires me." These words are spoken by the soul of the Emperor Justinian. Frank Napier, who died at the early age of forty-five, was stage director of the Old Vic Theatre from 1931 to 1934. He was well known in the profession for his technical knowledge and inventiveness, as shown in his two books, *Noises Off* and *Curtains in Stage Settings*. He acted in the first performance of T. S. Eliot's *Murder in the Cathedral* in 1935. In 1937 he was co-producer, with Laurence Irving, of *The Zeal of Thy House*, in which he also acted. In 1939 he played the part of Mephistopheles in *The Devil to Pay*.

2. The tradition that the name "Lichfield" meant "field of corpses" was widespread but the generally accepted modern explanation is different. "The name 'Lichfield' ('Lyccidfelth' is the earliest known spelling) indicates land attached to Lwytcoed, the Celtic name for the nearby town of Letocetum. . . .Caer Lwycoed means the defended fort or town of the grey wood." (J. Grould, *Archaeology and Development*). I am indebted to Prebendary E. C. C. Hill for this information.

3. I an indebted to Andrew Lewis for this explanation of the Roman legal terms "exceptio" and "replicatio," which seem to be implied in Dante's use of the word "replico."

4. The Reverend Lorna Dazeley has drawn my attention to the theory of Abelard (1079–1142): "For Abelard the work of the Cross is purely exemplarist. Christ's suffering and death is a supreme example and a message of divine forgiveness, which stirs men's hearts to repentance." Abelard was condemned by the University of Paris, and Dante, who could have read his writings, may have disapproved of him, for he makes no mention of Abelard in any of his own works. At all events, it is emphasis such as Abelard makes on forgiveness and repentance which some readers find missing in Dante's formula.

5. The Reverend Dr. Brian Horne informs me that Hans Urs Von Balthasar, author of *The Glory of the Lord*, has said: "The Cross of Christ, in all its reality, is met nowhere in the *Divine Comedy*." And he goes on:

The lack of Christological (and thus also of trinitarian) influence on the *Inferno* (the inscription above the gate is far from being sufficient) has its effect on *Purgatorio*, which places greater emphasis on the moral restoration of man than on the imitation of Christ and the inexorable confrontation with his Cross. Above all, it affects *Paradiso*, where the reality of Christ as universal mediator is almost entirely absent. Glory here is indeed the glory of a Heaven aflame with the Eros of God, but the distinctively Christian quality of this—God's descent into death and Hell, his humiliation to the point of complete kenosis, God taking our place and bearing the sin of the whole world—this kind of glory does not come into view." (P. 101)

6. *Introductory Papers on Dante*, p. 82.
7. Ibid., p. 183.

8. *Purgatorio* V, 85–129.

9. These lines, set to music by Antony Hopkins, were sung by the choir. Dante's words (Paradiso XXXIII, 1–6) are:

> Vergine madre, figlia del tuo figlio,
> umile e alta più che creatura,
> termine fisso d'etterno consiglio,
> tu se' colei che l'umana natura
> nobilitasti sì, che 'l suo fattore
> non disdegnò di farsi sua fattura.

10. While a pupil at the Royal College of Music Hopkins had been awarded the Chappell Gold Medal and the Cobbett Prize.

11. Chapter 19, pp. 237–39. Brabazon says also, "Her passion for Dante, intellectual though it might be, was as capable as any other passion of leading her astray."

12. I am indebted to Marcus Whichelow for permission to quote his words.

13. From a conversation with Norah Lambourne.

14. Norah Lambourne has spoken to me of Dorothy Sayers' strong visual sense and feeling for drama. This was evident in the 1949 production of *The Zeal of Thy House*, which Dorothy helped Christopher Hassall to direct.

15. Frank Napier had recently lunched with Dorothy Sayers to discuss the play. He was at that period acting the part of Bernard in Ronald Duncan's *This Way to the Tomb*.

16. On 27 August 1946 Dorothy Sayers wrote to Norah Lambourne:

I have been putting off and putting off writing to you in the hope of getting some definite news about *The Just Vengeance*, but circumstances have held us up. What happened was that Lord Vivian and Co. decided that it was a *big* job, and needed a really first-rate commercial producer to get all the necessary and complicated machinery working. It seemed to them and to my agents that the best possible person would be C. B. Cochran, so they duly approached him. He, it seems, was greatly interested—but immediately after dealing with the production of *Big Ben* he was hauled away to a nursing-home to have something snipped out of his inside. He is now much better, and has gone away for a rest—when last seen he was reported to be waving a copy of the play and declaring that he wanted very much to do it. . . . In the meantime the Bishop of London has been approached about funds and is keenly interested—and also (apparently) full of rather impracticable ideas about getting it done at St. Paul's. . . . Our own choice has fallen upon St. Marylebone Church, which is big, square, good for sound, and furnished with *two* galleries (dress and upper circle) and also reasonably free from traffic noises. And so we wait.

17. Antony Hopkins, *Beating Time* (Michael Joseph, 1982), p. 125.

18. 20 June 1946. The article is unsigned.

19. 17 June 1946. The article is signed "P.P."

20. I am indebted to Stewart Lack for allowing me to quote from his recollection of the play. He also writes:

The day was made all the more memorable in a personal way by my seeking out Norah before the performance and finding her ironing costumes, in which she was being assisted by Dorothy herself. The result was a long and fascinating chat, as the ironing proceeded, centering on Fenland churches, which both Dorothy and I knew well, and discussing the relative merits of various "angel roofs"—she preferring Upwell as against "my" March!

CHAPTER 7.

1. From a conversation with Norah Lambourne.

2. "The City of Dis," p. 128.

3. See chapter 5 herein, p. 67.

4. Much of the material for this lecture was incorporated in her article "The Writing and Reading of Allegory," in The Poetry of Search and the Poetry of Statement (Gollancz, 1963). See in particular pp. 217–20. T. P. Blackburn was an undergraduate then in his third year, though he had originally entered the college in 1939.

5. In Dante's Inferno the City of Dis (La Città di Dite) is a fortified city moated by the river Styx and enclosing the whole of Nether Hell. In ancient mythology Dis was the name of the god or king of the underworld. He was the son of Cronos and Rhea and the brother of Zeus. The underworld (Hades) was also called Dis.

6. I am indebted to Philip H. Vellacott for permission to quote from his two works. The quotation from Ironic Drama (Cambridge University Press, 1975), is to be found on pp. 7–8.

7. See "Holmes' College Career" in Unpopular Opinions (Gollancz, 1946), pp. 134–47. The article was first published in Baker Street Studies, edited by H. W. Bell (Constable, 1934).

8. The late Dr. R. C. Smail, Fellow of Sidney Sussex College, to whom I owe details of the meeting, told me that the fire was probably fuelled by logs from the college garden.

9. Creed or Chaos? and Other Essays in Popular Theology (Methuen, 1947). For the talk entitled "Creed or Chaos?" see pp. 25–46. It was delivered at the Biennial Festival of the Church Tutorial Classes Association in Derby and first published by Hodder and Stoughton in 1940.

10. It was republished in Unpopular Opinions, pp. 17–20, where it is dated 1940.

11. Among other writers of the period who were concerned with the relation between belief and behaviour were T. S. Eliot and Charles Morgan.

12. Unpopular Opinions, pp. 9–12.

13. First published by Methuen, it is included in Creed or Chaos?, pp. 65–88.

14. The classic example of this temptation (and one which Dorothy Sayers may well have had in mind) was Conan Doyle's surrender to public demand when he resurrected Sherlock Holmes.

15. For the recruitment of agents for Soviet Russia at Cambridge and in particular Trinity College, see Andrew Boyle, *The Climate of Treason: Five Who Spied for Russia* (Hutchinson, 1979).

16. Later published by Penguin Books (1965). The quotation is from p. 76 of this edition.

CHAPTER 8.

1. The epigraph to this chapter may be translated "And yet it does move." Galileo is reputed to have said this on being released from prison after recanting his theory that the earth moved round the sun.

2. I owe this information to Norah Lambourne, who showed me a snapshot of "the handsome tabby."

3. *Carducci: A Selection of his Poems, with Verse Translations, Notes and Three Introductory Essays* (Longmans, Green and Co., 1913); *The Poems of Leopardi, edited with Introduction and Notes and a Verse-Translation in the Metres of the Original* (Cambridge University Press, 1923).

4. The pupil referred to was Valerie Hallett, who took a distinguished first-class degree in French and Italian. Now Mrs. Valerie Minogue, she is Professor of Romance Languages at University College, Swansea. In the interests of historical accuracy, I should add that her recollection is not quite the same as mine. She writes, "I greatly enjoyed Dorothy Sayers' translation . . . but what I do seem to remember saying (and certainly thinking) is that I wondered whether Dante should really sound as racy and funny as he did in her translation."

5. Letter of 26 November 1949. "Oderint dum metuant [Let them hate so long as they fear]" is a saying quoted by Cicero in *Philippic* I, 14.

6. See chapter 5 herein, p. 65.

7. See *Dante Alighieri. The Divine Comedy. Text and Translation in the Metre of the Original* by Geoffrey L. Bickersteth (Basil Blackwell, Oxford, 1981), pp. xxxiii-xlv. See also my foreword to that edition, pp. vii-xiii.

8. Pp. xl-xli.

9. *Nine*, April 1956.

10. In "On Translating Dante," in *Dante: The Divine Comedy: A New Verse Translation* (Carcanet New Press, 1980), Sisson writes, "The real task is to give the matter of Dante, as one speaks most effectively. It will be obvious that the translations of Golding and Dryden follow this pattern, while those of Dorothy Sayers and Barbara Reynolds do not—if indeed these two could be said to write verse at all, in any but the most mechanical sense" (p. vi).

11. In *As Her Whimsey Took Her: Critical Essays on the Work of Dorothy L. Sayers*, edited by Margaret P. Hannay (Kent State University Press, 1979), pp. 133-49.

12. Oliver and Boyd, 2 vols., 1965–66. For the section on Sayers, see vol. 2, pp. 211–20.

13. Theodore Holmes' article appeared in *Comparative Literature* 9 (1957): 275ff.

14. Pp. 148–49. Dunlap also writes, "Whatever the reactions of her critics, she herself was never satisfied with the second-rate reading, scansion or image. I can judge her translation only as a reasonably informed reader of Dante's own language; in my view, there is great worth in the work" (p. 149).

15. In a letter to me dated 18 November 1949 Dorothy Sayers wrote, "I had to do a broadcast to Italy—in Italian! . . . under the vigorous direction of Orlando and his friends, and have remained mentally and physically unsettled ever since."

16. See, for instance, *Ode alla California*, with a preface by Mario Luzi (Editoriale Sette, Florence, 1984, 2d edition 1985).

17. Sinclair translates "colombi" as "doves," which would be "colombe." A "colombo" is a pigeon.

18. *The Daily Telegraph*, 1 December 1963. It was one of C. S. Lewis's last writings, completed shortly before his death on 22 November of that year.

19. In a letter to me, dated Christmas 1986, Ruggero Orlando wrote:

> Dante is a master in the stress on the seventh syllable: an *endecasillabo* [hendecasyllable] has two groups of five syllables, one at the beginning and the other at the end, and the sixth is in the middle, normally well stressed; when one puts the stress on the seventh, the line gets out of balance, like a horse whose jockey pulls himself forward, and it moves quick and forceful.

Concerning the abundance of pure rhymes in Italian as compared with English, he wrote, "Italian suffers from too many obvious rhymes, infinitives of verbs, abstractions (amore, onore, calore, timore, etc.), from which every real poet runs away. In the *Divine Comedy*, with growing practice, Dante's *rimario* becomes rare and difficult."

20. *Inferno* XX, 78. The line refers to the place where the river Mincio falls into the Po.

21. "Alive on men's lips" is a translation of the Latin "vivus per ora virum," a phrase taken from the epigram by Ennius:

> Nemo me lacrimis decoret nec funera fletu
> Faxit. Cur? Volito vivus per ora virum.
>
> [Let no-one adorn my funeral with tears nor accompany
> it with weeping. Why? I fly alive on the lips of men.]

CHAPTER 9.

1. Compare with this the flat rendering by C. H. Sisson:

The lovely planet which gives comfort in love
Was filling the whole eastern sky with laughter,
Hiding the Fish which followed in her train.

The words "che d'amar conforta" do not mean "which gives comfort in love." Despite the freedom of unrhymed verse, Sisson fails to make the Constellation of the Fishes plural.

2. William Anderson, *Dante the Maker* (Routledge and Kegan Paul, 1980), p. 281.

3. Letter dated 26 March 1946. For the "rushing up" of Mount Purgatory, see *Hell* XXXIV, 121–26 and p. 291n.

4. The drawing is a great improvement on the grotesque combination of drawing and diagram in W. W. Vernon's *Readings on the Purgatorio of Dante* (Macmillan, 1889), vol. 1, following p. xxxii). This squat monstrosity, like a wide-brimmed hat, rising in layers to a flat top, adorned as by a badger's brush with a single tree, which does duty for the Garden of Eden, had affronted Dorothy Sayers' imagination. So too had the drawing in Maria Francesca Rossetti's *A Shadow of Dante* (Longmans, Green and Co., London 1901), facing p. 107, which she described as "looking for all the world like a beastly bride-cake."

5. Temple Classics edition, *Purgatory*, pp. 12–13.

6. From a conversation with Dorothy Sayers.

7. M. A. Orr, *Dante and the Mediaeval Astronomers* (Gall and Inglis, 1913; new edition by Barbara Reynolds, Allan Wingate, 1955). It is mentioned in the list of "Books to Read," *Purgatory*, p. 388, where it is described as "quite the best guide available to Ptolemaic astronomy and to Dante's handling of celestial phenomena."

8. The episode of Manfred, "blond, handsome and of noble bearing," occurs in *Purgatorio* III. The reference to Milton which I had in mind was the line in *Samson Agonistes*: "O Dark, dark, dark, amid the blaze of noon!"

9. *Hell* XXV, 130–32.

10. "On Translating the *Divina Commedia*." The lecture was delivered at a course for Italian teachers of English organized by the British Council at Girton College, Cambridge. After Dorothy Sayers' death it was published in *Nottingham Mediaeval Studies* 2 (1958) and subsequently in *The Poetry of Search and the Poetry of Statement*, pp. 91–125.

11. Quoted in "On Translating the *Divina Commedia*," p. 107.

12. The great majority of her lectures on Dante were in fact written specially for the summer schools organized by the Society for Italian Studies. That is why she dedicated her *Introductory Papers on Dante* as follows:

252 Notes to Pages 143-59

To
the Organisers and Students of
the Summer Schools arranged by the
Society for Italian Studies
who so kindly encouraged me
to talk to them about
Dante

13. "The Translation of Verse," *The Poetry of Search and the Poetry of Statement*, p. 127.

14. She began the article but it was found unfinished after her death. See "Like Aesop's Bat," *Seven* (1980): 81–93.

15. July 1956. See also chapter 14, pp. 000 herein.

16. Volume 1, Italian-English, was published in 1962; volume 2, English-Italian, was published in 1981.

CHAPTER 10.

1. See Boccaccio, *Trattatello in Laude di Dante*, trans. Philip H. Wicksteed (Chatto and Windus, 1907), pp. 91–92.

2. Compare with Dorothy Sayers' versions Binyon's translation of the same lines:

"To the Father and to the Son and Holy Ghost
Glory!" burst forth from all the heavenly spheres,
So sweet, my spirit in ecstasy was lost.
What I saw seemed a smile of the universe,
So that the intoxicating ecstasy
Entered me both by the eyes and by the ears.

Dorothy Sayers commented:

The drunkenness seems literally to have gone to its feet, don't you think? But he has a thing about making the metre as rough and awkward as possible. And I do think one should avoid "intoxicating"—it does, after all, mean "poisonous." And he has fudged the first mention of drunkenness right out of existence. . . . "Inebriation" is, by the way, quite a common term in use among the mystics for this kind of experience, and I don't think one ought to refine it away.

3. To my delight, Gilbert F. Cunningham said that I had achieved my aim: "It may be said that, had the joint authorship remained undisclosed, the whole would readily have passed as Dr. Sayers' own work" (*The Divine Comedy in English: A Critical*

Bibliography, vol. 2, p. 211). Since Cunningham was not an ardent admirer of the Sayers translation, it is perhaps only fair to myself to add that he quoted eighteen lines of mine, on which he remarked: "These lines are of a quality to stand comparison with the best work of other recent translators in terza rima" (p. 219). There is here also an implied compliment to the translation by Dorothy Sayers of the first twenty cantos. The lines quoted by Cunningham are:

> As when the dome of air more lovely grows,
>   By Boreas serene and shining made,
>   When from his milder cheek he softly blows,
> Purging and scattering the murky shade
>   Wherewith the sky was stained until, made clean,
>   It smiles, with all its pageantry displayed,
> So did my understanding there grow keen
>   Soon as I heard her luminous reply,
>   And, like a star in heaven, the truth was seen.
> Her words, when they had ceased, were greeted by
>   A sparkling of scintillas in the spheres,
>   As showers of sparks from molten metal fly.
> Tracing each fiery circle that was theirs,
>   They numbered myriads more than the entire
>   Progressive doubling of the chess-board squares.
> I heard them sing Hosanna, choir on choir,
>   Unto the Point which holds them in the place,
>   And ever will, there where they ever were.
>   (*Paradise* XXVIII, 79–96)

The contemptuous Sisson has translated lines 92–93:

> There were so many that the number of them
> Was greater than all the combinations at chess.

That is not what Dante says. He says that the number of angels exceeded by thousands the total figure arrived at by the progressive doubling (i.e., geometrical progression: $1 + 2 + 4 + 8$, etc.) of sixty-four figures, which is the number of squares on a chessboard. The total goes into many millions. See my note, *Paradise*, Penguin Classics, p. 307.

4. There is a disputed reading of line 105. The Temple Classics edition reads *fama* (fame). Later editions read *fame* (hunger). Since Dorothy Sayers was using the Temple Classics edition I followed this.

CHAPTER 11.

1. This was first delivered as the Herford Memorial Lecture to the Manchester Dante Society on 14 March 1956. It was published in *Nottingham Mediaeval Studies* 2 (1958) and subsequently included in *The Poetry of Search and the Poetry of Statement*, pp. 45–68.

2. The passages mentioned but not quoted here were taken from: Traherne, *Centuries of Meditation* book iii, 3; Blake, *A Vision of the Last Judgment*; Browning, *The Ring and the Book* VI, 117–25; Tennyson, *The Holy Grail* lines 462–67.

3. Pamela Hansford Johnson, *Important to Me: Personalia* (London: Macmillan, 1974), p. 27.

4. The lines quoted are:

> E quant'io l'abbia in grado, mentre io vivo
> convien che nella mia lingua si scerna.

> [I am so grateful, that while I breathe air
> My tongue shall speak the thanks which are your due.]
>
> (*Inferno* XV, 86–87)

These words are spoken by Dante to Brunetto Latini, a Florentine author and man of learning whom Dante regarded as a teacher.

> Dimmi che è cagion per che dimostri
> nel dire e nel guardare avermi caro.
> Ed io a lui: Li dolci detti vostri
> che, quanto durerà l'uso moderno
> faranno cari ancora i loro inchiostri.

> ". . . pray make clear
> What cause thou hast to hold me—as I think
> Thy words and look attest—thus lief and dear."
> Then I: "Your verse, forged sweetly link by link,
> Which, while our modern use shall last in song,
> Must render precious even the very ink."
>
> (*Purgatorio* XXVI, 110–14)

This is a conversation between Dante and the poet Guido Guinicelli, the founder of the *dolce stil nuovo* (new sweet style) in love poetry, of which Dante became an exponent.

5. See "The Fourfold Interpretation of the *Comedy*," *Introductory Papers on Dante*, pp. 121–22.

6. The Affirmative Way found its fullest expression in its two greatest exponents, Aquinas and Dante, though each of them actually wrote at a time when the Negative

Way in fact became dominant. I am indebted to the late Patrick McLaughlin for this clarification.

7. See A. M. Hadfield, *Charles Williams: An Exploration of his Life and Work*, pp. 203–4.

8. P. 152. Patrick McLaughlin, who knew Charles Williams well, disagreed with Reilly. In his view, Williams' cast of mind was not "romantic," which suggested to him the disunion of the imagination from the intellect, allowing the imagination to operate apart from the control of the intellect.

9. *Further Papers on Dante*, pp. 183–204.

10. See chapter 3, p. 39 herein.

11. *Further Papers on Dante*, p. 196.

12. Author's preface, *Further Papers on Dante*, p. v.

13. Hone, p. 149.

CHAPTER 12.

1. *Inferno* V, 98–99. Francesca da Rimini thus refers to Ravenna, the city where she was born. The river in which the officers bathe, however, cannot be the Po. Much nearer Ravenna are two smaller rivers, the Ronco and the Montone and, to the south of the city, the Savio. (I am indebted to Philip L. Scowcroft for this information.)

2. *Further Papers on Dante*, pp. 78–101. Dorothy Sayers also mentions Eddington in *The Documents in the Case* and in the short story *Absolutely Elsewhere*.

3. Sir Arthur Eddington, *The Nature of the Physical World*, Gifford Lectures, 1927 (Cambridge University Press, 1928).

4. In the dialogue Dante quotes from three passages in his *Paradiso*:

> There and there only every longing has
>   Final attainment, perfect, ripe, and whole,
>   And there each part is where it always was,
> For it is not in space and has no pole.
> >   (XXII, 64–67)
>
> Nor has this heaven any other "where"
>   Than in the mind of God.
> >   (XVII, 109–10)
>
> Where centres every "where" and every "when"
> >   (XXIX, 12)

5. Published as *Further Papers on Dante*, pp. 148–82.

6. Boccaccio, for example, alleges this in his *Trattatello in laude di Dante*.

7. See appendix herein, pp. 223–35.

8. E. M. W. Tillyard, *Milton* (Chatto and Windus, 1946).

9. [I seemed to experience the height of bliss.]; *La Vita Nuova*, section III.

CHAPTER 13.

1. The words in the epigraph are spoken by the soul of Solomon in the Heaven of the Sun. Barbara Barclay Carter had visited all the places where Dante lived during his exile. She was accompanied on these journeys by her adoptive mother, Cecily Mary Marshall, one of the two people to whom the book is dedicated. The other is Don Luigi Sturzo, "whose encouragement urged it into being."

From 1924 onwards, when Don Sturzo made his home with her, thoughts about exiles must have been uppermost in her mind. There were so many. Opponents of Fascism who remained in Italy were imprisoned; others were murdered. Intrigue, betrayal, assassination must have been the subject of daily conversation in her household. Turning her mind to fourteenth-century Italy, she would have no difficulty in imagining the tensions, fears, disappointed hopes and privations endured by Dante. His dependence on hospitality, too, was something she understood at first hand, since, young as she was, she had been able to offer a revered friend, thirty years her senior, what Dante's protectors had offered him: a home. Don Sturzo must have been to her the father she had never known. Under his guidance she entered the Roman Catholic church. With his encouragement she created her portrait of the greatest of all exiles.

The book did not meet with the success it deserved. It has faults of style and was perhaps too learned. Nevertheless, it had sufficient quality to kindle the imagination of another creative writer.

2. Dante scholars are now agreed that Antonia and Beatrice are the same person, who, christened as Antonia, took the name of Suor Beatrice when she entered a convent in Ravenna after her father's death. The existence of Giovanni is problematical.

3. Some of his poems, composed under Dante's tuition, are still extant. See Catherine Mary Phillimore, *Dante at Ravenna* chapter 4.

4. Both these friends gave information about Dante to Boccaccio when he visited Ravenna.

5. There is a tradition that Giotto went to Ravenna for this purpose, but there is now no trace of his work there.

6. See sections XXXV–XLII of *La Vita Nuova*, trans. Barbara Reynolds, Penguin Classics.

7. In the *Convivio* Dante asserts that his love for the Donna Gentile prevailed over his love for Beatrice, as may be seen, he says, by reference to the end of the *Vita Nuova*. This statement cannot be reconciled with the end of the *Vita Nuova* as we have it.

8. Magdalene College, Cambridge is spelled with a final "e," Magdalen College, Oxford is not.

9. Patrick McLaughlin had tried to persuade her to allow him to drive her to Ravenna. I had tried to persuade her to go with me and my husband to Florence. She seemed tempted but was too busy and too tired.

10. *La Vita Nuova*, section XI.

11. Pp. 256–57. The words "after he has written the *Commedia*" are misleading. The emotional crisis occurs when he has not yet finished the *Purgatorio*.

12. *Ship Without Sails*, part 3, chapter 7, p. 369.

13. Part 1, chapter 3, p. 27.

CHAPTER 14.

1. It is there entitled "Dante the Maker"; pp. 21–44.

2. See chapter 8, p. 115 herein.

3. "Dante the Maker," p. 21.

4. Wiliam Anderson has told me that he felt "the Maker" summed up the theme of creativity in his book.

5. See *La Vita Nuova*, sections XVIII–XIX.

6. See Barbara Reynolds, "The *Aeneid* in Dante's Eyes," *Proceedings of the Virgil Society* no. 5 (1965–66): 1–13.

7. See chapter 8, p. 112 herein.

8. Quoted by Brabazon, p. 226. The letter is dated 13 August 1943.

9. Quoted by Brabazon, pp. 262–63.

10. See *Seven: An Anglo-American Literary Review*, vol. 3, pp. 9–18.

11. "intellectual light" . . . "full of love."

12. *Introductory Papers on Dante*, pp. 99–100. The passage continues: "The widespread disinclination today to take Hell and Heaven seriously results, very largely, from a refusal to take *this* world seriously."

13. *Further Papers on Dante*, p. 151.

14. Patrick McLaughlin also wrote: "Dorothy did not 'hide behind' the intellectual; she simply came from a different stable from that of Charles Williams, C. S. Lewis and John Wren-Lewis. For her the thrill of communion with God was felt in the intellect."

Compare with this the following comment by Martin Stannard on Evelyn Waugh:

The priest and the artist-craftsman, Waugh believed, were engaged on similar tasks. Their business was the organisation and elucidation of the disparate fragments of daily existence within a wider perspective. But for all that, the act of faith, that leap beyond the fallible intellect, was undeniable and recognised by Waugh as a fundamental precept of his new philosophy. A man of his acute intellect could never desert logical analysis. He merely re-directed it from the natural to the supernatural. From this point the supernatural became his new reality and he delighted in the scope this provided for anti-rationalist argument. Life on earth could now quite happily be reviewed as an empty charade. All forms of humanism which attempted to rationalise it were equally absurd. "Modernist" writers and painters, psychoanalysts and economists were, in his opinion, pretending to plumb the depths of reality in isolated ponds.

Evelyn Waugh: *The Early Years 1903–1939* (Dent, 1986), p. 231. I am indebted to Professor Brinley Thomas for calling my attention to this quotation.

15. New York, Abingdon Press, n.d. Published in England under the title *Speak What We Feel*, S.C.M. Press, 1964.

16. For Dorothy's statement that dogma was the most exciting study in the world, see "The Greatest Drama Ever Staged" and "The Dogma is the Drama" in *Creed or Chaos?* pp. 1–6; 20–24.

17. *Introductory Papers on Dante*, pp. 119–20.

18. "Lay," II, *Op. I*, p. 21.

19. *Modern Language Review* (July 1956): 30. Colin Hardie, a distinguished classical scholar, Fellow of Balliol College, and Fellow and Tutor in Classics, Magdalen College, Director of the British School in Rome, member of the Oxford Dante Society, was also a member of the Inklings. He is the author of numerous learned articles on Dante. His review of *Further Papers on Dante* was published in *Italian Studies* 13 (1958).

20. *Il Mattino* (Naples) 9 April 1958.

Principal Sources

PUBLISHED

Brabazon, James. *Dorothy L. Sayers: The Life of a Courageous Woman*. London: Gollancz, 1981.

Durkin, Mary Brian. *Dorothy L. Sayers*. Boston: Twayne, 1980.

Hannay, Margaret P., ed. *As Her Whimsey Took Her*. Section III, *Translation*. Kent, Ohio: Kent State University Press, 1979.

Hone, Ralph E. *Dorothy L. Sayers: A Literary Biography*. Kent, Ohio: Kent State University Press, 1979.

Sayers, Dorothy L. *Further Papers on Dante*. London: Methuen, 1957.

_____. *Introductory Papers on Dante*. London: Methuen, 1954.

_____. *The Poetry of Search and the Poetry of Statement*. London: Gollancz, 1963.

_____, trans. *The Comedy of Dante Alighieri the Florentine: I. Hell; II. Purgatory; III. Paradise* (with Barbara Reynolds). Harmondsworth, Middlesex: Penguin Books, 1949, 1955, 1962.

UNPUBLISHED

Correspondence between Dorothy L. Sayers and Geoffrey L. Bickersteth, Norah Lambourne, C. S. Lewis, Ruggero Orlando, Barbara Reynolds, E. V. Rieu, Wilfrid Scott-Giles, Charles Williams, and others. All letters except those of Dorothy Sayers to Charles Williams, which are in the Marion E. Wade Center, are in private ownership.

INDEX

Barbara Reynolds was for twenty-two years Lecturer in Italian at the University of Cambridge and retired as Reader in Italian Studies at the University of Nottingham. In addition to completing the translation and commentary for the Penguin edition of *Paradise*, Dr. Reynolds has translated Dante's *La Vita Nuova* and Ariosto's *Orlando Furioso* for the Penguin Classics. She is also the General Editor of *The Cambridge Italian Dictionary*.